WHITED SEPULCHRES

Judgment Must Begin at the House of God

AN EXPOSÉ BY

ALBERT & AIMEE ANDERSON

© 1996, 2001 by Albert & Aimee Anderson. All rights reserved.

No part of this book may be reproduced, stored in a retrieval system, or transmitted by any means, electronic, mechanical, photocopying, recording, or otherwise, without written permission from the author.

ISBN: 0-7596-6366-1

This book is printed on acid free paper.

First published in 1996 by ALBERT E. & AIMEE D. ANDERSON PUBLISHING, 904 Seattle Avenue, Ellensburg, Wash. 98926

Slightly Revised Edition

Printed in the United States of America.

1stBooks - rev. 11/6/01

The main source of Scripture quotations used in this book is the King James Version of the Bible.

We have taken the liberty of correcting some of the grammatical errors in letters and documents we have received. We have also chosen to omit some phone numbers and addresses. However, in taking these liberties it has in no way changed the meaning of the content therein.

A GENERATION OF VIPERS (a sequel to WHITED SEPULCHRES) on occasion, refers to page numbers that are in the <u>First Edition</u> of WHITED SEPULCHRES.

<u>PLEASE NOTE</u>: Due to the slight revisions in this current <u>Revised Second Edition</u> of WHITED SEPULCHRES, page numbers may not be the same in both Editions. Thus, in A GENERATION OF VIPERS when reference is made to page numbers in WHITED SEPULCHRES it is referring to the page numbers that are in the <u>First Edition</u> of WHITED SEPULCHRES.

Anyone desiring a copy of the **First Edition** of **WHITED SEPULCHRES**, please contact Albert and Aimee Anderson. (Phone 509-962-9011)

"Woe unto you, scribes and Pharisees, hypocrites! for ye are like unto whited sepulchers, which indeed appear beautiful outward, but are within full of dead men's bones, and of all uncleanness.

"Even so ye also outwardly appear righteous unto men, but within ye are full of hypocrisy and iniquity."

(Matthew 23:27,28)

People in the Kittitas Valley of
Central Washington witnessed
events unfold like those in
a Hollywood script; but
those events were
all too real.

DEDICATION

This book is dedicated to our Wonderful Heavenly Father,

who has always been and is so faithful and gracious to us.

Also, we dedicate this book to all those people who were so

deeply wounded "in the house of the Lord" at

Kittitas and Ellensburg, Washington.

Albert and Aimee

ACKNOWLEDGMENTS

We wish to express our profound appreciation and thanks to the following:

Myron and Jean Rachinski, Bonnie Clement, Pairlee Treat, Wanda Cotton, Jerry and Phyllis Marchel, Anita Kazee, Mike and Iva Steigleder, Jim and Sherry Boswell, Bob and AnnaMae Cousart, Jim Brown, Ruth Townley and Kennon Forester, who have been so helpful to us while we were documenting this true story and for giving us their statements to use.

Larry Thomas for writing the Foreword.

Bonnie Clement for permission to use her writings: *Beware the Wolves* and *Wolves Among the Flocks*.

Keith Love and the Ellensburg Daily Record for giving permission to reprint articles (concerning the Care-Net Outreach problems and the Kittitas Assembly of God turmoil.)

Most of all, with great thankfulness, we acknowledge the profound truths from the inspired Word of God, the Holy Bible.

SPECIAL THANKS

To our wonderful Lord and Saviour for His faithful, loving, patient, and persistent dealings in our lives, to make us more like Him.

To Olaus and Minnie Filan, Aimee's deceased father and mother, and Albert and Hazel Anderson, Albert's deceased father and mother. Albert and Aimee are grateful to the Lord for the godly influence their parents exerted on them. They feel blessed and enriched and are thankful for their heritage, knowing their parents are "at home" with the Lord.

To our dear children: our daughter Deborah and her husband Larry; our daughter Rebecca and her husband David, our daughter Mary and her husband Joseph, our daughter Eunice and her husband Emil, our son Mark and his wife Emily, and our son Jonathan — for standing by their Dad and Mom, in the darkest hours with their love, prayers, and encouragement.

To our seventeen precious grandchildren: Larissa, Matthew, Charity and her husband Tyler, Starr, Benjamin, Tyler, John, Jordan, Joseph, Jameson, Kendrin, Emil, Kristina, Breanna, Jordan, Zackary, Alexa, and our great-grandson Tristan, who continue to give their Grandpa and Grandma so much love and joy.

To our daughter Deborah and her husband Larry, and to our youngest son Jonathan, for working side by side with their Dad and Mom - helping them in ministry at the Ellensburg First Assembly of God.

To Bill Roberts, a dear friend of the Anderson family, for his loyalty, encouragement, and standing with us through difficult times.

And, to my beloved husband, Albert, I wish to include words of extra gratitude for his constant inspiration, encouragement, earnest prayers and his loyal, faithful and devoted love for his ever-loving wife, Aimee.

TABLE OF CONTENTS

PREFACE xvii

INTRODUCTION xxi

FOREWORD xxv

PROLOGUE xxix

SECTION 1.
    CHURCH BRAWL 1

SECTION 2.
    FORMAL CHARGES 81

SECTION 3.
    BLENDED INTRIGUE 221

SECTION 4.
    LAW OF THE HARVEST 417

PREFACE

The church must set forth the highest standards of righteousness and holiness for others to follow. "Righteousness exalteth a nation, but sin is a reproach to any people." (Proverbs 14:34)

Formal charges against several Northwest District Council church officials and executive presbyters were brought to the General Council of the Assemblies of God Executive Presbytery in accordance with the Northwest District and General Council bylaws on June 7, 1994. These valid charges of serious wrongdoing were whitewashed, ignored, and set aside as unimportant by both the Northwest District Council of the Assemblies of God executive presbytery and the General Council of the Assemblies of God executive presbytery.

Because of this cover-up by church officials, who were unwilling to clean up the corruption within their own camp, we believe it is God's time for the ministers and laity to become aware of the corruption within the church leadership so a real housecleaning can begin.

"For the time is come that judgment must begin at the house of God: and if it first begin at us, what shall the end be of them that obey not the gospel of God. And if the righteous scarcely be saved, where shall the ungodly and the sinner appear?" (I Peter 4:17, 18; cf. Ezekiel 9:6)

Thus this book, **WHITED SEPULCHRES**, has been written and published in order to expose the corruption within the church officiary so the church can be purged and cleansed and God's blessings can once again fall on the church.

The sin of Achan had to be dealt with and done away with before God's blessings upon the Israelites could continue. The same is true in the Assemblies of God. After the corruption was cleaned out of Achan's tent and Achan's sin was judged, God's blessings again flowed (Joshua 7:1, 7,10-13, 20-23) "And the Lord said unto Joshua,

'Fear not, neither be thou dismayed.'" (Joshua 8:1)

The enemy of the Church of Jesus Christ is waiting to lure any and all he can into his trap. "And be not conformed to this world: but be ye transformed by the renewing of your mind, that ye may prove what is that good, and acceptable, and perfect, will of God. For I say, through the grace given unto me, to every man that is among you, not to think of himself more highly than he ought to think; but to think soberly, according as God hath dealt to every man the measure of faith." (Romans 12:2-3)

We have included the content of the actual documents, either in full or in part, to portray the true story in a factual way. Thus, you the reader can readily see and understand the full scope of some of the things that have been taking place among The Assemblies of God church leadership, both on a District and National level.

The personal conversations that are used are true and correct to the best of our ability as they were promptly recorded after they took place. Real names of people and places have been used throughout this book except in *"Beware The Wolves"* and *"Wolves Among The Flocks"*.

In some of the materials used, we have taken the liberty to correct minor typographical errors, misspelled words, etc.

The motivation in telling this true story is to alert the church and public that leadership can go wrong. Sounding an alarm can help to protect the innocent. It can also serve as a warning to all Christians that we dare not compromise the truth of the Gospel. Redemption can only occur when truth is declared or made known. Again, as the Bible says, "Judgment must begin at the House of God."

"If my people, which are called by my name, shall humble themselves, and pray, and seek my face, and turn from their wicked ways; then will I hear from heaven, and will forgive their sin, and will heal their land." (II Chronicles 7: 14)

Revival cannot take place when deliberate violations of Biblical principles are being committed and defended. Thus, our hearts' desire and prayer is for a real awakening and sincere repentance among the Church leadership and laity!

We need to pray with the Psalmist David, "Search me, O God, and know my heart; try me, and know my thoughts; And see if there is any wicked way in me, and lead me in the way everlasting." (Psalm 139:23-24)

We trust that you will read this book prayerfully, asking God to expose and rid His church of corruption, wherever it is found, so His blessings will flow abundantly once more.

Aimee Filan Anderson

INTRODUCTION

Without question, any level of Christian leadership is an awesome responsibility. Failure here produces waves of destructive influence that cannot be measured. The "called" ministry, whether pastoral or strictly executive and administrative, deals in the currency of eternal souls. Thus a spiritual, yet practical, idealism must guide all leaders in their sphere of ministry. The Apostle Paul states this succinctly in 2 Corinthians 6:3 when he says: "Giving no offence in anything that the ministry be not blamed."

While every Christian's life is an open letter, "known and read of all men," any appointed or elected position of church leadership carries with it an additional weight of accountability and responsibility. It is here that godly standards of practical righteousness must come under even closer scrutiny, in part because of the potential influence and high visibility. Even greater must be the understanding that it is the living, eternal and infinitely holy God Who is being served; and He is the judge, not finite man. It is before the eyes of a largely unbelieving and Christ-rejecting world that we live out our lives. Many look for flaws in professing Christians (especially leaders) in order to bolster their reasons for rejecting the Gospel; and, at the same time, they find another opportunity to blaspheme God.

This is aptly illustrated in the Old Testament. It was Nathan, the prophet, who said to King David, following his sins of adultery, murder, and lying (2 Samuel 12:14), "...by this deed thou hast given great occasion to the enemies of the Lord to blaspheme..." Obviously, David's kingly position, influence and visibility, only compounded the awful effects of his sin. Though forgiven, he reaped the bitter results of those sins the rest of his life. The question may be asked: Has the dispensation of grace diluted or changed this principle? Certainly not, for it is Paul in writing to Christians who exhorts, "Be not deceived; God is not mocked: for whatsoever a man soweth, that shall he also reap." (Galatians 6:7). Again, the destructive influence upon other souls cannot be calculated.

All of this brings us to the reason for this book. It has not been an easy task. There is no joy in exposing sin and wrongdoing; but silence only allows the leaven of corruption to spread. No doubt, the camp will be divided. Some will defend those exposed in their sin; others will rejoice that wrong is uncovered. Jesus said, "For there is nothing covered, that shall not be revealed, neither hid, that shall not be known." (Luke 12:2)

The Biblical purpose for making sin known is for redemption; in order that those involved in wrongdoing may be corrected and their sin judged, as well as serving to warn others to walk a higher road.

Every effort has been made to be absolutely factual. First-hand witness and certified documentation substantiate the story told. This account centers around the search for truth and righteousness which must prevail at all levels in the Body of Christ. There must be ONE standard for laity and leadership. If something is wrong for the person in the pew, then it is equally wrong for the one in leadership. If we are to be successful in winning souls to Christ, one requirement is absolutely essential: there must be consistency between the doctrines we teach and preach and the walk we walk. "If we talk the talk, we must walk the walk." This should be with no difference between laity and leadership. The world has little defense against purity of doctrine lived out in practical and holy living. We may be ever so correct in doctrine; but without application of truth in everyday living, our teaching is worthless — yes, even destructive. Perhaps Paul summed it up in revealing his own passion, "And herein do I exercise myself, to have always a conscience void of offence toward God, and toward men." (Acts 24:16)

Again, it was Paul who exhorted, "Examine yourselves, whether ye be in the faith; prove your own selves." (2 Corinthians 12:5). Surely, each one of us as believers need often to "examine" ourselves; both as to acceptance of truth and our display of the same. Therefore read this book, not to condemn a person, but with the heart-cry, "Search ME, O God, and know MY heart: try ME, and know MY thoughts: And see if there be any wicked way in ME, and lead ME in the way everlasting." (Psalms 139:23-24) (Emphasis the writer's)

We are all pilgrims; we have not arrived. No person is an island to himself. We need at times the rebuke of a brother. Sin needs to be confronted. Eternity is too long to assume all is well if indeed it is not. Better to be ashamed NOW where remedy is possible than to stand ashamed before God in eternity when no recourse is granted.

To laity and leader alike then ... read on, knowing that "...every one of us shall give an account of himself to God." (Romans 14:12)

Rev. Albert E. Anderson

FOREWORD

Albert and Aimee Anderson have done a great service in writing this book. And like all who stick their necks out in the interest of truth, they have paid dearly for their efforts. Their David-and-Goliath struggle against a denominational hierarchy has taken its toll. They were removed from their church and Albert's health has declined because of the struggle.

This book is more than an expose' of one scandal, in one denomination, in part of the country. It is autopsy on the politically correct, politically powerful and politically motivated church of today. Although not trained as journalists, these pastors have done first-class investigation and fine reporting. Their facts are so well verified and the documentation so overwhelming, that a first-year law student could win an easy conviction if the matter was taken to court. And some of these matters may yet be decided by a judge. There is much more at stake here than just ecclesiastical improprieties. Several law enforcement agencies, both federal and state, are still involved in the investigation.

WHITED SEPULCHRES not only exposes this particular problem, but turns a spotlight on the crisis of integrity in the church today.

Rev. Larry Thomas
Publisher, *The Inkhorn*

BUILDING FOR ETERNITY

We are building every day,

A temple the world may not see;

Building, building every day,

Building for eternity.

...N. B. Sargent

PROLOGUE

To: General Council of the Assemblies of God and
Credentials Committee of the General Council
1445 Booneville Avenue
Springfield, MO 65802-1894

Subject: Petition to the General Council of the Assemblies of God; asking for an investigation into the manner in which the Northwest District Council of the Assemblies of God Presbytery and Northwest District Council Credentials Committee handled information given them regarding The Care-Net Outreach and the Kittitas Assembly of God.

(A copy of this petition and supporting documentation is being simultaneously furnished to the Northwest District Council of the Assemblies of God by certified mail.)

Date: May 10, 1994

INTRODUCTION:

I Peter 4:17 - "Judgment must begin at the house of God." The church needs to clean up their own camp and get rid of the corruption from within before they can point fingers at the world and accuse them of being corrupt and evil. Too many times church people live a double standard, which brings confusion to the world.

In 1992, Myron and Jean Rachinski responded to Rollin Carlson's request for help and gladly became involved with Care-Net. They fulfilled his demands until they felt they could not continue physically and financially. They were used and spent, and taken advantage of.

Myron and Jean Rachinski appealed to Albert and Aimee Anderson for help in solving the problems they were having with Rollin Carlson, Randy and Vicki Bale, and Care-Net.

The Andersons alerted Don Strong, Elmer Kirschman, Warren Bullock and Frank Cole of the unfair and unjust treatment of the Rachinskis by Rollin Carlson and Care-Net.

The Andersons saw no constructive response to their requests for help.

In November and December 1993, articles in the Ellensburg *Daily Record* revealed the turmoil, taking place in the Kittitas Assembly of God. The Andersons' hearts went out to the injured people with great sympathy, especially to the recently widowed woman, Pairlee Treat.

The Bible says, "Ye shall not afflict any widow." (Exodus 22:22) "Plead for the widows." (Isaiah 1:17) "Oppress not the widow." (Zechariah 7:10) "Honor widows that are widows indeed." (I Timothy 5:3)

Pairlee Treat along with her daughter and many other wonderful people were cruelly excommunicated from the Kittitas Assembly of God Church and made a public example. What wrong or sin did they commit except to question the pastor, Gary Jeffery?

Threats have been made by Northwest District Officials against Albert and Aimee Anderson and against Robert and AnnaMae Cousart for defending and befriending these excommunicated and rejected people.

Furthermore, the Andersons believe the people who give money to churches and ministries have a right for full disclosure. The public needs to see the books on Care-Net and the Great Commission Partners. Full disclosure of the financial records of the Northwest District of the Assemblies of God needs to be given to all the ministers and their churches. Full disclosure was requested by one of the ministers at the Northwest District convention in April 1994. The officials in charge refused the request.

How can we expect our government to be open with their books if our own District officials are unwilling to be open with the District's financial records? It's time to stop hiding and begin to be open and above board in all things.

May we, the church, show by example how to live honest, exemplary lives above reproach.

CHRONOLOGICAL ORDER OF EVENTS:

December 18, 1990 - Frank E. Cole and Elmer Kirschman signed a Certificate of Affiliation as a Home Missions Assembly with the Northwest District Council of the Assemblies of God. The certificate reads, "This is to certify that the Care-Net Outreach of Everett, State of Washington, has entered into fellowship with the Northwest District Council of the Assemblies of God, with right to proper representation in district affairs so long as maintaining a scriptural standard in teaching and doctrine." (Exhibit A)

May 20, 1991 - Kittitas County records show a Deed of Trust was executed between The Care-Net Outreach and the Northwest District Council of the Assemblies of God for $135,000.00, for the purchase of land in Kittitas County.

September 18, 1991 - Minutes of the Kittitas County Board of Adjustment read (in reference to Care-Net's application for conditional use of the Care-Net land), "CARLSON agreed this was a complete withdrawal and said he would start the process from the beginning including new fees." (Exhibit B) (According to the Kittitas County Planner, Rollin Carlson has never reapplied for the conditional Use Permit. Yet, six months after his withdrawal of the application, on March 6, 1992, he showed the Care-Net video to over

2,000 men at a men's retreat in Yakima. The video stated that Care-Net is a non-profit corporation licensed in the State of Washington and promoted it as a rehabilitation facility for men in transition.)

September 25, 1991 - The *Daily Record* printed an article about Care-Net pulling its application for a proposed guest ranch and rehabilitation center on land zoned Agricultural 20. The same issue of the paper printed a letter from Rollin Carlson where he stated, "The Care-Net Ranch voluntarily withdrew its conditional use application September 18, because of the need to clarify its purpose in construction and land use. Our intent is to be committed to the current (county) Ag/20 zoning." (Exhibit C)

February 9, 1992 - Myron and Jean Rachinski first attended Ellensburg First Assembly of God Church in the morning. On the way out of the church, Jean gave Aimee Anderson a blue Care-Net brochure and told the Andersons they were with Care-Net. The brochure contained photographs and a write-up about the people involved at the Care-Net Ranch. On the reverse side was a copy of the Certificate of Affiliation with the Northwest District. (Exhibit A) The brochure held the following statement:

> *Help provide 100 beef stock cows for the Care-Net Ranch in Kittitas, WA. Each year the offspring from this herd of cows will create a perpetual source of funds for the Care-Net ministry to needy Men-In-Transition.*
> *The contribution needed is $700.00 per cow. Come to the*

Men's Retreat with your check filled out.

February/March, 1992 - During February a friendship developed between the Andersons and the Rachinskis. The Rachinskis shared how Rollin had approached them about coming to Kittitas to be a part of the Care-Net Ministry. He told them their starting pay would be $200.00 per week plus their home and food. They were excited about being involved in this ministry.

March 6, 1992 - Albert Anderson and several other men from Ellensburg First Assembly attended the Men's Retreat in Yakima where over 2,000 men from the Northwest district gathered. In this service, the promotional video about Care-Net was shown.

Rollin Carlson and Myron Rachinski were on the platform promoting the Care-Net Outreach Ministry for men located at the Kittitas Care-Net Ranch.

March-July, 1992 — About this time Jean Rachinski began to really open up to the Andersons. Problems were developing between the Rachinskis and Care-Net. They did not receive the raise in salary they were led to believe would be forthcoming. Jean Rachinski told Aimee that Rollin would lay two $100.00 bills on a sheet of paper and run a copy off on the copy machine. He then had Myron sign this sheet of paper as a receipt for the money paid him for services rendered to the Care-Net Ranch. Jean said Rollin later told them that he was giving them the $200.00 per week out of his pocket as a personal contribution or gift. Jean also told the Andersons that Rollin required them to attend his church in Everett. If it was impossible for them to get to Everett, then they were expected to attend Kittitas Assembly of God with the rest of the Care-Net people, including Randy Bale (ranch director at Care-Net) and Vicki, his wife, and children. Later, Randy became a member of the Administrative Board at Kittitas Assembly, and Vicki became the treasurer of Kittitas Assembly. The Bales had advised the Rachinskis not to attend Ellensburg First Assembly of God.

June 11, 1992 - Albert and Aimee Anderson had a 10:00 a.m. appointment at Care-Net Ministries with Myron Rachinski and John Dudley, a resident at Care-Net who was there for rehabilitation. Albert had been asked by Myron to help counsel John and to baptize John in water. Albert had tried to phone Rollin before going out to Care-Net, but had not been able to reach him.

Albert and Aimee ate dinner with the Rachinskis and stayed at Care-Net until approximately 1:00 p.m. They talked to Myron and Jean about taking the youth group service on Wednesday evenings. Later the Rachinskis told the Andersons they could not take the youth group because Rollin wanted them to drive the men at Care-Net every weekend to Everett to attend Rollin's church.

Later, after the visit, Albert reached Rollin by phone. He told Rollin about the request for baptism, and Rollin replied that Care-Net was his responsibility, not the Andersons', and that he would do the baptizing.

August 1, 1992 - The Andersons ate dinner with the Rachinskis, who were moving back East. Myron Rachinski told the Andersons many concerns they had about Care-Net and the way Rollin Carlson did things. Later Aimee phoned Alfred Hansen, a former District presbyter and friend, and told them about Rollin and Care-Net. She asked him for advice on whether to contact Don Strong. He thought the Andersons could trust Don Strong to handle the situation properly.

August 6, 1992 - About noon the Andersons had an appointment to meet with Don Strong at Vantage in order to discuss Care-Net. They had lunch and were together almost two hours. The Andersons shared their concerns about the insurance, Rollin Carlson, and the way Myron and Jean Rachinski were paid and treated.

September 14, 1992 - Some days earlier Albert had phoned Joe Carlson (Rollin's brother) and asked to speak with Rollin. At that time Albert asked Rollin several questions about Care-Net. Rollin Carlson unexpectedly stopped by the Andersons' home. During Rollin's visit, Albert and Aimee asked him several questions. He made the following statements:

    a. Rollin and his wife agreed to give a contribution of $200.00 per week to Myron at Care-Net.

    b. Rollin said he told the insurance company all about his accident and that he couldn't do his work at the ranch and had to hire Myron. Rollin told the Andersons that the insurance company told him it was okay for him to be reimbursed for the money he had to pay Myron to do his job at Care-Net Ranch.

    c. Rollin said he didn't have any of his cattle out at Care-Net. Later he said he or his son had one or two or so there.

September 20, 1992 - Myron Rachinski wrote a "To Whom It May Concern" letter explaining the circumstances surrounding their employment at Care-Net. (Exhibit D) He mailed the letter to the Andersons requesting them to get it to the proper people. The letter reads in part as follows:

> Pastor Carlson called me and told me that the Insur. Co. was going to pay him back the money he had given me because of his car accident he had in '91 in which the doctor told him not to work because of the injury to his wrist or something like that, and he related to the Insur. Co. that is why he had to hire me to work at the ranch. He also said, that the receipts I have been signing were for the church record and the Insur. Co. didn't need to know anything about them. He told me that the Insur. Co. was going to call me and confirm the fact that I have been working and for how much.
>
> The Agent asked me what I did at the ranch, what I received for payment, when did I start, did Pastor Carlson work at the ranch, and did I have any record of what I had been paid.
>
> I remembered in Pastor Carlson's office after all this was done and I was getting my next wks. pay, he asked me if I had a problem with that. I told him, no. In my heart I didn't feel good about it and told my wife that there are probably some facts that we weren't aware of and

> *him being our pastor, we passed it off as being okay."*

September 28, 1992 - Don Strong visited the Andersons in their home. They gave him Myron Rachinski's "To Whom It May concern" letter. He promised to give it to the District officials. During the course of the conversation, Don told the Andersons that this is one time when Frank Cole was right. Frank had not wanted Rollin to start Care-Net, but because of pressure by Rollin and others, he gave in to it. Later Don revealed that their church had given thousands of dollars to Care-Net.

October 15, 1992 - After several attempts to reach Don by phone, the Andersons were finally able to talk with him after a ministers' and wives' luncheon in Yakima. Don told Albert and Aimee Anderson that he did not give the letter to the District Officials. When Aimee told him that he promised to give it to them, Don told her he didn't have time. In addition, Myron wrote another letter to Rollin that sounded "different." Don also said that if the Andersons did anything about it, he would not back them and they would look questionable. The Andersons thought Don was acting strange, either afraid or angry, and that he wanted to get away from them as soon as possible.

April 1, 1993 - Kittitas County records revealed a Deed of Trust was executed between the Care-Net Outreach and the Northwest District Council of the Assemblies of God for $350,000.00.

July 9, 1993 - Aimee tried to reach Elmer Kirschman by phone about concerns surrounding Care-Net, but failed to reach him.

July 19, 1993 - Aimee talked with Elmer Kirschman on the phone and told him about the "To Whom It May Concern" letter from the Rachinskis and asked what they should do with it. He told them to send it back to the Rachinskis, that there was "no need to get the Andersons' hands dirty." He did not seem interested in doing anything about it.

November, 1993 - The Andersons read in the Ellensburg *Daily Record* about the troubles in the Kittitas Assembly Church. At this time, Aimee Anderson called Pairlee Treat, one of the wronged people from Kittitas Assembly. Pairlee had attended Ellensburg First Assembly occasionally in the past. Pairlee told her story to the Andersons.

December, 1993 - The Andersons informed Frank Cole and Warren Bullock about the unjust treatment the Kittitas Assembly people were receiving.

December 2, 1993 - Albert and Aimee Anderson had a phone conversation with Warren Bullock at the Northwest District. They expressed their concerns about Care-Net and the trouble at the Kittitas Church. They told him about some of the wrongs concerning Rollin Carlson and Care-Net. Bro. Bullock asked them to send documentation. The Andersons sent him copies of Rachinskis' "To Whom It May Concern" letter and the Ellensburg *Daily Record* articles (Exhibits E and F) about Kittitas Assembly. The Andersons never received a response from Warren Bullock on this material.

December 11, 1993 - Andersons received the Care-Net brochure in the mail soliciting funds for the ministry at the ranch. The impression given is that the Care-Net Ranch is a rehabilitation facility servicing several people at a time. (Exhibit G)

December 14, 1993 - Albert and Aimee talked with Frank Cole on the phone. They expressed their concerns about Rollin Carlson, CareNet and the situation at the Kittitas Assembly of God. Frank Cole appeared not to know much about what was going on. He asked Albert to mail him the papers that were sent to Warren Bullock. The letter and newspaper articles were mailed to him also. (Exhibits E and H)

Again, the officials of the Northwest District did not respond to the Andersons' plea for help. Furthermore, the Northwest District has not been in compliance with Article X, Section 5.a of the Bylaws of the General Council of the Assemblies of God which state:

> *The superintendent of the district in which the alleged offense is reported to have occurred, and/or an appointed representative(s) shall conduct the investigation to determine their source and validity... (1) Interview with complainant(s). The persons involved shall be interviewed in order to ascertain the facts in the case and the reasons underlying the persistence of the reports or complaints.*

December 22, 1993 - The Andersons received a letter from Frank Cole in which he wrote: "I attended services at Kittitas last Sunday and I had dinner with Pastor Jeffery. Things are much quieter and we continue to be in prayer that the matter will be settled soon." (Exhibit I) There was no mention about CareNet in the letter.

January 7, 8 and 10, 1994 - Rollin Carlson attended the hearings concerning the Kittitas Church at the Kittitas County Courthouse. Rollin told Aimee that Frank Cole sent him to the hearing in Frank Cole's place since, he said, Frank could be subpoenaed to court. Since Randy Bale, one of the board members at the Kittitas Assembly, was also the manager and counselor at Care-Net Ranch, Rollin's presence at the hearings as a Northwest District representative was a conflict of interest and in violation of Article 3, Section 8 of the Northwest District Bylaws which read:

> *District officers who have an interest or relationship that biases, or appears to bias, a decision-making process shall disqualify themselves in matters of ministerial credentials and discipline, or disciplinary intervention in local assemblies when family, staff, close friendships, or business and pastoral relationships are involved.*

Furthermore, Rollin Carlson is the Care-Net pastor and was Pairlee Treat's former pastor at the Ellensburg First Assembly in the 1960s, and he has known Jerry Marchel from boyhood.

February 17, 1994 - Aimee phoned the Care-Net number. Jeff, a resident from Whidbey Island, answered the phone. He said he had lived there about two months and expected to be there possibly up to one year. He told Aimee that he had an alcohol problem and was getting help. Aimee asked Jeff if Jason, the counselor at Care-Net, received a salary. He told her he receives $300.00 a month as a blessing. Jeff also said they (Care-Net) were almost finished with the new bunkhouse that would house 9 to 10 men. Aimee asked him how a person could get to live at the ranch. He told her to talk with Rollin Carlson.

Aimee phoned Anita Kazee at the Kittitas County Commissioner's office (509-962-7571) and gave her the information that Jeff at Care-Net had given over the phone. She had already been doing some checking since she had seen the Care-Net video and brochure a few days earlier. She said the records show that Rollin Carlson and Care-Net had never received a variance or permit to operate the way the video and brochure indicated.

February 19, 1994 - Aimee called Jean Rachinski and talked about an hour. Some of the things she told Aimee included the following: Rollin did not want to go solo; he wanted the District to back him up. He hired Myron for Care-Net and paid him with offerings. Jean sewed the drapes for the multi-purpose conference room, which was finished, and in use the first part of 1992. Rollin went ahead with building the steel granary for supplies without getting a permit because he said he felt it was the work of God or God's work. They had two travel trailers on Care-Net property, but had to take them off (she did not say why). Sometimes Rollin took cattle to his property on the Coast and sold them over there. At times, twelve to fifteen men came to work at the ranch. When the Rachinskis and Bales had their problems, Jean said Rollin wanted to smooth it over because he said it would be a problem for Care-Net. She also mentioned one of the residents at Care-Net, Ed Morgan, was allegedly a wanted man. He left one night and never came back.

February 26, 1994 - At a conference held at Central Washington University, Albert and Aimee Anderson talked with Warren Bullock.

They gave him a copy of the conditional use application (Exhibit J), minutes of Kittitas County Board of Adjustment (Exhibit B), newspaper clippings about the "Rehab Ranch Is Put On Hold" (Exhibit C), and Rollin's letter to the County Planner stating he would abide by the Ag 20 zoning. (Exhibit K) He said Rollin asked to borrow money in 1993 from the Northwest District for Care-Net in 1993, but the District officials turned him down. He made no mention of the $350,000.00 Deed of Trust between The Northwest District and The Care-Net Outreach, dated April 1, 1993.

Albert told Warren that Rollin told him Care-Net has four boards: Everett Bethany Church Board, Care-Net board, Northwest District Home Missions Board, and the Northwest District Presbytery. Warren agreed that was correct, however, he further said the District officials are not given financial accounting information from Care-Net.

February 28, 1994 - Mr. Kruger, a builder for the Northwest District, told Aimee that they were almost through with another bunkhouse that would house ten men. He said that Care-Net was a rehabilitation ranch for men.

Later the same day Aimee Anderson and AnnaMae Cousart talked with Don Strong and Dale Carpenter. They told them that Rollin and Care-Net were operating illegally in that they had not received the proper permits. Aimee told them to talk with Warren Bullock if they wanted more information.

April 4, 1994 - Frank Cole wrote a letter to Robert Cousart, and sent a copy of the letter to Albert Anderson. (Exhibit L) The letter says, "non-members of Assemblies of God Churches do not have voice or vote in any business meeting." Later the letter says, "ministers shall refrain from taking any attitude toward disciplined members that would tend to nullify the action of the Credentials Committee." Further, it says, "Non-compliance with the foregoing shall be subject to censure or charge which may necessitate the recall of his/her credentials. I am hereby notifying you that unless you withdraw from participation in this conflict, whether by meeting, phone or letter, it will be necessary for you to meet with the Ministerial Relations Committee." The disciplined members who had their memberships removed from Kittitas Assembly are on one hand considered dissident members and on the other hand as non-members.

April 5, 1994 - In a phone call to the Internal Revenue Service, the person on the phone said Care-Net is not listed as a non-profit corporation. In another call to the Secretary of State, the person on the phone said Care-Net is not listed as a non-profit tax-exempt corporation licensed in the State of Washington.

April 14, 1994 - A check of Kittitas County records revealed property taxes on the Care-Net-owned land in Kittitas County are delinquent. A one percent was added the end of March. One half of the 1994 taxes will be added at the end of April, and a penalty will be added in May.

April 25-28, 1994 - At the Northwest District Council Convention, an emergency resolution revealed that, "the District has a _deficit_ in net assets of $3,481,324." The resolution further said, "The plan also calls for the District to be reorganized into two separate corporations. The corporation handling the loan fund functions would have a net worth of approximately 0. The new corporation handling the church and other ministry functions would have a _deficit_ of approximately $3.8 million." (Exhibit M)

May 2, 1994 - Don Strong phoned and asked if he could see the Andersons. He went to their home and stayed about an hour and a half. The topics of conversation centered on Care-Net and Kittitas Assembly's problems and the involvement of the Andersons in these two situations. Albert told Don that he had received the letter written to Robert Cousart and said, "I took his letter as a subtle hint or threat." Don indicated that it was not so subtle.

May 4, 1994 - Aimee Anderson phoned the Great Commission Partners, Assemblies of God Foundation, 1600 North Boonville Avenue, Springfield, MO 65803-2730. Phone 1-417-865-4880. The person with Great Commission Partners said that the money that is given to Great Commission is put in a trust fund and cows are given cost free to their ranchers. Care-Net was one of their ranches and was somewhat like a hybrid — on one hand it's a ranch and on the other hand it's a rehabilitation ministry for men under IRS Code 501-C-3. According to the person on the phone, Great Commission Partners and Care-Net were started in 1993. Randall Barton, an attorney, is the president of the Assemblies of God Foundation. The Andersons were informed by a friend that Randall Barton used to work for Care-Net in the State of Washington.

May, 1994 - *Mountain Movers*, Assemblies of God Division of Foreign Missions magazine, had a full-page advertisement inside the front cover for Great Commission Partners. The advertisement states, "A minimum of 25 percent of the net gain has been earmarked for investment in the lives of young people at Assemblies of God colleges. The remaining 75 percent will go to the ministry designated by the rancher or farmer who raises the livestock." (Exhibit N)

WE, THE UNDERSIGNED, HEREBY request that the General Council of the Assemblies of God and the Credentials Committee of the General Council conduct a full investigation into Rollin Carlson's actions, both as a Presbyter and Official of the Northwest District and as the President and Pastor of Care-Net Outreach. We also request that a full investigation be made into the reasons why officials of the Northwest District of the Assemblies of God (including, but not limited to, Frank Cole, Warren Bullock, Elmer Kirschman, Dale Carpenter and Don Strong) have not acted upon the information given them over a period of time since September 1992. General Council Bylaws, Article X, Section 4.d reads:

> *Responsibility of General Council Credentials Committee. In the event a district fails to take action within 90 days after a matter has been referred to it, it shall be the responsibility of the General Council Credentials Committee to see that action is initiated.*

WE, THE UNDERSIGNED, HEREBY state that the above events are true and correct to the best of our recollection.

Dated this 10th day of May, 1994.

Albert Anderson
Pastor, Ellensburg First Assembly

Aimee Anderson
Wife of Albert Anderson

Section 1.

CHURCH BRAWL

ALBERT & AIMEE ANDERSON

The Gate at the End of Things

Don't try to kid yourself with the thought

You can do as you please all the while;

Don't think you can kick the poor fellow who's down,

While you climb to the top of the pile.

Don't think you can fool all the folks all the while;

You may do it sometimes, that is true;

They will find you out in the end every time.

The only one you fool is you.

And you will learn what sorrow it brings

At the gate that stands at the end of things.

...Unknown

ALBERT & AIMEE ANDERSON

On Sunday, June 13, 1993, two women were publicly accused of unspecified sins at the end of a sermon on church discipline. The congregation was informed that these women would no longer be attending the Kittitas Assembly of God, and that no one from the congregation was to have anything to do with them until they repented.

Bonnie Clement, a member of Assembly of God churches in Montana and Washington since 1980, and of the Kittitas Assembly since 1992, stayed neutral until evidence gathered from several sources indicated the pastor was behaving inappropriately in the situation created by his expulsion of the women. The following was written to be used as a warning to other churches that might find themselves in a similar circumstance.

Beware the Wolves!

They come into God's flock in sheep's clothing. They are often hard to detect until it is too late and irreparable damage has been done.

The following is a true account. Names have not been used to protect the people involved.

They were young and enthusiastic, the pastor and his wife. They came with a vision for church growth and for a dynamic youth outreach. They seemed to be just what the quiet country church needed, and they were voted in by a large majority.

In the following months the youth group tripled in size. Teens who had been unruly in Sunday School suddenly became committed to Christ. A drama team was started, and several well-done skits and plays were performed, both at the home church and in neighboring towns. New people began attending services and members were added, swelling the congregation. The little church loved its new pastor and expressed their love in tangible ways. They believed they had a true man of God whose desire was to further the Kingdom of Christ.

The first indication many in the body had that anything was amiss happened one Sunday immediately after the sermon. The Pastor had just finished preaching about the sin of an immoral man in the Corinthian church. He emphasized that disciplinary action in the church was for the purpose of bringing people to repentance, forgiveness and restoration to the fellowship of Christians. Further, references to the immoral sin were continually made in the sermon. At the end he named two women, an elderly widow and her daughter, and said they would not be attending the church anymore. He said the board and he met and requested that the two women appear before them to face charges of habitual lying and gossip. They refused to come; so the board agreed the two women should no longer be allowed to worship at the church. One board member, however, stood and stated that he had not been in agreement with the action that was taken.

The next few months saw a widening split develop in what had once been a loving, united fellowship of believers. A few who had known the women for many years, were dismayed at what had taken place and left the church to worship elsewhere. Those who asked the Pastor what these women had done were told they were habitual slanderers and gossips and that the people were not to have any dealings with them until there was repentance and asking of forgiveness. After a two-and-half months silence, the widow wrote a letter telling her side of what had transpired between her and the Pastor. Not only did he not tell her what her "crime" was, he not gone to her, as Matthew 18:17 admonishes, and furthermore, told her she had a lying spirit and needed deliverance. This same woman only a few months before had been praised from the pulpit for her evangelism. Many felt a great injustice had taken place and petitioned the local district to send a mediator to help settle the matter.

The meeting which was called with the district representatives was clearly one-sided. The only issue that was allowed to be discussed was whether the pastor and board had acted rightly in disciplining the women. The church by-laws were the ruling document, even though it is clearly stated in them that the Bible was the overruling authority in all matters. It was apparent Matthew 18:17-19, as well as other Scriptures, had not been followed. Several voting members attending the meeting asked that the two women be allowed to come to the meeting to face their accusers. The request was denied. Anyone who wished to speak for mercy and love to be shown the women were interrupted by the officiating district representative and told they were either out of order or to sit down and be quiet. One of these members was eighty-year old saintly woman. Those who backed the pastor's and board's action were allowed to speak freely. Several people left the meeting crying and angry.

Members who had been staying neutral about the situation began to ask questions of the women who were being "disciplined" and of the board member who had not agreed with the action taken. There were disturbing discrepancies between what the pastor had said and what the women and the board member revealed. Then the board member, a man who had been attending and serving in the church nearly fifty years, received a certified letter stating that the Pastor and board had reviewed his lifestyle and conduct and decided that he was found to be "out of harmony" with the leadership of the church. Therefore, his membership was removed from the church roster. Because the man's wife had refused to attend the church since the public excommunication of the two women, she also received a certified letter removing her name from membership. Another long-time member, a police woman whose job required her to work Sundays, received a letter telling her she was no longer on the church membership roster, and her husband was told his membership was in danger. These two people had spoken up at the meeting in favor of letting the two women come before the body. A couple, in their 80's and founding members of fifty years, were told by the pastor that they were not in harmony with him and therefore would not be allowed to teach the adult Sunday School, greet people at the door, or engage in any other ministry. The remaining board members had not been told this action was going to be taken.

Young people had begun leaving the church during this time. When asked why, they would not say at first. However, little by little stories began leaking out — about guilt trips, intimidation, confidences being used against them in front of the whole group, being told to swear to keep secret the things "God revealed" to them in meetings, and fear of what the pastor's wife would do if they ever told anyone what was going on. Adults hinted at being told they would die if they did not align themselves with the pastor, and of being afraid of confronting the pastor with the actions taken against long-time members.

A couple of weeks before Thanksgiving, a group of ousted members and others who had left the congregation because of the pastor's actions, attended a service to show support for the members who had received letters removing them from membership. Three of the group tried to ask the pastor a question, and he immediately closed the service. The frustrations of dealing with months of unanswered calls and pleas for help, caused tempers to rise. A scuffle broke out in the sanctuary between the pastor's followers and the people who had been trying to get a resolution to this problem, which had so completely split the church. No one was hurt; however, the police were called and took statements. The pastor disappeared and never spoke with the officers who responded.

Two weeks later twelve of the group who had attended the service were served with petitions for restraining orders. The petitions initiated by the pastor and signed by him under oath and penalty of perjury, contained outrageous and slanderous lies. Later, at a deposition, the pastor again lied under oath. The matter was heard in the district court and took two and a half days. In the end, the judge dismissed all but one of the restraining orders. That one he issued only because the man did lay a hand on the pastor before the scuffle broke out. The judge, in his closing statements, told the pastor that several of his statements in the petitions had been fabrications.

The group has continued to try to talk with the district officials, and has been blocked at every turn. In the meantime, the pastor is still continuing to hold office at the church, and there appears no disciplinary action is going to be taken against him by the higher church officials. We find it hard to believe that the hierarchy is blinded to what is going on. Recently, another couple who have walked with the Lord many years and who have stood up and told the pastor he is in the wrong have received letters removing them from membership.

Why did it take so long for people to catch on to what was happening in this church?

Wolves who come into God's flock in sheep's clothing can be very subtle and clever. On the surface, it is difficult to detect a wolf. Sermons will be Scripturally correct. At first, there is praise for the gifts different members exhibit, and people feel this man really recognizes the contributions they make to the church. The few disturbing things that do reveal themselves are often passed off as, "I must have misunderstood what he said," or "he didn't really mean what I heard," or "I must have been wrong on that point." When the youth began leaving, at first it was easy to say that they weren't really committed to serving God. A few families had left early on, but no one seemed too concerned about them. After all, people can come and go in a church.

Is this a cult, which has invaded this little church?

Maybe. It has several earmarks of being one. Then again, it may be a matter of a young, inexperienced pastor and his wife becoming drunk with the power they seem to be able to wield over people. It is possible one of the new families who came to the church befriended them and indoctrinated the Pastor and his wife with some off-the-wall teaching they had experienced. God knows what happened; we may never know. We only know what has happened and continues to happen is not of God. It is of the devil and of the flesh.

How can you protect your church from experiencing the devastation this church has experienced?

Following are some warning signs this church did not recognize quickly enough:

1. When asked what he meant by "discipleship" during the interviewing process, the pastor ignored the question and quickly moved on to something else.

2. Shortly after becoming Pastor, he announced from the pulpit that Monday was his day off and the only day he and his wife could get away. In itself, this was not, an unreasonable request. However, it was soon followed by a statement that if anyone wanted to see him, an appointment had to be made and that he wanted to be called only in "dire emergencies." In the history of this particular church, the pastors were always available if someone wanted to drop in and say "hello" or to discuss a problem or just visit a while.

3. Several people were told, by the pastor that he "had a vision from God that they were having problems in their marriages." They were then told to make appointments

for "in-depth counseling" sessions with him and his wife. One of the women who went to one of these counseling sessions, suddenly found herself resenting the children she was ministering to in her home. Her ministry was the only opportunity many of them had to learn about Christ and God's love. As a result, her ministry came to an abrupt halt and some of these kids are beginning to get into drugs and gang activity.

4. Board members were told they would die if they aligned themselves with those who were being "disciplined" or did not go along with what the pastor wanted to do.

5. Young people were angry at what took place in meetings with the pastor and his wife, but they were afraid to talk about it. They expressed fear of what would happen to them.

6. Confidences told the pastor and his wife were used against the very people who told them as a means of guilt and intimidation.

7. Love was freely talked about and verbally expressed in services, but was not acted out in the everyday world.

8. People were told not to discuss with any outsiders what "special revelations" God gave them because the "people out there would not understand."

9. People who disagreed with the pastor over anything were targeted for disciplinary action or removal of membership.

10. A core group of "disciples" would give stock answers to questions about what was happening. The words would be almost

identical among the core group, especially the more serious lies.
11. There was an uneasiness about some of the early activities in the church, and an unwillingness to believe something wrong was taking place.

12. Worship services were orchestrated by a "worship team." Spontaneous worship became a thing of the past.

13. There were many discrepancies between what the pastor said people did or that he did in trying to solve problems and what these people would relate. One serious incident was a report he made to the police that his life had been threatened. That never happened. Another serious thing was saying he had gone several times to the women he accused of lying and gossiping. He never did.

14. The pastor's followers directed a spirit of outright hostility toward anyone who disagreed with the pastor or questioned the things he did.

15. Members were encouraged to over commit their time to the church until there was little time left for family and friends.

16. The pastor wanted total submission to his authority. Anyone who did not submit to him was in disharmony and risked being removed from membership.

We hope this will never happen in your church, and this is not intended to start a witch-hunt. But we do live in the latter days, and Jesus did warn us that there would be those who would deceive even the elect if possible.

Since this is a situation that is really happening and there are a lot of innocent people who have already been hurt by these things, I have not used my name, nor the names of the church and town and of the people involved. However, because cults like those led by Jim Jones and David Koresh get started by similar situations, it is important that God's people be warned of the danger their church may face if there is not proper discernment of the spirits, especially when a new pastor and/or new families come to the congregation from outside the area.

At the present time, another church in the little town has opened its doors and hearts to those of us who are no longer welcome at the church which had been our church home for many years. They have prayed for and with us and have involved us in their fellowship meetings and are welcoming us to participate in any ministries in which we would like to be involved. Most of us will never go back to the first church. Some of us are already getting involved in the second church. There is still a lot of grieving with the accompanying denial and anger over the loss of what had been such a warm, friendly congregation and over the loss of long-time friends who are under the pastor's control and who no longer dare to speak with us.

We continue to pray for those involved in the deception, especially for the young people who are being misled and for the elderly who gave of their time and tithes to the church and supported it with their prayers for decades.

The advice we offer is this: Know what the Bible says about God, His love, and what is expected of us as Christians. Be filled with the Holy Spirit and sensitive to the inner warnings the Spirit gives you about certain people, places, activities, publications and ministries. And above all, pray for wisdom and discernment and love and forgiveness if you ever find yourself faced with a similar set of circumstances. Be prepared to help those who become hurt and confused by wolves in sheep's clothing. They will be in need of Christian love practiced, not just talked about.

****

WHITED SEPULCHRES

Wanda Cotton, one of the women who had been accused of serious sin, gave the following statement as to what transpired between her and Pastor Gary Jeffery:

****

On June 6, 1993, I went to choir practice after being absent for three weeks due to illness. Before choir, they asked for prayer requests. I asked for prayer for Ruth Townley, who had been seriously ill for several months. In fact, she had been in the emergency room at the hospital the day before for six hours. I also asked for prayer because I was not feeling well. The pastor, Gary Jeffery, and one of the other choir members, Patty Carney, said, "Well, nobody knew about Ruth." My reply was, "I'm confused about what constitutes an emergency. The original prayer chain has been disbanded and there were only five left. We have been told not to call unless it was a dire emergency." Patty said, "I call about everything." They were getting ready to pray for me and Ruth when Pastor stood up and said, "Come with me to my office, Wanda." I was following him to his office, and he said over his shoulder before we reached his office, "You sound like you have a bee in your bonnet." I said, "I suppose I do." We walked on into the office, and he said, "What's your problem?" I said, "It's poor Ruth. Nobody's visiting her except me and Anita. You never come to visit me unless I have a dinner." "Whose problem is that?" he asked. I said, "Yours, Pastor. You should be visiting everyone in the church at least once every two months." He said, "Since you're so unhappy, find another church." I did not get prayed for. I walked out.

On June 10, 1993, at 9:00 a.m. the pastor called me and requested that I come before the board that night. I already knew what he had said to my mother Wednesday evening, June 9. I said, "I don't think so. Not after what you said to my mother, who is 72 years old." He said, "I'm real sorry to hear that. You are aligning yourself with a lying spirit." I said, "I don't think so," and I hung up.

ALBERT & AIMEE ANDERSON

This was the last conversation I had with Gary Jeffrey until Sunday, November 14, 1993. At least four or five weeks before the above events, this pastor had praised me from the pulpit for my hospitality (he had been teaching on the gifts of the Spirit), and commended my mother for her evangelistic efforts. Just the week before he had been at my house for banana splits.

****

WHITED SEPULCHRES

Anita Kazee had been a member of the Kittitas Assembly Of God several years. Dismayed by the events surrounding her friends, Wanda Cotton and Pairlee Treat, she wrote the following letter:

****

August 13, 1993

Gary Jeffery
Kittitas Assembly of God
212 N. Main Street
Kittitas, WA 98934

Gary:

If causing faction, division and pain because of gossip are reasons to disfellowship someone from the church body, then I submit that you practice what you preach — as you are guilty of causing more factions, pain and division and generating more gossip than Pairlee or Wanda and all of us put together could have caused ... and you did it from the pulpit in the name of God. What used to be a family is now a divided, upset, confused people who don't even speak to one another.

I also submit that you tried and convicted a widow and a fatherless woman on gossip. Our constitution states that even murderers are "presumed innocent" until PROVEN guilty and they have the right to "...be informed of the nature and cause of the accusation; to be confronted with the witnesses against him; to have compulsory process for obtaining witnesses in his favor..." — they are not convicted on "hearsay". Only in civil infractions are they presumed guilty if they do not appear and that's because the accused is the one who requests the hearing and then if they do not appear they are found "committed"; however no one is called to a hearing in a court of law without knowing what they have been charged with ... and they are given days and even months to prepare their defense. Please do not confuse the world's justice system with the Kittitas Assembly, the secular system is fair and upholds our constitutional rights. Gary, if you are going to make public statements about our justice system, tell the whole story and not just the part that justifies your deeds — Washington state does not recognize "No Contest"; however as you stated, these are the rules of the Kittitas Assembly — which obviously don't have to comply with the Bible, the Constitution, or the State of Washington.

    I also submit that not one of you men on the board would have allowed your wife or daughter to go before a board without your being present — and you would have never allowed Gary to talk to your wife the way he talked to Pairlee and Wanda. You would have told him that if he had anything to say to your wife, he could say it to you. You know that this is true, yet you ordered two women that have no husbands or fathers to stand in their defense to appear within 12 and 24 hours before a board of all men, not even given the right to know what they were charged with or to face their accusers or have witnesses on their behalf. How many of your wives or other women would have come before the board under those circumstances? Gary, how convenient and how well planned — you knew that they would be too upset to appear, and it worked. You worked out your plan quickly to achieve the results that you wanted. If the board really wanted to know the truth, each board member could have called and asked...I asked and I know the truth and the "lying spirit" is certainly not in Pairlee. Why does she have to go behind closed doors? Scripture does not say that you have to go before the "church board" — it says you go before the Body. What are you afraid of the Body hearing? Even the day after your "sermon", Del Kazee and Jerry Marchel went to you and stated that Pairlee and Wanda would be willing to come before the board if they could have just Jerry and Del there for moral support. The end result was that you stated "you'll do it my way and my way only and if you don't like the way this one is run there are

WHITED SEPULCHRES

other churches out there." Seems like anyone who tries to help gets the same answer.

Pairlee and Wanda do not know what they have done and you did not tell them or go to them 3 or 4 times about anything. And if you "disfellowshipped" them to "protect a family in the church" or "protect the accusers" (now isn't that an impartial, loving, statement) as was stated by you and Donna, then why don't they go ahead and do the dastardly deed — what have they got to loose now? This is all such a joke; a very, very cruel joke at the expense of those I love very much. Two people that have been there through the deep valleys of my life and many others in the church, they have always helped and loved and been a part of our body for many years — or at least they thought they were. I am very angry to see them wounded so deeply. I guess this goes along with our "throw away" society where "compassion and unconditional love" aren't considered.

I submit to you that you have ripped our body apart — this same body that the Bible states is one of another and if one suffer we all suffer - this same body that you preached on for weeks on the importance of each "part" — is now bleeding to death internally, while you continue to say everything is just fine.

This is not from God. God would not do this to his children. Jesus said "he that cometh unto me, I will no wise cast out." The Holy Spirit does not bear witness that this is of God. This is of man and it is wrong even to the ungodly...and it is such a good witness to the love of Jesus to all the unsaved. If you wanted to know what was "really" happening to the church body and would sincerely ask so people would not be afraid to tell you what they thought for fear of being told to find another church, as we were and Wanda was — you would know that things aren't just fine. But it seems the truth is not what you want, what you want is control and blind obedience and those that disagree are expendable. It appears that "freedom of speech" is also abridged in the Kittitas Assembly as people are afraid if they express their feelings they will be accused of "gossiping" and we all know what happens to those kind of people — public humiliation and excommunication. Do you know anyone that hasn't ever gossiped? I don't.

I also want to say that there is not a better Christian man or qualified, dedicated Board Member than Jerry Marchel. He shows his faith by his deeds. Anyone can give "lip service", but there is not one person in this church that Jerry has not helped — day or night he is there and not just when it's convenient and looks good...that's why the people go to him and elected him to represent them on the Board for the past 6 years. He shows his faith by loving and helping and not by judgment and self-righteousness. I am so thankful for men like Jerry — for as much as being on the board means to him and no matter how much pressure was put on him to vote your way, he chose to leave the board rather than compromise his sense of righteousness or compassion for his sisters in the Lord. How dare anyone question his salvation.

How could anyone, particularly a church board, sit in judgment on anyone else without any sound evidence — only hearsay. Because until it has been proven, that is exactly what it is...gossip and hearsay and it would seem to me that any person, especially a "Pastor", would have told anyone that came to him with something against his brother to "go to your brother and tell him, don't tell me. And then if he doesn't listen, come to me and I will go with you as a witness." You just don't hear one side before you pass judgment...and that's what you did or actually the board didn't even hear the accusations, they just judged. Pairlee doesn't have enough time in the world to live out the hurt you have caused her — you maligned her character, convicted and executed and then you say you want a hearing...why bother, the damage has been done. Sounds familiar doesn't it...seems like Jesus had one of those same hearings before those "great men" of God — the Pharisees.

WHITED SEPULCHRES

I know that I should not write this letter in anger...but God knows I'm angry, so why lie...I am so angry at what you did to our body...it will never be the same again. I think if Jesus were here, he would tell all those without sin to cast the first stone. As for me, I will take my place among the sinners, because I am one, and Jesus had more tolerance for sinners — even the woman he found committing the act of adultery than he did for the Hypocrites in the church.

Who's next on your list? If it's me, I'll save you the trouble. I want my name removed from that building's membership...I do not want anyone to know now or down through time, that I was ever associated with such heartless cruelty. My heart has no desire to stay in a place where loved ones are callously "thrown away" with no regard for their pain or well being, and you just keep on going like they never existed. Jesus says I came to give life and that more abundantly...and the enemy comes to kill, steal and destroy. Let's call it by name and this certainly is not life more abundantly for Pairlee and Wanda or anyone else that has any compassion or love in their heart for one another. We suffer with them. But of course, it didn't happen to your wife or daughter, so I guess it doesn't concern you.

Gary, if you can stand at the pulpit and tell everyone why Pairlee and Wanda "won't be coming back to this church" without their knowledge or permission, after preaching a sermon on a son sleeping with his mother to make your point of how we must expel the immoral brother, I want you to do the same for me with my permission ... but read my letter — I don't want people assuming that I too must be immoral.

Don't bother to call me before your tribunal. I am not accountable to you.

Anita Kazee

cc: John Konvalin, Randy Bale, Jerry Marchel, Jake Harris, Dale Carpenter, (with tape on sermon) and selected others.

****

ALBERT & AIMEE ANDERSON

After two months of silence, except for confiding in a few select friends from the church, Pairlee wrote the following letter, telling her side of what happened:

****

August 28, 1993

Gary Jeffery
Kittitas Assembly of God
212 S. Main
Kittitas, WA 98934

Gary:

I've given lots of thought before writing this letter, but I feel the church must hear my story. I want the people to know that without any provocation or wrong doing on our part, you have taken such extreme spiteful action against me and my daughter, Wanda. I also want you to know that my rebuttal does not lend any credence to what you have done. You have done wrong.

The night in June when you called me on the phone at 6:00 p.m. telling me to come to a "Board" meeting the next night, I refused because you refused to tell me why. Only after I pressed you for a reason, did you tell me anything. Then in <u>anger</u> you told me what you thought was wrong with me...you accused me of having a "lying spirit" and that I had slandered everyone in the church. This was such a false accusation!

I said, "Pastor, this is not true."
Then you said, "Woman, you have been living under a lying delusion for years."
I asked you to come and talk to me and I said, "I'll go before the church."
You said, "No, you'll come before the Board." Then you said, "do you know what this means?"
I said, "No, I don't know."
You said, "If you do not submit and come before the Board and let us deliver you of this evil

spirit, it means you will never be allowed to step your foot inside the church again."
 I said, "Pastor, you can't do this."
 You said again, "don't you let me ever see you step your foot inside the church again."

The next day you called my eldest daughter, Wanda, and told her to come to the Board meeting. When she refused, you said to her, "I'm sorry you choose to align yourself with an <u>evil spirit,</u>" meaning me, her mother. Of course you had already the past Sunday ordered her to find another church because she had asked you about going to visit Ruth Townley, a sick older woman in the church and told you that you should visit everyone in the church. But for you to use a conniving, conspiratorial approach to try and put a wedge between me and my daughter was so wicked and cruel!
 You've told people in the church that since I didn't submit and come before your men of the Board, that God had shown you I was going to DIE...THAT MY HEART WOULD JUST STOP AND I'D JUST DROP DEAD! Why do you want me to die? Why did you want Wanda and me out of the church? It is not true that I'm "possessed with a lying spirit" or that I've "slandered anyone." This is a falsehood. Why are you saying such things? Is it to bring the people under fear, so they will obey you when you decide to call them before the "tribunal"? How can this be of God? Now if you, as my pastor, had come to me 3 or 4 times as you said you did and that you have "done everything correct scripturally" then why don't I know about it?
 <u>You know, and I know, and God knows</u> you have not done so — you never came to me. NO, NOT ONE TIME DID YOU COME TO ME TO SAY I HAD DONE ANYTHING WRONG OR THAT YOU OR ANYONE ELSE HAD OUGHT AGAINST ME! AND YOU NEVER CAME TO ME <u>WITH ANYONE ABOUT ME.</u> You brought Jerry Marchel to my house one night to tell me how very <u>wrong he was</u> and how Jerry had sinned. You never once even by remote inference said I had done anything wrong, nor did you tell me that you had "eight things against me in the record you kept about me." You've only told this to other people

and in the sermon you preached on June 13th, "The Excommunication Day" when you publicly before the entire church and community, maligned, castigated, slandered and defamed my name and my daughter Wanda's name. That Ex Post Facto Exposition you called a sermon in which you used scripture to accuse, demean, demote, demoralize, damn and disgrace us. You accused us of horrible habitual sin using the scripture about the "man sleeping with his father's wife"! How could you by inference and suggestive insinuation imply we were guilty of sin, let alone such gross, horrible, detestable sexual sin!

I recall many times in your past sermons you have said how so very mean you used to be and how you would do such mean, cruel, hateful things to people — and all this even though you were a Christian. Well, when did you change? Seems to me this mean thing is your worst one yet.

How could you judge me as unfit and unworthy of taking communion on that last Sunday I was allowed to be in church (you told people because I took communion that was "your sign" you had to put me out of the church). Why? What a dreadful thing you have done. What irreparable damage you have done to the entire church and to us. I trusted you. I thought you were my pastor. I thought you cared for me and my family. But how mistaken I have been. You've told people you've had things on me from "day one" and how you have it all "down in your computer." You've also said you came here on a special mission and that you were "gonna die here." Is your mission here for the purpose of casting out of the church all of the faithful Christians? Those that have walked with the Lord many more years than you have lived? And all those who would stand against error and false teaching?

How could you be so mean and brazen on Sunday the 13th of June to tell the entire church that by our not coming before your "Board" and I quote you, "Your God appointed, Holy Spirit filled, speaking in tongues, Board," that it meant we were guilty? No, we are not guilty...YOU ARE GUILTY because you have not done what God's word says to do. How did *you think you could be God and judge, convict, condemn, slander (libelous slander at that) and execute and cast out two of God's children from the Body of Christ and that there would be no repercussions? Do you think this is going to cause a mighty move of God and that all the people in the church will suddenly become perfect? And that people were going to just begin to flow into the church? But in your excommunication sermon you said that when this all begins to happen you would cast others out of the church.*

Who will be next? How many more are on your list? Because you said you are getting rid of all the "old leaven" — or did you mean the "older people," like me? God did not appoint you a judge or convictor. No. That is the work of God and the Holy Spirit. Not you!

Did you use me and Wanda as your first example so as to put dreadful fear into the people's hearts so they would never dare to question nor disobey you? So they would know what to expect from you, their pastor, who can wield such power. To deny anyone the right to come to church, which is a public place operating as a tax free, open door house of worship for "whosoever will may come". The church I thought was for all members and non-members alike. I am not a member, yet you have denied me the right to come. With all you have done to me and Wanda how can any one of your followers feel safe and secure? How can they not fear that they too will be subjected to public ridicule and humiliation and excommunication? Is anyone safe with you in power?

You stood there on June 13th and told the people an intentional untruth, absolute falsehood, when you said "<u>they</u> will say we threw them out of the church," when that is exactly what you did. Of course, you threw me out over the phone and you threw Wanda out of the church behind closed doors where, as planned, there were no witnesses. As you said in your condemnation sermon, "I set this up on purpose". It sure was a set up. But, God, who sees all and knows all, is our judge, not you, Gary Jeffery! And, God will surely hold you accountable for all the discord and upheaval you have caused in the church.

You have turned friends and fellow believers against one another and instructed them to avoid, shun and not even eat with us! How could you show such disrespect to me, a recent widow and elderly woman? Have you no respect for others at all? Not to mention no love, which is the very essence of God.

You said you were "turning me over to satan and that after I was out in the world and out of the church, and away from Christian fellowship, I'd come to my senses." Was this another fear tactic? <u>I've not been away from God, for He holds me in the hollow of His Hand</u>.

What gross fear you have put on people. You have put Big Stumbling Blocks before so many of the young tender lambs who have just come to know the Lord Jesus. Seems it's time for the "millstone to be hanging".

How wrong you were to take God's Holy Word out of context, wresting the scriptures for your own aims and purposes to make you seem so right and others so wrong. When you made the decision privately to throw us out of the church and then call your board together and say it was for the purpose of "affirming our decision". How ludicrous, how absurd.

The board are men, some of whom I've known and highly respected for years. Men who I know love God. Men who always endeavor to do what is right and pleasing before God, but somehow you got them to go along with you without even knowing what your charges against me were, that is, all except Jerry Marchel, who would not vote me out. If you had truly wanted to do the right thing, you would have come to me, as the Bible instructs, but you did not.

The people should know that when you came here you were committed from the start to eliminate, cast out and disfellowship certain people. You came with a biased attitude against some of us. Did you listen to gossip against us? You have been a good actor. You let us believe you loved us, but you *have betrayed many and have engendered division, schism, bitterness, murmuring, and strife within the Body of Believers at Kittitas Assembly. Did you think Wanda and Pairlee were so insignificant and unimportant that God nor anyone else would care? Or that your actions against us would not affect others? How can it ever be healed? How can it ever be resolved?*

My trust is in God, who is the Judge of <u>all</u> and the rewarder of them who diligently seek Him. My Faith, my confidence is in Jesus, who will never leave me, nor forsake me, for He is my Savior and My Redeemer.

Pairlee

cc: John Konvalin, Randy Bale, Jake Harris, Jerry Marchel, Pastor Dale Carpenter and selected others

****

ALBERT & AIMEE ANDERSON

Although Jerry Marchel continued to attend services at the Kittitas Assembly, his wife, Phyllis, had refused to take part in that church until the wrongs against Pairlee and Wanda were corrected. The following letters were written by her to the pastor and the board:

****

September 29, 1993

Dear Pastor Jeffery and Board,

After much prayer and listening to God through "His Word", I cannot meet with you until the oppression that you have imposed on a 72 year old, grieving, (lost her husband eleven months before) widow woman has been corrected.

Zechariah warned the people about oppressing widows, orphans, foreigners and the poor. The message God gave through Zechariah, was for them to be merciful and kind to everyone. For them to stop oppressing the widows, orphans, foreigners and the poor or God's great wrath would come down on them. (Zechariah 7:8-14)

In the book of James, God the Father says that the Christian who is pure and without fault, is the one who takes care of widows and orphans.

I cannot take part in this church until this sin has been corrected.

I love all of you,

Phyllis Marchel

P.S. Please post this letter on the back bulletin board, so the congregation will know why I'm not attending. Thank you.

****

WHITED SEPULCHRES

Phyllis Marchel wrote the following letter to Executive Presbyter Dale Carpenter the very next day:

****

September 30, 1993

Pastor Dale Carpenter
The Stone Church
Yakima, WA

Dear Pastor Carpenter:

When I talked to you on the phone a couple of weeks ago, you told me to stay in the Kittitas Assembly of God Church. Because of the circumstances that are going on there, as a Christian, I cannot be a part of the sin that has and is being committed there.

My husband Jerry and I were married in the Kittitas Assembly of God Church thirty-seven years ago. Jerry has attended that church since he was a small boy.

We have always loved and backed the Pastors of this church. We are still good friends with former Pastors and their families. The Dittys, Johnsons, Cousarts and the Fountains. Pastor Gary Fountain and his wife Debbie, along with their children were here from Homedale, Idaho, a couple months ago, where Pastor Fountain is Pastoring. We had a birthday party for Debbie and Rachel in our home while they were visiting us.

I asked Jerry to stop at the church and leave a copy of this letter. I'm enclosing one for you with Pastor Jeffery because I had tried to talk to him on the phone a while back, explaining what I thought about the circumstances going on in the church. He said, "it really doesn't matter what you think, we're moving on."

He said he was sent to this church on a mission and he was going to accomplish it!

Jerry left the letter with him yesterday. Pastor Jeffery said to Jerry, "It is over, give me the letter and take a hike buddy!"

A petition will be sent to you shortly with signatures. This petition is only for your help in getting this church back in God's will.

Sincerely,

Phyllis Marchel

****

WHITED SEPULCHRES

Phyllis attempted to read the following to the congregation of the Kittitas Assembly during the October 13, 1994 special business meeting at the church, but was rudely interrupted by Don Strong, one of the Northwest District presbyters officiating, and was forbidden to continue:

****

On the evening of Thursday, June 10th, I was sitting in our living room talking to my sister who was visiting from out-of-town.

Jerry came home from the board meeting and I knew something was wrong by the look he had on his face. I asked him what was wrong, and he said, "It's awful, I can't talk about it," and he went into our bedroom. I got up and went in to talk to him, and he was sitting on the edge of the bed crying. I put my arms around him and said "what's wrong honey?" He said, "I can't talk about it—it's so awful."

I went back into the living room and called one of the other board members, John Konvalin, to see what had happened. John said, "Phyllis, my stomach is in knots and I can't even look up. I'm so upset, but I can't talk about it. You had better call the Pastor."

I didn't because it was getting so late and I thought I had better wait until the next day.

The next morning, Pastor Jeffery called me and said he wanted to talk to me about the meeting the night before. I told him, "Yes, I want to know what had happened." He told me to get my Bible, that he was going to read to me the Scripture that he had read to the board regarding the issue on Pairlee and Wanda. I got my Bible and followed along as he read. Then I said, "Pastor, what was Jerry so upset about? Jerry told me it had happened at the end of the meeting." Pastor said, "I'll get to it in a minute, I have a few more scriptures to read!" When he was finished I said, "What was Jerry so upset about?" Pastor Jeffery said, "Well, God has revealed to me that if Pairlee doesn't repent and come before the board and myself, she is going to die." Then I said, "Pastor, wait a minute. I believe God's scriptures, but you're just a man and you say, 'God told you Pairlee is going to die?' I've known other Pastors who have been in the wrong — 2 of them being Jimmy Swaggart and Jim Baker." I said, "Pastor, I only go by God's Word."

Pastor Jeffery then said, "Well, it's good you feel that way, but I'm just warning you, so when it happens you won't be shocked, but Pairlee is going to die, her heart is just going to stop, not a heart attack — God is just going to kill her."

Sunday, June 13th the sermon was on church discipline and that Pairlee and Wanda would no longer be coming back to this church.

Pastor had said it was not a matter of option — but a condition — that they had to come before him and the board.

Pastor Jeffery said, "the bottom line is Pairlee and Wanda will not be coming back to this church."

I was upset over this whole thing. I love Pairlee and Wanda. They've always been loving and kind to me. They're not perfect — neither am I or any of you.

I've prayed much over this situation. I've read God's Word and I'm so impressed that a wrong has been done to Pairlee, a widow who lost her husband Otis eleven months before and to Wanda who was still grieving over the loss of her dad. God kept reminding me of His great love for us and that we were to love one another.

I didn't go to church for 2 weeks. I stayed home and watched TBN, the Christian Broadcasting station on television.

Pastor Jeffery called me after the second week and asked if I was alright. I said, "Yes, I'm alright." He asked again if I was alright. I repeated the same thing, "I am fine." When he asked the third time, I said, "Well no, Pastor, I'm really not alright, I believe the situation with Pairlee and Wanda was handled wrong." I told him, "I have prayed much and read God's Word and that very morning while I was praying, God brought to my mind the fruit of the spirit which is, "Love, Joy, Peace, Patience, Kindness, Goodness, Faithfulness, Gentleness and Self-Control." I said, "Pastor, I don't believe this was done in gentleness and kindness. I believe it was handled wrong."

Pastor Jeffery's voice got stern and he said, "It really doesn't matter what you think, it's not going to change a thing. We're moving on."

Phyllis

****

ALBERT & AIMEE ANDERSON

Bonnie Clement mailed the following letter to all members and frequent attendees of the Kittitas Assembly of God after the October 13, 1993 business meeting with Northwest District Presbyters Dale Carpenter and Don Strong. (Two months later, under oath during a deposition one of the board members, said this letter caused souls to be lost.)

****

October 15, 1993

Dear Brothers and Sisters in Christ:

> *"What does the Lord require of you? To act justly and to love mercy and to walk humbly with your God. (Micah 6:6-8) NIV*
>
> *"A new command I give you: Love one another. As I have loved you, so you must love one another. By this all men will know that you are my disciples, if you love one another. (John 13:34-35) NIV*

I am sick at heart over what transpired in the meeting Wednesday night, October 13. God's Word admonishes us to love one another, to act justly, to love mercy and to walk humbly with Him. All four admonitions were violated at that meeting.

There were many of us voting members — who attended that meeting hoping that Wanda's and Pairlee's side of the sin they have been accused of would be faced openly in front of the church. So that the membership — not just the Administrative Board — could make a determination of what course of action should be taken, if any, against these two women. Instead, the only issue, which was allowed by the Presbyters was whether or not the Pastor and the Administrative Board followed the by-laws correctly.

I would like to point out that the section of the By-Laws, which was used referred to the discipline of members. If Wanda and Pairlee were not and are not members, then the issue should not be whether the Pastor and the Administrative Board had acted correctly according to the By-Laws, since the By-Laws did not pertain to them. The issue should have been to let these two women appear before the church — voting membership, not just a small group of leaders — to face their accusers, to repent if they were in the wrong, and to be reconciled with the body of Believers. The Presbyters, the Pastor and the Administrative Board did not act justly, nor did they love mercy, for if they were obedient to those admonitions, Wanda and Pairlee would have been called in, as many voting members repeatedly requested during the meeting. Why has this issue been skirted time and time again? Are the leaders afraid that they may have acted wrongly against these women?

There is not one person in this congregation who is without sin. If we are to be obedient to our Lord, we must humble ourselves before Him and be willing to let the truth — no matter how painful it may be — be told, from both sides. What has happened to Wanda and Pairlee and the way the meeting was conducted Wednesday night are not examples of obedience to love one another as Christ has loved us.

If this had been a case of discipline done entirely as God has ordained in His Word, Kittitas Assembly would not be in the turmoil it is today. Godly discipline done in love reconciles, strengthens, and pulls together congregations. This so-called "discipline" has had the opposite effect. There is something very wrong here. There is something very wrong when young people who had been on fire for the Lord are confused over what is happening and begin dropping out. There is something very wrong when people who have been members of Kittitas Assembly for many years are being wounded by words said to them by their pastor. There is something very wrong when Godly parents tell their children not to come to Kittitas Assembly any more.

In the name of Christ, I implore everyone — the Pastor, the Administrative Board, the Presbyters, members and non-members alike, whoever has been part of or touched by this situation — to examine our actions in light of Scripture. Let us be willing to humble ourselves before the Lord with broken hearts over what has been happening in our body of Believers; and let us confess and repent of our individual sins, ask forgiveness of God and of each other, and be reconciled to one another. Let us stop this attack of Satan on Kittitas Assembly by removing ourselves as the implements of that attack.

In the Name of Jesus Christ, our Lord and Savior,

Bonnie Clement

****

WHITED SEPULCHRES

Jerry Marchel had verbally resigned from his position on the Administrative Board of Kittitas Assembly of God, but he had continued to attend church regularly every Sunday. At the urging of concerned former members and attendees, he submitted the following letter:

****

October 25, 1993

Gary and Donna Jeffery
Randy Bale
Jake Harris
John Konvalin

I hereby rescind my verbal resignation from the Administrative Board of Kittitas Assembly of God. That verbal resignation was said out of dismay and fear over the decision made about Pairlee Treat and Wanda Cotton. As I have been voted to serve on the Board by the voting membership of Kittitas Assembly of God, I believe I can best serve that membership by remaining on the Board and not letting my feelings interfere. Furthermore, no written recognition has ever been made regarding my verbal statement.

As a member of the Administrative Board of Kittitas Assembly of God, I am seeking a way in which the rift that has occurred in the congregation over the decision made by the four of you can be mended. There are distressed people on both sides of the issue, good Christian people who are hurt and saddened by what has taken place. This should not be! The meeting held October 13, 1993, with Dale Carpenter and Don Strong did not resolve the problem; it only inflamed it. I have been contacted by several concerned voting members and non-voting regular attendees. We desire that there would be a meeting of everyone, including Pairlee Treat and Wanda Cotton, so this issue can be discussed in an open, loving and forgiving atmosphere.

ALBERT & AIMEE ANDERSON

    Therefore, on behalf of all concerned members and non-member attendees of Kittitas Assembly of God, the four of you are invited to meet with us on Thursday, November 11, 1993, at 7:00 p.m., in the Community Hall in Kittitas. We have chosen the hall as a neutral place for all concerned because of the sensitive nature of what has happened and the number of people who have been hurt, who have no desire to enter the church building under the present circumstances.

    Please call me at 968-3406 and let me know that you will attend this meeting. Our only desire is to bring restoration and reconciliation to the body of Believers at Kittitas Assembly of God.

Sincerely in the Name of Christ,

Jerry Marchel

cc: Dale Carpenter
   Northwest District Council of the Assemblies of God
   General Council of the Assemblies of God

****

WHITED SEPULCHRES

The following article appeared in the Friday, November 26, 1993 issue of the *Daily Record*, the local newspaper published in Ellensburg, Washington. Mr. Keith Love graciously gave us permission to reprint this and other articles concerning this situation.

****

CHURCH SQUABBLE ERUPTED INTO ALTERCATION AT Sunday service

By Mike Johnston
City Editor

A five-month long church dispute spilled into the public arena when City of Kittitas police were called to the Assembly of God Church shortly before noon on Nov. 14. The visit was in response to a fight reported during the Sunday morning worship service.

As a follow-up to that incident, two city officers were instructed to standby at the city police station last Sunday in case there was another disturbance, but the worship service concluded without incident, according to Kittitas Mayor Mel Wilson.

Officer Vernon Rosa said that when he and Reserve Officer Gary Moore arrived at the church Nov. 14 the altercation was over. Rosa took statements from 12 people and said there were no injuries.

Rosa said he was later contacted by the church's pastor, Gary Jeffery, who told him he had been assaulted and threatened, but wanted to check with his attorney before deciding whether to pursue assault charges. After speaking with an attorney for the region's Assembly of God churches, Jeffery decided not to pursue charges.

"I'm into peace and restoring people," Jeffery said. "I want peace and harmony in the church. It's too bad that some (people) created an environment of fear and violence."

But others believe it's the pastor and board's past action that is the root of the problem.

A group of about 17 former church members and others came to services that morning at the church on Main Street in Kittitas, intending to read letters to the congregation.

The letters had been sent from Jeffery and church board members to former board member Jerry Marchel and his wife, Phyllis. They state that their church memberships had been revoked by the board due to their disagreement with church leadership.

One letter alleges that actions by Jerry Marchel were having an adverse effect on the church: "What you have chosen to do is to malign and degrade the ministry here." Marchel denies the allegation.

Jerry Marchel, 58, said he and others disagree with the way the pastor and church board excluded two women, Pairlee Treat and her daughter Wanda Cotton, who were not members, from attending the church. Marchel said the women never knew who was accusing them of misconduct.

Treat, 71, said she has attended the church for 14 years. Cotton, 52, has attended for four years.

According to Jeffery, church rules were followed and efforts to meet with the two women privately have not been successful.

"All we want is a fair hearing before both members and non-members for the people who have been accused," said Anita Kazee, a former member who called police from the church during the Nov. 14 service. "We have not had due process of law. We want a chance to have the people hear the accusers face the accused."

"We just wanted to let others know the truth about what's been going on," said Jerry Marchel. "A lot of people didn't know what had happened to me and my wife. We're not in rebellion, we just don't agree with kicking a widow and her daughter out of the church. But I really don't believe anyone wanted what happened after we tried to read the letters in an orderly way."

Others, including Pastor Jeffery and board members, saw the actions at the Sunday service as a disruption to the service. Jeffery said he told those who wanted to read the letters from the board to Marchel, that they were out of order. When they insisted the letters be read, he declared the service over and asked people to join him in prayer.

There are different versions as to what occurred at the service, but most reported there was shouting and some brief grappling, pushing and shoving. People on both sides claim they were physically assaulted, though not seriously.

Jim Boswell, Marchel's son-in-law from Snohomish, said the pastor kneeled in prayer after dismissing the service and he bent down to talk to him. He said the only time he touched the pastor was when he put a finger under his chin and lifted his face up so the two could see eye to eye.

"That touching him wasn't an assault," Boswell said. "If he calls it an assault he's wrong." He also denies that he verbally threatened Jeffery.

Boswell also claims that he was assaulted by someone, though he has not pressed an assault complaint either.

Jeffery declined to comment on why the two women were not allowed to attend services or why the Marchels' church membership was taken away. He said it was a confidential church matter.

Marchel claims he and his wife were removed from membership because they disagreed with the pastor and the board's action. One former church member said attempts are being made to call in district or national Assembly of God leaders to mediate the situation.

"It's an internal church difficulty created by some disgruntled people who don't like me as a pastor," said Jeffery. "The whole thing is very sad, very sad." Jeffery, 39, has been the pastor at the church for a year and eight months. He has been an Assembly of God Church minister since 1974.

****

At the request of Jeff Slothower, Attorney, Phyllis Marchel wrote down her reasons for attending the Kittitas Assembly of God Church on November 14, 1993:

****

Jerry and I had received certified letters on Monday, November 8th, telling us our memberships were removed from the church. My removal was because I was not in harmony with the leadership of the church. Jerry's letter stated that Jerry had a bad life style and because of his conduct his membership was removed.

Iva Steigleder had called me on Friday, November 12, telling me that Pastor Gary Jeffery had notified them on the phone that, because Iva and her husband, Mike, were not in submission to his authority, all their privileges were taken away. Iva could no longer teach the adult Sunday School class or greet people at the door. Mike was no longer grounds or building overseer.

Jerry said, "he was still going to church on Sunday." He had attended that church since he was a little boy and he was going back. I had not attended that church since August 8th, but Jerry had been going almost every Sunday.

I told Jerry I was afraid for him. I thought Gary Jeffery might have him bodily thrown out. I decided I would not let him go alone. I would go in support of Jerry and also to tell the people in the congregation what Pastor Gary Jeffery had done to Iva and Mike Steigleder.

I told our children and some of our friends that I was going to go to church to support Jerry. He had never done anything wrong and Pastor Gary Jeffery had been treating Jerry badly ever since Jerry would not vote to have Pairlee and Wanda kicked out of the church.

****

Two days after the scuffle took place at the Sunday service, Don Strong, Sectional Presbyter of the Northwest District of the Assemblies of God, Randell Bale, board member at the Kittitas Assembly, and Gary Jeffery, pastor, wrote the following letter to Jim Hansen, Attorney:

****

KITTITAS ASSEMBLY OF GOD
P. O. Box 929, 212 Main Street
Kittitas, WA 98934

November 16, 1993

Rev. Jim Hansen, Attorney
Assemblies of God
P. O. Box 699
Kirkland, Washington 98083

Dear Jim,

Choice greetings! I have stayed overnight at Kittitas A/G parsonage with Pastor Gary and Donna Jeffery and we are writing this letter to inform you of the events that happened during the Sunday morning service, November 14th.

Pastor Jeffery called me Sunday afternoon and told me what had happened so I left immediately and was with them in the service last night. We had a great, great service last night and the church is full of good people and the blessing of God is there! We need your council as to what we should do in regard to what happened in the morning service.

To give you some background, Pastor Jeffery and the Official Board disciplined a sister who is a non-member last June and she has pretty much stirred up everything since that time. This lady, Pairlee Treat, has been the source of most of the trouble in the Assembly of God churches in the area for the past 20 to 30 years! The Board invited her to a special hearing and she refused to come. Instead, she wrote letters to the congregation and young people and gathered others around her in an all-out effort to force Pastor Jeffery to leave Kittitas. After several Board meetings, Pastor Jeffery called me. Dale Carpenter and myself went up for a special business meeting on Oct 20th. We had all three Board members speak and went through the entire matter and found the Pastor and Board had stayed within the By-laws and the Word of God on every instance. The meeting was for the members only but some of these non-members insisted on staying and caused us some difficulty in the meeting. Pastor Carpenter and I concluded almost all the membership and all three Board members were 100% behind Pastor Jeffery.

One of the Board Members who resigned on June 19th, in protest of the disciplining of this woman wrote a letter to the Church and Board stating that he was rescinding his resignation and would be to the Board Meeting on November 2nd. He showed up at the Board Meeting and the board members refused to let him stay. A group of 17 people came to the Sunday Morning service yesterday. 12 of these 17 people have never been members of Kittitas Assembly of God. Of the remaining 5, 1 resigned their membership on August 16, and the former board member and his wife had their names removed on November 2nd, after his angry attack toward the Pastor and Board. These 17 people all jumped up in the middle of the service and began yelling at the Pastor, Board Members and other people. Pastor Jeffery and Jake Harris echoed the same for a congregational prayer and the pianist went up and began playing choruses. The angry people swarmed to the platform, pulled at the piano player on the bench, turned off the mics and grabbed Pastor Jeffery. All of the supporting people pretty well held their cool, did not hit anyone and made a circle around the Pastor in prayer. Some of the 17 people began hitting and shoving people and so someone went out and called the police. Pastor Jeffery went back to his office and 7 of these people followed him in and cornered him and threatened his life. The police came and talked to some of the people. As I said before none of them attended the Sunday night service and the glory of God was manifested in a most unusual way.

Jim, we need your council. We don't know what to do. The whole Board and congregation, Pastor Jeffery and his wife, Donna, are all determined to go forward with this remaining church of about 80 people. There seems to be no way that we can make peace with these 17 people since they want the removal of Pastor Jeffery. This has happened so many times in the past that the congregation and Board feel they cannot go on if they lose another Pastor.

Should a restraining order be given to these people? We are very reluctant to do this because new people are coming into the church and a spirit of revival prevails. But we are concerned about this threat on Pastor Jeffery's life because it was made by one of these people who is unstable and has been known to carry a gun at times. Pastor Gary is not afraid and has a peace about continuing on as Pastor of this Church. As his Presbyter, I am very concerned about this whole matter and this threat in particular. We are sending copies of this letter to Brother Cole and Brother Carpenter. We need wisdom from all three of you! We look forward to hearing from you hopefully this week before Sunday!

I remain prayerfully yours and have asked Pastor Jeffery and one of the Board Members to sign this letter with me attesting to it's accuracy.

Sincerely,

Rev. Don Strong

DS/dj
Randell W. Bale
Gary E. Jeffery

****

ALBERT & AIMEE ANDERSON

On November 19, several people from the Kittitas Assembly of God signed a letter addressed to both the Northwest District and the General Council of the Assemblies of God. This letter was mailed on November 22, 1993. Members still in good standing, together with members who had been removed from the church roster and concerned non-members, signed the letter. This letter read as follows:

****

November 19, 1993

Rev. Elmer E. Kirschman
Secretary-Treasurer
Northwest District Council of the
Assemblies of God
Box 699
Kirkland, WA 98083-0699

AND

Rev. Thomas E. Trask
General Superintendent
General Council of the Assemblies of God
1445 Booneville Avenue
Springfield, MO 65802-1894

Dear Rev. Kirschman and Rev. Trask:

We prayerfully and respectfully come to you requesting your help in settling a serious dispute which has resulted in a division in the Kittitas Assembly of God. We also request intervention, putting this church under Home Missions rule, until this dispute can be settled. (Article VI.A, sections c. and d. of the Bylaws of the Northwest District Council) Of those who have signed this letter, some of us are (or were until recently) voting members and others are not voting members, but have been part of the Kittitas Assembly for many years. Our status is indicated after our names. Some who have been voting members for many years have had their membership removed in recent weeks because they were "not in harmony" with the pastor.

There is evidence that the pastor, Gary Jeffrey, is using dictatorial authority, intimidation and condemnation to get people in the church to do things his way (Article VI.A, sections c. and d. of the Bylaws of the Northwest District Council). Those who do not agree with him are accused of being out of harmony, aligning themselves with evil spirits, and even told they will die if they do not submit to his authority. Furthermore, they are having their membership and/or ministry suspended.

There appears to have been a rush of new memberships in recent months of people who will support the pastor, while people who have been voting members for several years are having their memberships removed. We request that an investigation be made to determine who were voting members as of the last business meeting in February, 1993. We also request that all new memberships that have been given since February, 1993, be put on hold until the following events can be looked into:

Following is a summary of events which have occurred since June, 1993:

June 6, 1993

Wanda Cotton confronted Gary Jeffrey about not visiting a member of the church, Ruth Townley, who had been ill for several months. He told Wanda to find another church. (Exhibit A)

June 10, 1993

The pastor and board members met in an emergency meeting to discuss the expulsion of Wanda Cotton and her mother, Pairlee Treat. He told the board that the women had been engaged in slander and gossip, and that he had tried to talk with them about it. He wanted them to come before the board and face charges. Since they refused to come, he considered them to be in rebellion and therefore should not be allowed to fellowship at Kittitas Assembly until they repented. He told the board God told him Pairlee would die if she did not submit to him and the board. Jerry Marchel disagreed with the severity of the action and pleaded with the pastor to counsel with the women. Jerry was told that if he aligned himself with Pairlee, he was aligning himself with an evil spirit and would die. Jerry Marchel verbally resigned from the Board.

June 13, 1993

Gary Jeffrey preached a sermon about sin in the Corinthian church — sin of fornication. He also emphasized that the sinning person was cast out of fellowship with the purpose of bringing him to repentance, forgiveness and reconciliation. Immediately afterwards he announced that Wanda Cotton and Pairlee Treat would not be attending Kittitas Assembly any more because they were in sin and refused to meet with the Administrative Board regarding their sins of gossip and slander. He again emphasized that the purpose of church discipline was to bring repentance and reconciliation and to eventually restore the sinning ones to fellowship. He also said the Board had been in total agreement with him on this action. Jerry Marchel, a member of the board at that meeting, stood and said he had not agreed with this action taken against the two women. Del Kazee, an adherent member and long-time friend of the women, wanted to know exactly what these two women had done which warranted such severe action. The pastor would not say, only that there were eight or nine things, which he had on his computer.

August 13, 1993

Anita Kazee wrote a letter protesting the procedure used to expel two women from the church. A copy of this letter is attached. (Exhibit B)

August 29, 1993

Pairlee Treat broke her silence and sent a letter to the pastor, board and selected other members of Kittitas Assembly of God. This letter refutes the story told by Gary Jeffrey from the pulpit. (Exhibit C)

September 14, 1993

A petition requesting help from the Presbyters was drawn up and signed by twelve voting members still on the church roster and by Anita Kazee, who had resigned her membership because of the June 13th announcement. This petition requested help from the District in mediating the situation for the purposes of healing and reconciliation. This petition was hand delivered to Dale Carpenter's secretary at The Stone Church in Yakima. (Exhibit D)

September 16, 1993

The board members announced from the pulpit that they requested a special meeting with the District Presbyters. The time and date would be announced by letter.

September 29, 1993

Phyllis Marchel wrote a letter to the pastor and board expressing her anguish over the treatment of Pairlee. She told them that she could "not take part in this church until this injustice had been corrected." She asked that this letter be posted on the bulletin board in the church. It was never posted. A copy of this letter, as well as a copy of a letter to Dale Carpenter and a copy of some journal-type entries made by Phyllis during this time are enclosed. (Exhibits E, F and G)

ALBERT & AIMEE ANDERSON

October 5, 1993

 Letters were mailed to members announcing a special business meeting. (Exhibit H)

October 13, 1993

 Dale Carpenter and Don Strong met with the Kittitas Assembly voting members. They stated they were there at the request of the pastor and the board. They further said they had received a petition, but because there were not enough signatures by voting members and one signature was by a person who had resigned, the petition was not valid. (At the time the petition was signed, there were 38 or 40 voting members; twelve signatures would have constituted 30 percent, enough to meet the requirements of the by-laws of both Kittitas Assembly and the Northwest District.)
 The only issue the Presbyters would allow discussion on was whether the pastor and board had followed proper procedure in disciplining Wanda Cotton and Pairlee Treat, according to the By-laws of Kittitas Assembly of God. Several people, voting members and a few adherent members who attended, asked that Wanda and Pairlee be allowed to come before the body to face their accusers. Matthew 18:17-19 was quoted to back this request. The request was denied. Heated discussion followed, but the Presbyters were unbending. Those in support of the pastor's and board's action were allowed to speak; those who asked for disclosure of the truth were told to sit down and be quiet. Iva Steigleder, a godly woman of 80 and one of the founding members of Kittitas Assembly, wanted to share a message she believed was from the Lord. She was told she could do so later on in the meeting. A few minutes before 9:00 p.m., Don Strong announced he saw no problem and the matter was settled as far as he was concerned. He said the pastor and board had acted properly. Iva Steigleder again stood and asked to share the message she had, and was told she had already spoken and was told to "sit down and be quiet."

When the Presbyters were asked to heed Matthew 18:17-19, they refused, saying the only issue was whether the board and pastor had followed the Kittitas Assembly Constitution and Bylaws, which the voting membership had voted in.

October 15, 1993

A letter from Bonnie Clement was sent to everyone in the church, asking for examination of what took place October 13 in light of Scripture. A copy of this letter and some of the responses are attached. There is an unsettling similarity to several of the responses. (Exhibits I, J, K, L and M)

October 25, 1993

Jerry Marchel sent a letter to the pastor and board rescinding his verbal resignation. He said he resigned because of fear of the pastor's statement that anyone who did not agree with the pastor on the discipline of Wanda and Pairlee would die. Furthermore, since Jerry had been voted into office by the congregation, he felt he could better serve the people by staying on the board. (Exhibit N)

November 2, 1993

Jerry Marchel attended the board meeting. The pastor told him the letter rescinding his resignation didn't mean a thing. Jeff Gorman, not a board member, took over the meeting at that point and accused Jerry of being ignorant. Approximately thirty minutes of that meeting was captured on tape.

November 7, 1993

Jerry Marchel received a certified letter signed by Gary Jeffrey stating that his membership at Kittitas Assembly of God "has been removed per Church By-Laws Article II, Section 5 (D)." The reason for this action was stated as a "review of (his) conduct and lifestyle as a member" revealed that he had chosen to "malign and degrade the ministry" and that his attitude at the membership meeting with the District Officials was "deplorable." (Exhibits O and P)

November 12, 1993

Mike and Iva Steigleder received a call from Gary Jeffrey. They were told since they are not in harmony with the church leadership, Iva would no longer be allowed to teach the adult Sunday School class or be a greeter at the door on Sunday mornings. Mike was told he would no longer be allowed to be in charge of maintenance of the grounds. At least two of the board members, John Konvalin and Jake Harris, did not know this action was going to be taken. Mike Steigleder is one of the founders of Kittitas Assembly of God and he and his wife have been faithful members for fifty years.

November 13, 1993

Jerry Marchel's daughter called the pastor and tried to talk with him about the letter her parents received. Gary Jeffrey refused to discuss it with her and hung up.

November 14, 1993

Several people who had stopped attending Kittitas Assembly because of the situation with Wanda Cotton and Pairlee Treat attended the service to lend support for Jerry and Phyllis Marchel and for Mike and Iva Steigleder. After the worship songs, Jerry's son, Chris, daughter Sherry Boswell and son-in-law Jim Boswell stood and asked to read the letters which had been sent to their parents. Gary Jeffrey told them they were out of order and to sit down. When they did not sit down, he dismissed the service. Pleas were made for the congregation to listen to what was going on, what was happening to people who had been members ever since the early days of the church. People in support of the pastor's actions surrounded him. He did not acknowledge nor answer any questions put to him. One of his supporters grabbed Jerry Marchel's son-in-law, Jim Boswell, and Jerry's son, Chris, was shoved off the stage. The ensuing scuffle knocked over microphone stands and the podium.

The police were called and took a report on what happened. This was not what anyone wanted. Emotions were running high because several attempts to talk with the pastor and board and board members were met with refusal to discuss the situation or with outright rudeness. People on both sides of the issue did and said things which were not glorifying to God.

Besides the above listed events, some of the teens who left the church several months ago have begun to come forward with some disturbing stories about what took place in the Sunday School, Youth Group and Drama Team meetings. Donna Jeffery is the youth pastor, and, from what these young people have told, has used guilt, condemnation and intimidation to make the young people "toe the line." One time she held up her dog and said she loved the youth so much she would be willing to slit her dog's throat to prove how much she loved them. One 15-year-old girl, Katie Letson, was detained in the pastor's house for approximately one hour and not allowed to leave while both Gary and Donna Jeffery "disciplined" her by yelling and screaming at her. This was done without her mother's knowledge nor permission. Another young girl, a foster child who had been placed with Jerry and Phyllis Marchel, was provoked by Donna Jeffery. Donna told Phyllis that she was trying to get her so angry that "she would have to be held down until all the anger got out of her." She also said it might be necessary to restrain the girl all night. Some of the youth left the church after being told by Donna that if they "weren't totally committed," they could leave. Things told Donna in confidence were used against the ones who confided in her in public humiliating scenarios and guilt trips during Sunday School or Youth Group meetings.

As a result of the events over the past several months, several families have left Kittitas Assembly, some to worship elsewhere, and others, sadly, to worship nowhere. All told, approximately sixty people have left the fellowship, almost half of which are teen-age or younger.

We do not sign this letter lightly. All of us are saddened by what has been happening to Kittitas Assembly of God. What had been a loving church family has been split into two opposing factions. Angry words have been uttered by both sides. The elderly who have made Kittitas Assembly their church home for 30, 40 or 50 years are sickened and saddened by what has happened. Some young people who had been on fire for the Lord have had their faith badly shaken.

We don't know for sure if the Jefferys and the "inner circle" are the beginnings of a cult movement, but there are many similarities to cult activities in what has been taking place. People are afraid to speak up; they say they have been sworn to secrecy or that the pastor has great power and they are afraid of him.

We ask that Kittitas Assembly be placed under Home Missions rule while the Northwest District Council and/or the General Council in Springfield investigates these things. We also ask that all resignations and removals of membership and new memberships be considered null and void retroactive to February 1, 1993. Please give the people who were part of the voting membership prior to that time a chance to help restore order to this church.

Prayerfully in Christ's Name,

(Signatures were on attached pages)

****

WHITED SEPULCHRES

On Wednesday, December 1, 1993, the following article appeared in the Daily Record, Ellensburg, Washington:

****

Church pastor seeks anti-harassment order
By Mike Johnston, City Editor

A pastor at a church in Kittitas is seeking anti-harassment orders against 12 former church attendees in connection with a dispute in which some people have disagreed with the church board's handling of church discipline.

Pastor Gary Jeffery's court petition claims the orders are needed to protect him from harassment and threats like those he contends occurred when the church's Nov. 14 service was disrupted by those opposing the board's actions. He claims assaults occurred during the scuffle, although no criminal charges are being pursued by those on both sides of the dispute.

Jeffery, pastor and board member of Kittitas Assembly of God church, last week filed in Kittitas County Lower District Court a petition asking Judge Tom Haven for nine orders that would restrict the 12, including a member and some former church members and others, from contacting or communicating to him, his wife and children.

The orders also would bar the 12 from keeping the pastor and his family under surveillance and would prohibit them from going within 300 feet of the pastor's home and his work-place -- the Kittitas Assembly of God Church building. The orders would be effective for one year.

A Friday court hearing on Jeffery's petition was cancelled, according to a district court official, and a new hearing date has not been set in the civil legal proceeding.

According to court papers filed by Jeffery, he has been urged to obtain the orders by church families and by state Assembly of God Church leaders. In his court petition, Jeffery claims that actions since spring 1993 by some of those named have led him to believe they are threatening the peace of the church and his life.

"I wouldn't be doing this if I didn't have a fear of harassment to myself, to my family and to the rest of the church," Jeffery said earlier this week. "I want a safe environment to worship." He said two-thirds of the voting membership of the church have expressed support of gaining the civil restraining orders.

But some of the 12 named in the petition claim the pastor's concerns in his court papers are unfounded and many of his allegations, they contend, are untrue.

"I don't see any truth in the document," said Pairlee Treat, one of those served with court papers who is seeking legal advice in the matter. "There is absolutely no truth in it, not one iota."

Treat and her daughter, Wanda Cotton, are the center of the dispute as a result of the pastor and board agreeing to exclude the two women, who are not members from attending the church. The women claim no one in the church has come forward to inform them of the specific allegations against them, when they occurred and who was making them. Several people named by Jeffery share the same concern and are seeking mediation of the dispute through state and national Assembly of God officials.

Bonnie Clement, one of those named in Jeffery's filing, said she continues to be a member of the church and said his court documents may contain some truth, but contends most of it is either exaggeration or outright falsehoods.

Del and Anita Kazee, former church members also named by Jeffery, claim the document has many untrue statements taken under oath.

"Under no circumstances did I make a threat to him whatsoever," said Del Kazee about Jeffery's allegations. Kazee said Jeffery is telling lies in the document in connection with his alleged actions. His wife is seeking legal counsel in the matter.

WHITED SEPULCHRES

On January 7, 1994, the following front-page article appeared in the Daily Record:

****

Kittitas pastor requests anti-harassment orders
By Mike Johnston, City Editor

A hearing began in Kittitas County Lower District court this morning on a Kittitas church pastor's request for court orders against 12 former churchgoers and others barring them from having any contact with him and keeping them out of the church building.

Pastor Gary Jeffery, of the Kittitas Assembly of God Church, filed a petition in late November requesting the court to grant nine anti-harassment orders that would prohibit the 12 from keeping the pastor and his family under surveillance and would bar them from going within 300 feet of the pastor's home and workplace -- the Kittitas Assembly of God Church building

The hearing began at about 10:15 a.m. after an almost 45-minute pre-hearing conference between Jeffery and his attorney Rick Bueschel, and the 12 people, represented by attorney Jeff Slothower, and Judge Thomas Haven.

Jeffery is seeking the orders in a civil case because of a dispute in which some people disagreed with the church board's handling of church discipline. Jeffery is a member of the church board.

The orders, if granted by Judge Haven, also would restrict the 12 from contact with the pastor, his wife and children. If approved, the orders would be effective for a year.

The 12 include a current member, former members including a former church officer, non-member attendees of the church, and relatives.

Named in the petitions are: Bonnie Clement, Wanda Cotton, Jim Scones, Pairlee Treat, Bill Peterson, Chris Marchel, Jim and Sherry Boswell, Jerry and Phyllis Marchel, and Del and Anita

Kazee. Except for the Boswells who live in Snohomish, those named live in or near the city of Kittitas.

The first witness called by Bueschel was former church member Steve Lyons, who continues to attend the church. Lyons said that Jerry and Phyllis Marchel warned him last summer that Jeffery was running a cult at the church and that it may be following what has been called the "Shepherding Movement" out of Southern California.

Jeffery's petition claims the orders are needed to protect him from harassment and threats like those he claims occurred on November 14, 1993, when a church service was disrupted by people opposing a recent church board action. He claims he and others were assaulted during the scuffle.

During opening statements, Slothower said, "this is an action that shouldn't be before the court." He said testimony would show his clients' actions do not constitute harassment as outlined in state statute.

In his petition, taken under oath, Jeffery claims a group of about 10 persons have "planned together to use violence to disrupt church services." He also claims he has had his life threatened and some of those named in his petition want him to leave the community. Jeffery, 39, became the pastor of the church in March 1992.

At the center of the dispute is an announcement by Jeffery in June 1993 at a church service that Pairlee Treat, and her daughter Wanda Cotton, had been excluded from attending services due to unspecified wrongdoings. The two women, and others named in the anti-harassment petition, claim they were denied a fair hearing to answer the allegation. They say no one in the church has come forward to inform them of details of the specific allegations against them.

Jeffery and board members claim all church rules were followed in the disciplining process, and in subsequent church membership revocations arising from individuals not agreeing with actions by the church leadership.

Some of those named in the petitions have stated many of the pastor's concerns in the court papers are unfounded and many of the allegations are untrue. In previous statements, they contend the pastor was never threatened and there was never any plan to disrupt church service. They said their efforts to get a fair hearing before the church board about their concerns with the pastor's actions have been thwarted. They have appealed for mediation in the dispute to state and national Assembly of God officials, but have received no reply.

Testimony was still being taken at press time. The hearing was expected to continue well into the afternoon.

★★★★★★★★★★★★★★★

On January 8, 1994, the following article appeared in the Ellensburg Daily Record:

****

Kittitas Church dispute continues at court hearing
By Mike Johnston, City Editor

A regional Assembly of God official on Friday accused a group of disgruntled churchgoers in Kittitas of bypassing the local church's authority in bringing allegations of improper behavior against the church's pastor.

The statement came from Don Strong, an Assembly of God Church district leader from Pasco, during a daylong hearing in Kittitas County Lower District Court. Pastor Gary Jeffery is seeking anti-harassment orders against the group. He claims there is a planned effort to remove him from the church and community, and cites a Nov. 14 disruption as an example.

The incident brought Kittitas police to the small church and was depicted in court testimony on Friday as an organized effort by a group of disgruntled churchgoers and others who refused to follow church rules in expressing their opposition to the pastor and the actions of the church board.

But other testimony, brought out under questioning by the group's attorney, painted a picture of former church members and non-members as being denied a fair hearing before the congregation, and being ignored by district and state Assembly of God officials. They say that is contrary to what the Bible says about resolving conflicts.

Judge Thomas Haven heard testimony during the civil proceeding Friday and Saturday. The anti-harassment orders being sought would bar 12 people from having any contact with Jeffery or his family, or from coming near the church.

The 12 are: Bonnie Clement, Wanda Cotton, Jim Scones, Pairlee Treat, Bill Peterson, Chris

Marchel, Jim and Sherry Boswell, Jerry and Phyllis Marchel, and Del and Anita Kazee.

After Jeffery's attorney, Rick Bueschel, presented his case with a long list of witnesses on Friday, the group's attorney, Jeff Slothower, brought his main witness, Chris Marchel. Chris Marchel said he and others went to the Nov. 14 service only as a show of support to his father and mother, Jerry and Phyllis Marchel, whose church membership had been revoked. He said he decided to attend the service only the night before and decided Sunday morning to stand and read the letters revoking his parents' membership Sunday morning. He said the letters stated his father had a "bad lifestyle" and his mother was "not in harmony" with the church leadership.

"I wanted to make sure they didn't physically throw my parents out of the church," Marchel said. His parents had previously disagreed with the pastor and board's action to exclude Pairlee Treat and her daughter Wanda Cotton from the fellowship of the church for unspecified wrongdoings.

Marchel also said in court he went to the church because Jeffery had taken away from members Mike and Iva Steigleder their long held church responsibilities due to disagreements with the church leadership.

Marchel said he and the others had made no plans to disrupt the service. He said he took a "verbal whipping" when Jeffery pointed at him and shouted, "You're out of line, brother, sit down." He said his intent was to inform people at the service what had been done to his parents by the church board.

Rev. Strong said he and another district official met Oct. 13, 1993, with members of the church about allegations against the board and pastor. A petition outlining the allegations was submitted, but it was denied for the lack of one signature, Slothower claimed.

Strong said only members can speak at such membership meetings so non-members and others were out of order when they interrupted to speak. He said nothing was found that indicated the pastor or the board did anything wrong in disfellowshipping Pairlee Treat and Wanda Cotton, non-members but regular church-goers. This also applied to the revoking of the Marchel's membership and others.

Earlier testimony by board member Randy Bale said disfellowshipping was a Biblical practice used if someone refused attempts to settle disagreements. It didn't mean Treat and Cotton couldn't come to church, but that members shouldn't go out of their way to be friendly or have contact with them.

Bale said disfellowshipping occurred after the two women refused to come before the church board to deal with allegations against them. It was brought out that they refused because the board would not allow two non-members to accompany them to the board meeting.

Strong said the group with the petition were attempting to bypass the church board. But attorney Slothower said the path of the disgruntled church-goers was a "circle" -- they had no standing before the board or the church membership because they were not members and couldn't speak, but they are still required to go through the board to have their grievances officially recognized.

Strong didn't clearly answer whether or not he conducted an independent investigation of the allegations in the petition, but later said he did receive a few phone calls and letters on the matter.

****

WHITED SEPULCHRES

Monday, January 10, 1994, the *Daily Record* ran the following article:

****

Kittitas churchgoers, pastor trade charges at court hearing
By Mike Johnston, City Editor

Allegations that threats were made in June, 1993 against the life of a Kittitas church pastor were flatly denied Saturday by two former churchgoers during a daylong hearing in Kittitas County Lower District court.

Under cross examination, the pastor, Gary Jeffery of the Kittitas Assembly of God church, acknowledged he didn't mention the death threat to his church board on the day the threat was made, didn't publicly reveal it until he brought legal action against the two men in late November. In August he took part in the marriage of the daughter of one of the men he said threatened him.

The testimony came on Saturday, the second full day of hearing before Judge Thomas Haven in Kittitas County Lower District Court, on Jeffery's request for one-year anti-harassment orders against the two men and 10 others he claims want to oust him from his ministry. He also claims the church members and former members have threatened his life and assaulted him.

Jeffery, 40, said the group of 12 "planned together to use violence to disrupt church services," a disruption that brought Kittitas city police to the small church on Nov. 14, 1993. Several witnesses on Saturday acknowledged that many in the group had attended a Nov. 12 Bible study and did discuss problems at the church, but did not plan to violently disrupt church services.

The 12 named in Jeffery's petition attended the Nov. 14 service, but they contend their only intention was to read letters informing the congregation about how the church board had taken memberships and church responsibilities away from those opposed to the pastor -- not to cause a fight. They claim the board's actions were done improperly according to Biblical principles and the church bylaws.

Jeffery also testified that Jerry Marchel and Del Kazee had met with him privately on June 15, two days after he announced that the church board had excluded from the church Pairlee Treat and her daughter Wanda Cotton for allegedly gossiping and spreading dissention. The two men asked Jeffery to reconsider allowing the women to come before the board with two friends, rather than appear alone as Jeffery and the board required.

Jeffery refused to allow the women to be accompanied. Because the women refused to come earlier without being accompanied, the board "disfellowshipped" them, meaning church members were not to be friendly with them.

Jeffery said he remarked during his session with the two men that he was willing to "die for Christ" and "for righteousness" in the situation. He claimed that Marchel, opposed to the expulsion of the two women, said his "death for Christ" could be arranged and knew someone -- Jim Scones -- had done violence before.

Under cross-examination, however, Jeffery said he held hands and prayed with the two men after the meeting.

In later testimony, Marchel and Kazee denied they threatened the life of the pastor at the meeting and had never mentioned Jim Scones. Kazee said he recalls the pastor saying he was willing to die for something, but couldn't remember specifics.

Marchel also testified it was the board's intent to meet alone with the two women and "cast evil spirits out of them," what board members attempted to do to him at a later board meeting. Marchel also said Jeffery told him that Treat, 71, and Marchel might die as a result of their wrongdoing.

Several people complained that non-members had not been allowed to speak at an Oct. 13 meeting with regional Assembly of God officials, held to *review complaints against the pastor and board. Kazee said it had been a church tradition to allow non-members to speak in church membership meetings, and that it had seemed as if church officials had already made up their minds to support Jeffery. The officials said he had done nothing wrong.*

In other testimony, Debbie Letson, a former churchgoer, said she took her teenage daughters out of the church's youth group because of complaints she had heard that youth group members were required to show total submission to the group and Donna Jeffery, wife of the pastor.

Letson claimed the Jefferys held her 15 year-old daughter against her will for an hour during a so-called disciplining session. She claims they also yelled at her. Letson has referred the matter to Kittitas police and the county prosecutor's office is looking into the incident as possible unlawful imprisonment of a minor, she said.

****

Following is the document issued by Judge Thomas Haven after the two-and-a-half day hearing before him concerning the anti-harassment charges Gary Jeffery brought against twelve former members and non-members of the Kittitas Assembly.

****

LOWER KITTITAS COUNTY DISTRICT COURT
STATE OF WASHINGTON

GARY JEFFERY, Petitioner, Vs.	)) No.A93-68,A93-69,A93-70) A93-71,A93-72,A93-73) A93-75,A93-76
BONNIE CLEMENT, WANDA COTTON, JIM SCONES, PAIRLEE TREAT, BILL PETERSON, CHRIS MARCHEL, JERRY and PHYLLIS MARCHEL, DEL and ANITA KAZEE, Respondents.	)))) Findings of Fact,) Conclusions of law,) and Order Dismissing) Petitions)))))

Based on the testimony heard, the exhibits admitted into evidence and the arguments of counsel, the Court makes the following:

FINDINGS OF FACT

1. That the petitioner has failed to establish that the above named respondents constitute a group who "have planned together to use violence to disrupt church services" as alleged in paragraph 1.2 of the various petitions.
2. That the petitioner has failed to establish that any of the above named respondents threatened to kill the petitioner, as alleged

in paragraph 1.2 and 1.3 of the various petitions.
3. That the petitioner has failed to establish that the above named respondents "stormed the stage" of the Kittitas Assembly of God Church on November 14, 1993 as alleged in paragraph 1.3 of the various petitions.
4. That the petitioner has failed to establish that any of the above named respondents "trapped" petitioner in the church office as alleged in paragraph 1.3 of the various petitions.
5. That no other act by any of the above named respondents alleged in the various petitions constitute unlawful harassment as defined in RCW 10.14.020.

Based on the above Findings of Fact, the Court makes the following:

CONCLUSIONS OF LAW

That the Petitioner has failed to establish by a preponderance of the evidence that the above named respondents have committed acts of unlawful harassment or that good cause exists for the issuance of protection orders.

ORDER

Based on the above Findings of Fact and Conclusions of Law, the Court hereby dismisses the Petitions filed against the above named respondents.

January 10, 1994   JUDGE Thomas Haven

****

ALBERT & AIMEE ANDERSON

At the request of the twelve people he represented, Attorney Jeff Slothower wrote the following letter:

****

Lathrop & Winbauer
Attorneys at Law
Post Office Box 1088
201 West Seventh Avenue,
Ellensburg, WA 98926

Jeff Slothower

January 25, 1994

VIA FACSIMILE TRANSMISSION AND FIRST CLASS MAIL

Mr. Frank Cole, District Superintendent
Northwest District Council of the Assemblies of God
P.O. Box 699
Kirkland, WA 98083-0699

Dear Mr. Cole:

    I represent the twelve individuals who Pastor Gary Jeffry (sic) of the Kittitas Assembly of God Church attempted to restrain from attending the Kittitas Assembly of God church.
    Some of my clients, on November 22, 1993, sent to Reverend Elmer E. Kirschman and to Reverend Thomas E. Trask a letter with details of what had been transpiring since June of 1993 at the Kittitas Assembly of God church. On December 7, 1993, they received a response from Mr. Kirschman. Mr. Kirschman's response indicates that your office had the matter under consideration. To date, my clients have not had a response from you with respect to their letter. They would like a response and I, as their attorney, feel they certainly are due a response.
    Unfortunately, like a number of matters that end up in our courts, a great deal of the issues

were "tried in the press". As a result of this, I believe that this community's view of the Kittitas Assembly of God church and Pastor Gary Jeffry (sic), in particular, is less than favorable. In fact, at the trial, it became clear to all who were present, including the judge, that Pastor Gary Jeffry (sic) was being less than truthful. The evidence also indicated that Mr. Jeffry (sic) is currently under investigation by the local prosecuting authority. After the court made its decision, some of my clients were assured your representative, Mr. Carlson, who attended the trial, that the church would address their concerns and attempt to sort this matter out. I believe his exact words were "we (meaning the church) really blew this."

Needless to say, my clients, as long-standing members and adherents of the Kittitas Assembly of God church are deeply concerned about Pastor Jeffry's (sic) conduct, both in summarily dismissing various individuals from the church and his systematic removal or attempts to remove anyone who questions his running of the church and in particular, his motives. My clients are incensed that the church and the church's resources were used against them. My clients were required to expend money, time and emotional energy in responding to what amounted to unfounded accusations on the part of Pastor Jeffry (sic). They feel, at the very least, that the church should compensate them for what they have been made to endure.

Understand the position of my clients. They have been long-standing members and adherents to the church in Kittitas, have contributed spiritually, emotionally and financially to the church during their association with the church. And they now have a pastor at the church who has summarily removed them from the church, in violation of the church By-laws and brought them before a civil court to silence them when he was unable to do it himself, all the while utilizing the resources of their church against them. Mr. Jeffry's (sic) conduct amounts to defamation of my clients. Several of them will, in all likelihood, be commencing civil actions against Mr. Jeffry (sic) and, because he was acting under church auspices, even though he brought the action in his own name, my clients will be looking to you for compensation of their injuries.

I would strongly urge you to sit down with my clients, listen to their grievances and do something about Pastor Jeffry (sic) and his conduct since June at the Kittitas Assembly of God church.

Please direct your reply to me at the above address.

Very truly yours,

Jeff Slothower

JS:jcj008
cc:clients
Thomas E. Trask, General Superintendent, General Council of the Assemblies of God/via facsimile

****

WHITED SEPULCHRES

Following is the answer to the above letter:

****

NORTHWEST DISTRICT COUNCIL
of THE ASSEMBLIES OF God
Frank E. Cole, District Superintendent

February 10, 1994

Mr. Jeff Slothower, Attorney at Law
Lathrop and Winbauer
P.O. Box 1088
Ellensburg, WA 98926

Dear Mr. Slothower:

   I am responding to your recent correspondence. Historically, in the Assemblies of God, non members have not been afforded the right to voice or vote in membership matters. Most of our congregational bylaws indicate the same.
   The Kittitas situation is besieged by unusual and unordinary impact. Therefore, the normal ecclesiastical mediation/arbitration procedures have not been possible. It is my understanding that the same was cited by the court. However, we are willing to take a step beyond what has already been taken in an effort to bring matters to a conclusion for all concerned.
   I am asking you to set a meeting date, time and place for our officials to receive input from non members in the Kittitas situation. I feel that the meeting should be held in a neutral facility, not at the church. Please allow us three (3) date options for the purpose of schedule coordination. Please inform the persons you represent concerning the meeting which will be conducted as a hearing. Their statements should be presented in writing. At your approval, your clients will be allowed opportunity to read their statement. We will need five (5) copies of each statement handed to our

hearing chairperson prior to the statement being read.
 If you have any questions, please contact my office.

Sincerely,

Frank E. Cole
District Superintendent

gu
cc: Executive Presbytery
Thomas E. Trask, General Superintendent
Elmer E. Kirschman, District Secretary-Treasurer

****

Jeff Slothower's response to Frank Cole:

****

Lathrop & Winbauer
Attorneys at Law
Post Office Box 1088
201 West Seventh Avenue
Ellensburg, WA 98926

Jeff Slothower

February 15, 1994

VIA FACSIMILE AND FIRST CLASS MAIL

Frank E. Cole,
District Superintendent
Northwest District Council of the Assemblies of God
P.O. Box 699
Kirkland, WA 98083-0699

RE: Kittitas Assembly of God Church

Dear Mr. Cole:

I am in receipt of your February 10, 1994 letter. I have had an opportunity to review the letter with my clients and we are somewhat perplexed. Your letter indicates that you would be willing to meet with my clients, however you are going to conduct the meeting as a hearing. Under what authority is this hearing being conducted? I would appreciate it if you could provide me with the provisions in the Bylaws or other document that the church is relying upon as authority to conduct this "hearing".

Your anticipated cooperation is greatly appreciated.

Very truly yours,

ALBERT & AIMEE ANDERSON

Jeff Slothower

JS:jcj004

cc: clients
   Thomas E. Trask, General Superintendent
   Elmer E. Kirschman, District Secretary-Treasurer

****

WHITED SEPULCHRES

The last response received from the Northwest District:

****

Northwest District Council
Of the Assemblies of God
Frank E. Cole, District Superintendent

February 17, 1994

Mr. Jeff Slothower, Attorney at Law
Lathrop and Winbauer
P.O. Box 1088
Ellensburg, WA 98926

Dear Mr. Slothower:

Re: Kittitas Assembly of God
Your letter of 2/15/94

    We were under the impression that your clients were desirous of having an opportunity to be heard by official representatives of the Northwest District Council of the Assemblies of God. Our fax of February 10th entertained that possibility.

    However, since the Kittitas Assembly of God is a sovereign church, and there are no local church or district bylaws allowing for or authorizing meetings with non-members and since your letter raises questions about our authority to do so, we hereby withdraw our offer to meet with your clients.

    Our desire was not to add to any existing controversy, but our hope was that the results of such a meeting would restore peace to a troubled situation.

Sincerely,

Frank E. Cole
District Superintendent
gu
cc: Thomas Trask, General Superintendent and
     Elmer E. Kirschman, District Secretary-Treasurer

ALBERT & AIMEE ANDERSON

The Reverend Robert Cousart had been a former pastor of the Kittitas Assembly of God. When the hurting people of that church sought his advice, he listened and counseled with all who came to him. He wrote the following letter, pleading further with the district officials to listen to both sides of the issue.

****

March 14, 1994

Reverend Donald B. Strong
3517 N. Road 84 (117E)
Pasco, WA 99301-1665

Dear Don:

I feel compelled to write to you again concerning the handling of the Kittitas Assembly matter. As I expressed in my previous letter, I have always held you in high regard, and have appreciated your support down through the years.
However, I am extremely disappointed with the inappropriate manner in which this was handled. In the first place, you never tried to hear the other side of the story. You seemed intent on hearing and believing only Gary and Donna Jeffery and those loyal to them.
It disturbs me to hear from various District officials that they cannot talk to non-members. Non-members are people, too. They have souls. They need ministry and fellowship just as members do.
When there is a serious disagreement in a church and help is asked of the presbyters, I feel they need to be heard. Yet, they were given no opportunity to tell their side of the issue.
I have been a loyal member of the Assemblies of God for 50 years, an ordained minister since 1960, served as Secretary-Treasurer of the Alaska District Council for almost 10 years until resigning to return to pastoring. For these 50 years, I have whole-heartedly supported the

Assemblies of God, but with the way these matters have been mishandled, I am very distressed.

Your letter of November 16, 1993 to Reverend Jim Hansen, attorney for the Northwest District really disturbs me. You state concerning Pairlee Treat, that "This lady...has been the source of most of the trouble in the Assembly of God churches in the area for the past 20 to 30 years!" This is not true. You have not even tried to speak with her to get the facts.

Also in this same letter you state: "Pastor Carpenter and I concluded almost all the membership and all three Board members were 100% behind Pastor Jeffery." That may be true simply because Pastor Jeffery systematically removed from membership all those who did not completely agree with him.

You also state: "the former Board member and his wife had their names removed on November 2nd, after his angry attack toward the Pastor and Board." Jerry Marchel did not make an angry attack toward the Pastor and Board!

Your description of the events in the Sunday morning service on November 14 are slanted, especially when you state: "All of the supporting people pretty well held their cool, did not hit anyone..."

Let me quote from a letter drafted by Bonnie Clement signed by her and 10 others: "Pleas were made for the congregation to listen to what was going on, what was happening to people who had been members ever since the early days of the church. People in support of the pastor's actions surrounded him. He did not acknowledge nor answer any questions put to him. One of his supporters pushed Jerry Marchel's son-in-law, Jim Boswell. The ensuing scuffle knocked over microphone stands on the stage.

The police were called and came to the church, took statements and made a report on what happened. This was not what any one wanted. Emotions were running high because several attempts to talk with the pastor and board and board members were met with refusal to discuss this situation or with outright rudeness. People on both sides of the issue did and said things which were not glorifying to God."

I was not there, you might point out, but neither were you. We are both relying on what we have heard. We have heard both sides, and we have seen both sides in action. In the court proceedings Mike Kelly stated that Jim Boswell did not attack him first, but that he, Mike Kelly, had initiated the scuffle. Also, it was brought out in court that Ray Kelly had had Jim Scones in a choke-hold. So you see, Don, that all of the supporting people did not "keep their cool."

Years ago I was told that there are three sides to every story: your side, my side, and the right side. The problem here is that only one side has been heard by the district brethren.

Let me comment on Gary Jeffery's Declaration In Support of Anti-Harassment Order. First Gary certifies that a "group of approximately 10 persons...planned together to use violence to disrupt church services." I know for a fact that this is untrue! As is the charge that this group met together Friday, November 12, 1993, to plan a violent disruption of the Sunday, November 14, 1993 service at the church. I was invited to that meeting at which I led singing, Scripture was read, and a couple who had gone on a mission to Central America shared from their experiences. No planning for violent disruption of the church service.

Don, I have known Jerry Marchel for 14 years. He is a fine Christian man, with a loving attitude, very friendly, and throughout this whole ordeal, he has kept sweet and humble, oftentimes breaking into tears over what has happened. The statement that he had threatened Gary's life is a total fabrication.

I enclose copy of the FINDING OF FACT by Judge Tom Haven which plainly finds that the petitioner failed to establish that the respondents constitute a group who have planned together to disrupt church services. Also failed to establish that any of the respondents threatened to kill the petitioner.

How could you not meet with these people and try to bring about a reconciliation? How could you and the other district brethren even think about going to court against these people? It seems strange to me that in the December 26, 1993 issue of the Evangel the article OF COURTS AND CONFLICTS was printed. I feel that we have strayed far from the Biblical way of taking care of matters such as these.

I have been available to these dismembered Christians, though none of them attend my church and I will intend to minister to the bruised and hurting people around me because that is my calling.

I am loyal to the Assemblies of God as long as they continue to follow the Bible, but I cannot stomach this terrible travesty of justice. It is neither fair nor equitable.

It is still my wish that you would meet with these people who have been so grievously hurt and seek to undo the wrong that has been done both by Pastor Jeffery and the district officials.

There is much more I could say, but this letter is already too long. Please pray much about this situation and what God would have you to do.

Sincerely yours,

Robert E. Cousart
Box 930
Kittitas, WA 98934

cc: Dale Carpenter
   Frank Cole
   Warren Bullock
   Elmer Kirschman
   Rollin Carlson

****

ALBERT & AIMEE ANDERSON

As of the date this book went to press, Pairlee Treat and Wanda Cotton and the others involved in the Kittitas situation have not been contacted by District Officials to hear their side of what happened. No counter charges have been filed against the Assemblies of God for damages and in all probability will not be since most are more interested in obeying Scripture instead of seeking revenge. However, there are several people whose spiritual lives have been damaged by the events that took place, and several are still nursing hurt feelings, for themselves as well as for friends who have been hurt. The following, written by Bonnie Clement, sums up some of the feelings and results of all that has happened:

FORGIVE

Disbelief,
Anger over what happened
and that it happened
by the hands
of ones who claim
they were serving God.

Some were vocal
in their disbelief
and anger
and openly confronted
the wrongdoing
and let their feelings
be made known,
while others
hid their dismay
deep inside
and quietly drifted away,
their anger
burrowing deep
within.

WHITED SEPULCHRES

*For both the ones
who voiced their anger
and for those
who held it inside,
healing can only come
when they forgive
the ones who hurt them
and let the matter
rest in God's hands.*

*Some have been
able to do this
and have gone forward
in their walk with God—
while others
are holding on
to their anger
and are letting it
harden their hearts
and hinder their walk.*

Section 2.

FORMAL CHARGES

The Destiny of Man

How far may we go on in sin?
How long will God forbear?
Where does hope end, and where begin
The confines of despair?
An answer from the skies is sent;
"Ye that from God depart,
While it is called today, repent,
And harden not your heart."
...Dr. J. Addison Alexander

TAKE TIME TO BE HOLY

Take time to be holy, Speak oft with thy Lord;
Abide in Him always, And feed on His Word;
Make friends of God's children, Help those who are weak;
Forgetting in nothing His blessing to seek.

Take time to be holy, The world rushes on;
Spend much time in secret with Jesus alone;
By looking to Jesus, Like Him thou shalt be;
Thy friends in thy conduct, His likeness shall see.

Take time to be holy, Let Him be thy guide,
And run not before Him whatever betide;
In joy or in sorrow, Still follow thy Lord,
And looking to Jesus, Still trust in His Word.

Take time to be holy, Be calm in thy soul;
Each tho't and each motive Beneath His control;
Thus led by His Spirit To fountains of love,
Thou soon shalt be fitted for service above.

   William D. Longstaff

The following letter is the only written response received by the Andersons from the Northwest District relative to the May 10, 1994 "Petition for an Investigation." (Prologue)

****

Elmer E. Kirschman
Secretary-Treasurer
Northwest District Council of
The Assemblies of God

May 26, 1994

Al and Aimee Anderson
— — — Avenue
Ellensburg, WA 98926

Dear Brother and Sister Anderson,

   In light of certain difficulties occurring over a period of time, and certain complaints you've registered concerning the Northwest District's Executive Officers handling of problems, plus your endeavor to involve the General Council to attempt a solution, you are hereby requested by the District Presbytery to meet with the Executive Presbytery at their June 7, 1994 meeting at the Northwest District office in Kirkland at 2:00 p.m. for dialog.
   It is urgent that you honor this appointment. Should you choose not to honor our request, further steps will become necessary.
   As brothers and sisters in Christ, we're confident such matters can be brought to a satisfactory solution. We look forward to your response.

Sincerely,

Elmer E. Kirschman
Secretary-Treasurer

Gjb

ALBERT & AIMEE ANDERSON

****
Appointment Confirmation
Al and Aimee Anderson

_____Yes, we will plan to attend the interview with the Executive Presbytery on June 7, 1994 at 2:00 p.m. at the Northwest District office in Kirkland.

_____No, we will not be present at the June 7, 1994 meeting.

Reason for not attending _____

Northwest District Council of the Assemblies of God
P.O. Box 699, Kirkland, WA 98033

****

In response to Elmer Kirschman's May 26, 1994 letter requesting the Andersons attendance at the Executive Presbyter's meeting, on June 7, 1994, Albert and Aimee drove to Kirkland for their 2:00 p.m. appointment. They were kept waiting in the reception room for one hour past the scheduled time. While sitting in the foyer, Al Baunsgard approached them with greetings and told them he had to leave. Thus, the Andersons took this opportunity to give Al his charge packet since he had to leave early.

Greg Austin came out around 3:00 p.m. and led the Andersons into the room to meet with the eight District Officials. Those present were; Warren Bullock, Elmer Kirschman, Les Welk, Rollin Carlson, Dale Carpenter, Don Strong, Julius Jepson and Greg Austin.

From the first contact by phone from Warren Bullock, District Superintendent, Albert and Aimee understood that this meeting was to discuss Rollin Carlson and his dealings with Care-Net. Not so! Warren Bullock let the Andersons know in no uncertain terms that they were called in to discuss Albert and his credentials and to be interrogated.

The Andersons sensed and felt the cold and unfriendly atmosphere as the following conversation took place:

Aimee, "Can we tape this meeting?"
Dale, "Oh, no, we trust everybody around here."
Warren, "We're here to talk about you and your relational problem with the church. (Albert understood this to mean his credentials were in question.) Have you heard the name Dick Clever?"
Albert, "If I answer that, it will just lead to something else."
Warren, "Have you talked to Dick Clever?"
Aimee, "We don't have to answer that."
Warren, (Pointing his finger at Aimee, very quick and angry said) "You be quiet, I'm not talking to you, I'm talking to him." Then he pointed his finger at Albert and asked, "What do you have to say?"

Albert, "The same as my wife. She's right."

Warren, "Well, it looks like we're through then."

Albert, "Yes, I guess we are."

Aimee, (leaning over toward Albert and reaching for the attaché case sitting on the floor) "Honey, before we leave, maybe now is a good time to give their packets to them?"

Albert and Aimee both leaned over and picked up the packets out of the attaché case and began passing them out to everyone. The men started to open them.

Warren, looked at the men moving to open their charge packets and said, "Don't open those now."

Aimee, "Les, Dale and this one is unnamed. I'm sorry we didn't know your name, Greg Austin. We have filed formal charges like Brother Wood told us to. And, the **charges** sent to the General Council Credentials Committee are **against** not only **Rollin Carlson**, but also against **Frank Cole, Warren Bullock, Elmer Kirschman, Don Strong, and Dale Carpenter.**

Warren, "Why us?"

Albert, "Because you didn't respond to our complaints and check into it like you should have. Because of the way you have handled information about Care-Net, Kittitas and Rollin."

Aimee, "Also, because of the threats we have received. Manuel Deeds said we are not on trial."

Warren, "What does he know? When did you talk to him?"

Albert, "We went to see him recently in Sunnyside."

Aimee, "He read everything, all the charges."

Warren, "Why did you refuse to come to the May 18th meeting?"

Albert, "I told your secretary that we felt we should wait until we received a response from General Council since you said you wanted to talk about Care-Net."

Julius, "Brother Bullock, maybe I can clear something up. Mrs. Anderson phoned me and I told her to bring everything about Care-Net. Maybe I misunderstood?"

Aimee, "That's right. I told him no one was paying any attention to us and he told us to bring everything. Besides, Manuel Deeds told us we were not on trial."

Albert, "May I say something to Rollin?"

Warren, "Yes."

Albert, "Rollin I'm glad you are here today because I wanted to tell you to your face, that I don't hate you. I don't even dislike you. I love you in the Lord. I just don't agree with some of the things you are doing."

Les, (After turning to Aimee he asks) "If it's as bad as you say, why isn't the County doing something about it?"

Aimee, "For one thing, Rollin tells them something else."

Albert, "May I read a letter from the County?"

Warren, (Nods his head)

Rollin, "What's the date of that letter?"

Albert, "June 3, 1994." (Number 23 in charge packet list)

Rollin, "I'm hurt that you didn't come to me first with that."

Aimee, (looking at Warren) "May I read a letter, too?"

Warren, (Nods his head)

Aimee, read Kennon Forester's letter about Rollin. "He had devalued the cost of the hay and increased the cost of the freight," in order to collect more from the insurance company. (Number 22 in charge packet list)

Rollin, "Well, he was just angry because we wouldn't buy any more hay from him."

Dale, "Aimee, you were all upset and talked to Don and myself about the Kittitas people. What does that have to do with you?"

Aimee, "I talked about Care-Net too and said Rollin and Care-Net were operating illegally."

Dale, "You just talked about the Kittitas situation."

Aimee, "Anna Mae Cousart and I were there and we talked about both Care-Net and Kittitas."

Don, "You lit into us."

Rollin, (Held up a pamphlet titled "Beware the Wolves") I understand you had some input into this."

Aimee, "We read it, but we didn't know anything about it until after it was finished."

Rollin, (reading from a list in his hand) "You've condemned me, you have been judge and jury, you've abused ministerial trust, you falsely accused, you've slandered, you've gossiped and sown discord among the brethren. You've spoken against my family and my father."

The Andersons felt like Rollin was throwing out a smoke screen to get them off the issue and didn't even bother answering the **false accusations** except the **false statement** about his father.

Aimee, "We love your father, and we never even thought about speaking against your father."

Rollin, "We might have to sell the ranch because of what you've done."

Dale, "People from your church are phoning us."

Albert, "About who?"

Dale, "About you." (This was expected after the petition was circulated.)

Aimee, "Some of our people said a Board member tried to pressure them into signing a petition, but they refused. A couple of our deacons said one of the District Presbyters told them to circulate a petition asking for Albert's resignation, even though there were no charges against him."

PLEASE NOTE: Compare the treatment to Pastor Albert Anderson with no charges against him, to the District's treatment of Pastor Gary Jeffery who committed gross sins which were proven in a court of law (related in "Church Brawl" section)

Warren, "We are going to close in prayer." He then prayed something about the truth coming out.

Albert and Aimee got up to leave. Everyone stood and Rollin followed them to the door.

Aimee, "Rollin, do you remember in our living room when you asked if I believed you?"

Rollin, "No, I don't remember that."

Albert, "It wasn't a good testimony for the Care-Net taxes to be delinquent."

Rollin, "There's nothing wrong with that. A lot of people do that all the time."

Aimee, "Have you talked to Oscar?" (Rairdan)

Rollin, "Oscar talked to me. I told him to go talk to Don."

On different occasions Oscar mentioned to the Andersons that he had visited with Rollin Carlson. Rollin Carlson pastored Ellensburg Assembly of God, some years ago before the Andersons moved there, and knew who he could talk to. It was quite certain to the Andersons that some of the District Officials in question wanted the Andersons out of the Ellensburg and Kittitas area. The two deacons, Paul Bennett and Dale Ball, told Albert Anderson that Don Strong told them (Paul and Dale) and Oscar Rairdan to circulate a petition asking for Albert's resignation as pastor, this in spite of the fact that there were no charges against him.

Warren, "If you want to continue talking, you'll have to go out."

Albert and Aimee said good-bye and left.

****

Following is a list of exhibits and documents enclosed in the original June 3, 1994 packet, followed with copies of those documents:

****

1. Formal Charges of Unchristian Conduct.

****

DATE: June 3, 1994

FROM: Albert E. and Aimee Anderson
        — — — Avenue
        Ellensburg, WA 98926

To: Northwest District Council
        Credentials Committee
        P. O. Box 699
        Kirkland, WA 98083-0699

                and

        General Council Credentials Committee
        1445 Boonville Avenue
        Springfield, MO 65802-1894

RE: Formal Charges of Unchristian Conduct

FOREWORD:

We prayerfully come to you, seeking your help in a situation, or rather a series of situations, which have occurred in the Northwest District of the Assemblies of God over the past two years. It has been brought to our attention by Rev. George O. Wood of the General Council that since the Northwest District believed it had received no formal charges against Rollin Carlson, there were no grounds for action on its part. Therefore, we wish to correct that oversight by filing herewith formal charges of unchristian conduct on the part of Rollin Carlson mainly, and of Don Strong, Frank Cole, Elmer Kirschman, Dale Carpenter, and Warren Bullock in varying lesser degrees.

As Christians, we are admonished very clearly by our Lord Jesus to be honest in all our dealings and to treat others as we ourselves would like to be treated. In the situations that have occurred in the Northwest District over the past two years, the above named men have withheld the truth from us and others and have tried to prevent the full investigation of Care-Net and of the situation at the Kittitas Assembly of God.

Officials of the Northwest District have backed the unchristian behavior of Rollin Carlson and Gary Jeffery on one hand. While at the same time they have attempted to silence us and Robert and Anna Mae Cousart, who have sought to find a solution to the wrongs we have witnessed and have heard from hurting, confused people who came to us seeking help.

Following is a chronological history of our attempts to seek a solution through the structure of the Assemblies of God, first through our own Northwest District, and secondly through the General Council. This history was presented as an eleven-page "Petition to the General Council of the Assemblies of God, asking for an investigation into the manner in which the Northwest District Council of the Assemblies of God Presbytery and Northwest District Council Credentials Committee handled information given them regarding Care-Net Outreach and the Kittitas Assembly of God." And was sent to both the General Council and the Northwest District by registered mail on May 10, 1994. We are again presenting that document with the addition of charges spelled out. We pray you will let God's truth be made known in your hearts.

CHRONOLOGICAL HISTORY AND CHARGES:

December 18, 1990 - Frank E. Cole and Elmer Kirschman sign a Certificate of Affiliation as a Home Missions Assembly with the Northwest District Council of the Assemblies of God. The certificate reads, "This is to certify that the Care-Net Outreach of Everett, State of Washington, has entered into fellowship with the Northwest District Council of the Assemblies of God, with right to proper representation in district affairs so long as maintaining a scriptural standard in teaching and doctrine." (Exhibit A)

May 20, 1991 - Kittitas County records show a Deed of Trust was executed between the Care-Net Outreach and the Northwest District Council of the Assemblies of God for $135,000.00, for the purchase of land in Kittitas County.

September 18, 1991 - Minutes of the Kittitas County Board of Adjustment read (in reference to Care-Net's application for conditional use of the Care-Net land), "CARLSON agreed this was a complete withdrawal and said he would start the process from the beginning including new fees." (Exhibit B) (According to the Kittitas County Planner, Rollin Carlson has never reapplied for the conditional Use Permit. Yet, six months after his withdrawal of the application, on March 6, 1992, he showed the Care-Net video to over 2,000 men at a men's retreat in Yakima. The video stated that Care-Net is a non-profit corporation licensed in the State of Washington and promotes it as a rehabilitation facility for men in transition.)

September 25, 1991 - The *Daily Record* printed an article about Care-Net pulling its application for a proposed guest ranch and rehabilitation center on land zoned Agricultural 20. The same issue of the paper printed a letter from Rollin Carlson where he stated, "The Care-Net Ranch voluntarily withdrew its conditional use application September 18, because of the need to clarify its purpose in construction and land use. Our intent is to be committed to the current (county) Ag/20 zoning." (Exhibit C)

February 9, 1992 - Myron and Jean Rachinski first attended Ellensburg First Assembly of God Church in the morning. On the way out of the church, Jean gave Aimee Anderson a blue Care-Net brochure and told the Andersons they were with Care-Net. The brochure contained photographs and a write-up about the people involved at the Care-Net Ranch. On the reverse side was a copy of the Certificate of Affiliation with the Northwest District. (Exhibit A) The brochure held the following statement:

> Help provide 100 beef stock cows for the Care-Net Ranch in Kittitas, WA. Each year the offspring from this herd of cows will create a perpetual source of funds for the Care-Net ministry to needy Men-In-Transition. The contribution needed is $700.00 per cow. Come to the Men's Retreat with your check filled out.

CHARGE: Rollin Carlson continued to solicit funding for Care-Net Ranch as a rehabilitation outreach, even though, because of strong public opposition, he withdrew his application for conditional use of the ranch property, and to date has not reapplied. Also, the video stated that

ALBERT & AIMEE ANDERSON

Care-Net was a non-profit corporation licensed in the State of Washington. To date, this is not true. This video was used by Rollin to solicit funds deceitfully; and without the proper land use permits, he is operating outside the laws of Kittitas County. These are actions no Christian should be guilty of.

February/March, 1992 - During February a friendship developed between the Andersons and the Rachinskis. The Rachinskis shared how Rollin had approached them about coming to Kittitas to be a part of the Care-Net Ministry. He told them their starting pay would be $200.00 per week plus their home and food. They were excited about being involved in this ministry.

March 6, 1992 - Albert Anderson and several other men from Ellensburg First Assembly attended the Men's Retreat in Yakima where over 2,000 men from the Northwest district gathered. In this service, the promotional video about Care-Net was shown.

    Rollin Carlson and Myron Rachinski were on the platform promoting the Care-Net Outreach Ministry for men located at the Kittitas Care-Net Ranch.

March-July, 1992 - About this time Jean Rachinski began to really open up to the Andersons. Problems were developing between the Rachinskis and Care-Net. They did not receive the raise in salary they were led to believe would be forthcoming. Jean Rachinski told Aimee that Rollin would lay two $100.00 bills on a sheet of paper and run a copy off on the copy machine. He then had Myron sign this sheet of paper as a receipt for the money paid him for services rendered to the Care-Net Ranch. Jean said Rollin later told them that he was giving them the $200.00 per week out of his pocket as a personal contribution or gift.

Jean also told the Andersons that Rollin required them to attend his church in Everett. If it was impossible for them to get to Everett, then they were expected to attend Kittitas Assembly of God with the rest of the Care-Net people, including Randy Bale (ranch director at Care-Net) and Vicki, his wife, and children. Later, Randy became a member of the Administrative Board at Kittitas Assembly, and Vicki became the treasurer of Kittitas Assembly. The Bales had advised the Rachinskis not to attend Ellensburg First Assembly of God.

CHARGE: According to Myron Rachinski, Rollin Carlson hired the Rachinskis to work on Care-Net Ranch and promised them a raise. Later, he called the $200.00 per week he gave them a "contribution" or "gift." In addition, he paid them by cash, running a copy of the money on a photocopier and having Myron sign it as a "receipt for money paid him for services." According to Myron's letter, Rollin did not keep his word about giving the Rachinskis a raise and he has apparently avoided withholding taxes and paying Social Security on the money, he was paying the Rachinskis. Even Jesus paid the taxes levied in his day.

June 11, 1992 - Albert and Aimee Anderson had a 10:00 a.m. appointment at Care-Net Ministries with Myron Rachinski and John Dudley, a resident at Care-Net who was there for rehabilitation. Albert had been asked by Myron to help counsel John and to baptize John in water. Albert had tried to phone Rollin before going out to Care-Net, but had not been able to reach him.

Albert and Aimee ate dinner with the Rachinskis and stayed at Care-Net until approximately 1:00 p.m. They talked to Myron and Jean about taking the youth group service on Wednesday evenings. Later the Rachinskis told the Andersons they could not take the youth group because Rollin wanted them to drive the men at Care-Net every weekend to Everett to attend Rollin's church.

Later, after the visit, Albert reached Rollin by phone. He told Rollin about the request for baptism, and Rollin replied that Care-Net was his responsibility, not the Andersons', and that he would do the baptizing.

August 1, 1992 - The Andersons ate dinner with the Rachinskis, who were moving back East. Myron Rachinski told the Andersons many concerns they had about Care-Net and the way Rollin Carlson did things. Later Aimee phoned Alfred Hansen, a former District presbyter and friend, and told him about Rollin and Care-Net. She asked him for advice on whether to contact Don Strong. He thought the Andersons could trust Don Strong to handle the situation properly.

August 6, 1992 - About noon the Andersons had an appointment to meet with Don Strong at Vantage in order to discuss Care-Net. They had lunch and were together almost two hours. The Andersons shared their concerns about the insurance, Rollin Carlson, and the way Myron and Jean Rachinski were paid and treated.

September 14, 1992 - Some days earlier Albert had phoned Joe Carlson (Rollin's brother) and asked to speak with Rollin. At that time, Albert asked Rollin several questions about Care-Net. Rollin Carlson unexpectedly stopped by the Andersons' home. During Rollin's visit, Albert and Aimee asked him several questions. He made the following statements:

   a. Rollin and his wife agreed to give a contribution of $200.00 per week to Myron at Care-Net.
   b. Rollin said he told the insurance company all about his accident and that he couldn't do his work at the

ranch and had to hire Myron. Rollin told the Andersons that the insurance company told him it was okay for him to be reimbursed for the money he had to pay Myron to do his job at Care-Net Ranch.
  c. Rollin said he didn't have any of his cattle out at Care-Net. Later he said he or his son had one or two or so there.

September 20, 1992 - Myron Rachinski wrote a "To Whom It May Concern" letter explaining the circumstances surrounding their employment at Care-Net. (Exhibit D) He mailed the letter to the Andersons requesting them to get it to the proper people. The letter reads in part as follows:

> *"Pastor Carlson called me and told me that the Insur. Co. was going to pay him back the money he had given me because of his car accident he had in '91 in which the doctor told him not to work because of the injury to his wrist or something like that, and he related to the Insur. Co. that is why he had to hire me to work at the ranch. He also said, that the receipts I have been signing were for the church record and the Insur. Co. didn't need to know anything about them. He told me that the Insur. Co. was going to call me and confirm the fact that I have been working and for how much.*
> *The Agent asked me what I did at the ranch, what I received for payment, when did I start, did Pastor Carlson*

> work at the ranch, and did I
> have any record of what I had
> been paid. I remembered in
> Pastor Carlson's office after
> all this was done and I was
> getting my next wks. pay, he
> asked me if I had a problem
> with that. I told him, no. In
> my heart I didn't feel good
> about it and told my wife that
> there are probably some facts
> that we weren't aware of and
> him being our pastor, we
> passed it off as being okay."

CHARGE: Rollin Carlson told Myron Rachinski the insurance company didn't need to know anything about the "receipts" he had been signing. It also appears Rollin tried to make the insurance company think he spent a lot of time at Care-Net Ranch actually working at ranching, and therefore, needed the Rachinskis' help while he was unable to do farm work because of the injury sustained in a vehicular accident. This is deceitful behavior and not becoming of a Christian, especially an ordained minister.

September 28, 1992 - Don Strong visited the Andersons in their home. They gave him Myron Rachinski's "To Whom It May concern" letter. He promised to give it to the District officials. During the course of the conversation, Don told the Andersons that this is one time when Frank Cole was right. According to Don, Frank had not wanted Rollin to start Care-Net, but because of pressure by Rollin and others, he gave in to it. Later Don revealed that their church had given thousands of dollars to Care-Net.

October 15, 1992 - After several attempts to reach Don by phone, the Andersons were finally able to talk with him after a ministers' and wives' luncheon in Yakima. Don told Albert and Aimee Anderson that he did not give the letter to the District Officials. When Aimee told him that he promised to give it to them, Don told her they didn't have time. In addition, Myron wrote another letter to Rollin, which sounded "different." Don also said that if the Andersons did anything about it, he would not back them and they would look questionable. The Andersons thought Don was acting strange, either afraid or angry, and that he wanted to get away from them as soon as possible.

CHARGE: Don Strong broke his promise to give the Rachinskis' letter to District Officials. Further, he threatened not to back the Andersons if they tried to do anything about it.

April 1, 1993 - Kittitas County records revealed a Deed of Trust was executed between the Care-Net Outreach and the Northwest District Council of the Assemblies of God for $350,000.00.

July 9, 1993 - Aimee tried to reach Elmer Kirschman by phone about concerns surrounding Care-Net, but failed to reach him.

July 19, 1993 - Aimee talked with Elmer Kirschman on the phone and told him about the "To Whom It May Concern" letter from the Rachinskis and asked what they should do with it. He told them to send it back to the Rachinskis, that there was "...no need to get the Andersons' hands dirty." He did not seem interested in doing anything about it.

CHARGE: Elmer Kirschman did not want to see the letter from the Rachinskis, even though there were some serious statements in it that concerned a minister in the Northwest District. Article X, Section 5.a of the Bylaws of the General Council of the Assemblies of God which state:

> *The superintendent of the district in which the alleged offense is reported to have occurred, and/or an appointed representative(s) shall conduct the investigation to determine their source and validity... (1)Interview with complainant(s). The persons involved shall be interviewed in order to ascertain the facts in the case and the reasons underlying the persistence of the reports or complaints.*

As of June 2, 1994, the Rachinskis have never been contacted by District Officials to verify their statements to us and in their letter.

November, 1993 - The Andersons read in the Ellensburg *Daily Record* about the troubles in the Kittitas Assembly Church. At this time Aimee Anderson called Pairlee Treat, one of the wronged people from Kittitas Assembly. Pairlee had attended Ellensburg First Assembly occasionally in the past. Pairlee told her story to the Andersons.

December 2, 1993 - Albert and Aimee Anderson had a phone conversation with Warren Bullock at the Northwest District. They expressed their concerns about Care-Net and the trouble at the Kittitas Church. They told him about some of the wrongs concerning Rollin Carlson and Care-Net. Bro. Bullock asked them to send documentation. The Andersons sent him copies of Rachinskis' "To Whom It May Concern" letter and the Ellensburg *Daily Record* articles (Exhibits E and F) about Kittitas Assembly. The Andersons never received a response from Warren Bullock on this material.

December 11, 1993 - Andersons received a Care-Net brochure in the mail soliciting funds for the ministry at the ranch. The impression given is that the Care-Net Ranch is a rehabilitation facility servicing several people at a time. (Exhibit G)

CHARGE: The Care-Net brochure uses a direct quote by Randy Bale, the ranch manager, which says in part, "Men are arriving and receiving supports and accountability in a loving ranch environment." Later this same brochure lists 1,202 meals served in October, making it sound as if a large number of men are being ministered to at Care-Net Ranch. If a large number of men are being ministered to at the ranch, then Care-Net is operating without the proper land use permits. If a large number of men are not being ministered to at the ranch, then the brochure is deceptive and is soliciting funds under false pretenses. In either case; this is not the type of activity Christians should be party to.

December 14, 1993 - Albert and Aimee talked with Frank Cole on the phone. They expressed their concerns about Rollin Carlson, CareNet and the situation at the Kittitas Assembly of God. Frank Cole appeared not to know much about what was going on. He asked Albert to mail him the papers that were sent to Warren Bullock. The letter and newspaper articles were mailed to him also. (Exhibits E and H)

Again, the officials of the Northwest District did not respond to the Andersons' plea for help. Furthermore, the Northwest District has not been in compliance with Article X, Section 5.a of the Bylaws of the General Council of the Assemblies of God which state:

> *The superintendent of the district in which the alleged offense is reported to have occurred, and/or an appointed*

> representative(s) shall conduct the investigation to determine their source and validity...(1)Interview with complainant(s). The persons involved shall be interviewed in order to ascertain the facts in the case and the reasons underlying the persistence of the reports or complaints.

CHARGE: Frank Cole and Warren Bullock were both informed about the situation at Kittitas Assembly, as well as concerns about Rollin Carlson and Care-Net, by the Andersons. Elmer Kirschman was informed by a petition, for help, from the Kittitas Assembly group in November 1993. (A copy of this letter is included here.) Yet, the petitioners from Kittitas Assembly have never been interviewed by Northwest District Officials in an attempt to discover what really happened. Only the word of Gary Jeffery and his followers have been heeded.

> December 22, 1993 - The Andersons received a letter from Frank Cole in which he wrote: "I attended services at Kittitas last Sunday and I had dinner with Pastor Jeffery. Things are much quieter and we continue to be in prayer that the matter will be settled soon." (Exhibit I) There was no mention about Care-Net in the letter.

CHARGE: Although Frank Cole had been informed about the injustices that had occurred at Kittitas Assembly, according to the excommunicated members, he has never contacted any of the people who had complained about Gary Jeffery.

> January 7, 8 and 10, 1994 - Rollin Carlson attended the hearings concerning the Kittitas Church at the Kittitas County Courthouse. Rollin told Aimee that Frank Cole sent him to

the hearing in Frank Cole's place since, he said, Frank could be subpoenaed to court. Since Randy Bale, one of the board members at the Kittitas Assembly, was also the manager and counselor at Care-Net Ranch, Rollin's presence at the hearings as a Northwest District representative was a conflict of interest and in violation of Article 3, Section 8 of the Northwest District Bylaws which read:

> *District officers who have an interest or relationship that biases, or appears to bias, a decision-making process shall disqualify themselves in matters of ministerial credentials and discipline, or disciplinary intervention in local assemblies when family, staff, close friendships, or business and pastoral relationships are involved.*

Furthermore, Rollin Carlson is the CareNet pastor and was Pairlee Treat's former pastor at the Ellensburg First Assembly in the 1960s, and he has known Jerry Marchel from boyhood.

CHARGE: Rollin Carlson should have removed himself from representing the Northwest District at the court hearings involving Kittitas Assembly of God. His involvement with CareNet and the ranch manager being a member of the Kittitas Assembly board constituted a conflict of interest.

CHARGE: The Northwest District has not dealt properly according to the bylaws in dealing with Gary Jeffery, who resorted to using the civil courts to try to solve his problem with those who questioned his actions. According to the people who were excommunicated, he did not try to talk

with any of the twelve people he accused of harassment, and the judge himself said his statements were fabricated in an attempt to have anti-harassment papers served on those twelve. He not only disobeyed Scriptures, he also disobeyed the bylaws of the Kittitas Assembly of God and he disobeyed civil law by lying under oath.

February 17, 1994 - Aimee phoned the Care-Net number. Jeff, a resident from Whidbey Island, answered the phone. He said he had lived there about two months and expected to be there possibly up to one year. He told Aimee that he had an alcohol problem and was getting help. Aimee asked Jeff if Jason, the counselor at Care-Net, received a salary. He told her he receives $300.00 a month as a blessing. Jeff also said they (Care-Net) were almost finished with the new bunkhouse that would house 9 to 10 men. Aimee asked him how a person could get to live at the ranch. He told her to talk with Rollin Carlson.

 Aimee phoned Anita Kazee at the Kittitas County Commissioner's office (509-962-7571) and gave her the information that Jeff at Care-Net had given over the phone. She had already been doing some checking since she had seen the Care-Net video and brochure a few days earlier. She said the records show that Rollin Carlson and Care-Net had never received a variance or permit to operate the way the video and brochure indicated they were.

February 19, 1994 - Aimee called Jean Rachinski and talked about an hour. Some of the things she told Aimee included the following: Rollin did not want to go solo; he wanted the District to back him up. He hired Myron for CareNet and paid him with offerings. Jean sewed the drapes for the multi-purpose conference room; which was finished and in use the first part of 1992. Rollin went ahead with building the steel granary for supplies without getting a permit because he said he felt it was the work of God or God's work.

They had two travel trailers on Care-Net property, but had to take them off (she did not say why). Sometimes Rollin took cattle to his property on the Coast and sold them over there. At times, twelve to fifteen men came to work at the ranch. When the Rachinskis and Bales had their problems, Jean said Rollin wanted to smooth it over because he said it would be a problem for Care-Net. She also mentioned one of the residents at Care-Net, Ed Morgan, was allegedly a wanted man. He left one night and never came back.

February 26, 1994 - At a conference held at Central Washington University, Albert and Aimee Anderson talked with Warren Bullock, and gave him a copy of the conditional use application (Exhibit J), minutes of Kittitas County Board of Adjustment (Exhibit B), newspaper clippings about the "Rehab Ranch Is Put On Hold" (Exhibit C), and Rollin's letter to the County Planner stating he would abide by the Ag/20 zoning. (Exhibit K) He said Rollin asked to borrow money in 1993 from the Northwest District for Care-Net in 1993, but the District officials turned him down. He made no mention of the $350,000.00 Deed of Trust between Northwest District and Care-Net Outreach, dated April 1, 1993.

Albert told Warren that Rollin told him Care-Net has four boards: Everett Bethany Church Board, Care-Net board, Northwest District Home Missions Board, and the Northwest District Presbytery. Warren agreed that was correct, however, he further said the District officials are not given financial accounting information from Care-Net.

February 28, 1994 - Mr. Kruger, a builder for the Northwest District, told Aimee that they were almost through with another bunkhouse that would house ten men. He said that CareNet was a rehabilitation ranch for men.

CHARGE: If Care-Net Ranch is a rehabilitation ranch for men, then Rollin is operating it as such without the proper county permits. If it is a regular working ranch, then is Rollin paying salaries, and if he is, is he withholding federal taxes and paying Social Security taxes, workman's compensation and medical benefits? According to Rollin's statement to Albert Anderson, Care-Net pays no salaries. If that is the case, how can it be a working ranch with hired help?

Later the same day Aimee Anderson and AnnaMae Cousart talked with Don Strong and Dale Carpenter. Aimee told them that Rollin and CareNet were operating illegally in that they had not received the proper permits. Aimee told Dale to talk with Warren Bullock if he wanted more information.

April 4, 1994 - Frank Cole wrote a letter to Robert Cousart, and sent a copy of the letter to Albert Anderson. (Exhibit L) The letter says, "non-members of Assemblies of God Churches do not have voice or vote in any business meeting." Later the letter says, "Ministers shall refrain from taking any attitude toward disciplined members that would tend to nullify the action of the Credentials Committee." Further, it says, "Non-compliance with the foregoing shall be subject to censure or charge which may necessitate the recall of his/her credentials.
I am hereby notifying you that unless you withdraw from participation in this conflict, whether by meeting, phone or letter, it will be necessary for you to meet with the Ministerial Relations Committee." **The disciplined members who had their memberships removed from Kittitas Assembly are on one**

hand considered dissident members and on the other hand as non-members.

CHARGE: Frank Cole threatened Robert Cousart (and Albert Anderson indirectly by sending him a copy of the letter) with recalling his (their) credentials if they did not withdraw from the conflict. According to the excommunicated people, at no time did Frank Cole conduct an investigation into the Kittitas situation either by interviewing the people who had complaints against Gary Jeffery's actions or having other District Officials interview them.

April 5, 1994 - In a phone call to the Internal Revenue Service, the person on the phone said Care-Net is not listed as a non-profit corporation. In another call to the Secretary of State, the person on the phone said Care-Net is not listed as a non-profit tax-exempt corporation licensed in the State of Washington.

CHARGE: The Care-Net video falsely states that Care-Net is a non-profit corporation licensed in the State of Washington. Rollin Carlson's use of this video to solicit funds is doing so under false pretenses.

April 14, 1994 - A check of Kittitas County records revealed property taxes on the Care-Net-owned land in Kittitas County are delinquent. A one percent was added the end of March. One half of the 1994 taxes will be added at the end of April, and a penalty will be added in May.

CHARGE: Rollin Carlson is giving a poor Christian testimony by allowing Care-Net property taxes to become delinquent. Northwest District executive officers, especially, should set a good example.

April 25-28, 1994 - At the Northwest District Council Convention, an emergency resolution revealed that, "the District has a _deficit_ in net assets of $3,481,324." The resolution further said, "The plan also calls for the District to be reorganized into two separate corporations. The corporation handling the loan fund functions would have a net worth of approximately 0. The new corporation handling the church and other ministry functions would have a _deficit_ of approximately $3.8 million." (Exhibit M)

May 2, 1994 - Don Strong phoned and asked if he could see the Andersons. He went to their home and stayed about an hour and a half. The topics of conversation centered on Care-Net and Kittitas Assembly's problems and the involvement of the Andersons in these two situations. Albert told Don that he had received the letter written to Robert Cousart and said, "I took his letter as a subtle hint or threat." Don indicated that it was not so subtle.

May 4, 1994 - Aimee Anderson phoned the Great Commission Partners, Assemblies of God Foundation, 1600 North Boonville Avenue, Springfield, MO 65803-2730. Phone 1-417-865-4880. The person with Great Commission Partners said that the money that is given to Great Commission is put in a trust fund and cows are given cost free to their ranchers. Care-Net was one of their ranches and was somewhat like a hybrid — on one hand, it's a ranch and on the other hand it's a rehabilitation ministry for men under IRS Code 501-C-3. According to the person on the phone, Great Commission Partners and Care-Net were started in 1993. Randall Barton, an attorney, is the president of the Assemblies of God Foundation. The Andersons were informed (by a friend) that Randall Barton used to work for Care-Net in the State of Washington.

May, 1994 - *Mountain Movers*, Assembly of God Division of Foreign Missions magazine, had a full-page advertisement inside the front cover for Great Commission Partners. The advertisement states, "A minimum of 25 percent of the net gain has been earmarked for investment in the lives of young people at Assemblies of God colleges. The remaining 75 percent will go to the ministry designated by the rancher or farmer who raises the livestock." (Exhibit N)

Not included in the original petition is information from Ken Forester, who sold hay to Care-Net Ranch, that Rollin Carlson requested the bill be made out in separate statements, one for the hay and one for the hauling. When Rollin paid him, he had made out two statements of his own, increasing the amount for the hauling and decreasing the amount for the hay. He told Ken that he would be collecting the cost of the hauling from the insurance company because he hurt his wrist. Ken is in the process of sending us a notarized statement.

CHARGE: Rollin Carlson was deceiving the insurance company as to the actual cost of the hauling. Not only was he being deceitful, but he was also setting a bad example of how Christians should act.

Also, a deacon of Ellensburg First Assembly told Albert Anderson in a board meeting that Don Strong told two of the deacons to tell Albert to resign. The reason given was "the church was not growing." Others in the congregation told the Andersons that at least one deacon was saying Don Strong told them to circulate a petition asking for Albert's resignation because "he had been there too long." These people refused to sign the petition. Later, in the Andersons' home Don Strong did admit that the deacons could have gotten the impression he was asking Albert to resign.

CHARGE: Don Strong acted unethically and irresponsibly in encouraging or seeming to encourage the removal of a minister who had no charges against him; yet, on the other hand, he completely backed a neighboring minister who had several charges against him.

In 1992, shortly after he saw the Care-Net video, Jim Brown, a builder, told us that he was contacted by Randy Barton, now president of the Assemblies of God Foundation, who asked him to build four bunkhouses to house both men and women for rehabilitation at Care-Net Ranch. Jim could not go along with the request, because he was asked to put the houses on blocks, which are illegal according to the local building codes.

CHARGE: Care-Net has not only tried to operate as a rehabilitation facility without the proper land use permits, it has also tried to construct buildings outside the local building codes. This is a poor witness from a Christian organization.

IN CONCLUSION:

I Peter 4:17 - "Judgment must begin at the house of God." The church needs to clean up their own camp and get rid of the corruption from within before they can point fingers at the world and accuse them of being corrupt and evil. Too many times church people live a double standard which brings confusion to the world. We trust you have seen that double standard in the foregoing chronology of events. The Assemblies of God have been used mightily by God in the spreading of the Gospel. However, in recent years, we have had the shameful excesses of Jim Bakker and Jimmy Swaggert connected with our movement. If we do not deal with dishonesty and deception ourselves and root it out, God will deal with it. He certainly will not bless our efforts until the evil is rooted out.

WHITED SEPULCHRES

We have come before you with these charges, not as a vendetta against any one or two people, but in an attempt to see some terrible wrongs righted. What has been happening with Care-Net and Kittitas Assembly is not glorifying to God. What kind of message are we sending a lost and corrupt world when Christians are engaged in deceitful activities? In a day when cults are running rampant, what kind of image are we portraying when we allow a minister to arbitrarily remove long-time members from a church because they question his actions and will not "submit to his authority?" We pray in the Name of our Lord Jesus Christ that you will see what has been happening and that you will take steps to correct the injustices that have occurred.

Albert E. Anderson, Pastor
Ellensburg First Assembly

Aimee Anderson
Wife of Albert E. Anderson

cc: Rev. Thomas E. Trask

****

2. Summary of the seventeen (17) charges.

****

SUMMARY OF FORMAL CHARGES

CHARGE No. 1: Rollin Carlson continued to solicit funding for Care-Net Ranch as a rehabilitation outreach, even though, because of strong public opposition, he withdrew his application for conditional use of the ranch property, and to date has not reapplied. Also, the video stated that Care-Net was a non-profit corporation licensed in the State of Washington. To date, this is not true. This video was used by Rollin to solicit funds deceitfully; and without the proper land use permits, he is operating outside the laws of Kittitas County. These are actions, no Christian should be guilty of.

CHARGE No. 2: According to Myron Rachinski, Rollin Carlson hired the Rachinskis to work on Care-Net Ranch and promised them a raise. Later, he called the $200.00 per week he gave them a "contribution" or "gift." In addition, he paid them by cash, running a copy of the money on a photocopier and having Myron sign it as a "receipt for money paid him for services." According to Myron's letter, Rollin did not keep his word about giving the Rachinskis a raise and he has apparently avoided withholding taxes and paying Social Security on the money he was paying the Rachinskis. Even Jesus paid the taxes levied in his day.

CHARGE No. 3: Rollin Carlson told Myron Rachinski the insurance company didn't need to know anything about the "receipts" he had been signing. It also appears Rollin tried to make the insurance company think he spent a lot of time at Care-Net Ranch actually working at ranching, and therefore, needed the Rachinskis' help while he was unable to do farm work because of the injury sustained in a vehicular accident. This is deceitful behavior and not becoming of a Christian, especially an ordained minister.

CHARGE No. 4: Don Strong broke his promise to give the Rachinskis' letter to District Officials. Further, he threatened not to back the Andersons if they tried to do anything about it.

CHARGE No. 5: Elmer Kirschman did not want to see the letter from the Rachinskis, even though there were some serious statements in it that concerned a minister in the Northwest District. Article X, Section 5.a of the Bylaws of the General Council of the Assemblies of God which state:

> *The superintendent of the district in which the alleged offense is reported to have occurred, and/or an appointed representative(s) shall conduct the investigation to determine their source and validity...(1)Interview with complainant(s). The persons involved shall be interviewed in order to ascertain the facts in the case and the reasons underlying the persistence of the reports or complaints.*

As of June 2, 1994, the Rachinskis have never been contacted by District Officials to verify their statements to us and in their letter.

CHARGE No. 6: The Care-Net brochure uses a direct quote by Randy Bale, the ranch manager, which says in part, "Men are arriving and receiving supports and accountability in a loving ranch environment." Later this same brochure lists 1,202 meals served in October, making it sound as if a large number of men are being ministered to at Care-Net Ranch. If a large number of men are being ministered to at the ranch, then Care-Net is operating without the proper land use permits. If a large number of men are not being ministered to at the ranch, then the brochure is deceptive and is soliciting funds under false pretenses. In either case, this is not the type of activity Christians should be party to.

CHARGE No. 7: Frank Cole and Warren Bullock were both informed about the situation at Kittitas Assembly, as well as concerns about Rollin Carlson and CareNet, by the Andersons. Elmer Kirschman was informed by a petition for help from the Kittitas Assembly group in November 1993. (A copy of this letter is included here.) Yet, the petitioners from Kittitas Assembly have never been interviewed by Northwest District Officials in an attempt to discover what really happened. Only the word of Gary Jeffery and his followers have been heeded.

CHARGE No. 8: Although Frank Cole had been informed about the injustices that had occurred at Kittitas Assembly, according to the excommunicated members, he has never contacted any of the people who had complained about Gary Jeffery.

CHARGE No. 9: Rollin Carlson should have removed himself from representing the Northwest District at the court hearings involving Kittitas Assembly of God. His involvement with Care-Net and the ranch manager being a member of the Kittitas Assembly board constituted a conflict of interest.

CHARGE No. 10: The Northwest District has not dealt properly according to the bylaws in dealing with Gary Jeffery, who resorted to using the civil courts to try to solve his problem with those who questioned his actions. According to the people who were excommunicated, he did not try to talk with any of the twelve people he accused of harassment, and the judge himself said his statements were fabricated in an attempt to have anti-harassment papers served on those twelve. He not only disobeyed Scriptures, he also disobeyed the bylaws of the Kittitas Assembly of God and he disobeyed civil law by lying under oath.

CHARGE No. 11: If Care-Net Ranch is a rehabilitation ranch for men, then Rollin is operating it as such without the proper county permits. If it is a regular working ranch, then is Rollin paying salaries; and if he is, is he withholding federal taxes and paying Social Security taxes, workman's compensation and medical benefits? According to Rollin's statement to Albert Anderson, CareNet pays no salaries. If that is the case, how can it be a working ranch with hired help?

CHARGE No. 12: Frank Cole threatened Robert Cousart (and Albert Anderson indirectly by sending him a copy of the letter) with recalling his (their) credentials if they did not withdraw from the conflict. According to the excommunicated people, at no time did Frank Cole conduct an investigation into the Kittitas situation either by interviewing the people who had complaints against Gary Jeffery's actions or having other District Officials interview them.

CHARGE No. 13: The Care-Net video falsely states that Care-Net is a non-profit corporation licensed in the State of Washington. Rollin Carlson's use of this video to solicit funds is doing so under false pretenses.

CHARGE No. 14: Rollin Carlson is giving a poor Christian testimony by allowing Care-Net property taxes to become delinquent. Northwest District executive officers, especially, should set a good example.

CHARGE No. 15: Rollin Carlson was deceiving the insurance company as to the actual cost of the hauling. Not only was he being deceitful, but he was also setting a bad example of how Christians should act.

CHARGE No. 16: Don Strong acted unethically and irresponsibly in encouraging or seeming to encourage the removal of a minister who had no charges against him; yet, on the other hand, he completely backed a neighboring minister who had several charges against him.

CHARGE No. 17: Care-Net has not only tried to operate as a rehabilitation facility without the proper land use permits, it has also tried to construct buildings outside the local building codes. This is a poor witness from a Christian organization.

****

3. May 22, 1994 letter to Albert and Aimee Anderson from George Wood in response to Albert and Aimee Anderson's Petition for Investigation.

****

THE GENERAL COUNCIL OF THE ASSEMBLIES OF God
1445 Boonville Avenue
Springfield, Missouri 65802-1894

George Wood   Phone 417-862-2781
General Secretary   Fax 417-863-6614

May 22, 1994

Rev. and Mrs. Albert E. Anderson, Pastor
First Assembly of God
701 Capitol Avenue East
Ellensburg, WA 98926

Dear Brother and Sister Anderson:

Greetings in the Lord!
I have received the letter which you have sent, as well as the enclosures.
Subsequent to receiving your letter, I have talked with your district superintendent, Warren Bullock. In my opinion, he has a very satisfactory explanation for all the questions which you have raised.
Brother Bullock indicated to me that he extended an opportunity for you to meet with him, Rollin Carlson, and Elmer Kirschman to attempt to resolve the issues which you have raised. He had indicated to you that this would be an informal session in which you could be free to ask Brother Carlson any questions you would like. He indicated to me that you declined to attend that meeting. I would encourage you to consider the matter and be present at such a session, in the spirit of Matthew 18.
It is also my understanding that you have never formally placed charges with the district against

Rollin Carlson. You have brought certain documents and verbal statements and letters to the district regarding feelings you have on the Rollin Carlson matter -- but you have not explicitly laid before the district charges against Rollin Carlson as a minister.

On the district's part, they have felt they have provided you satisfactory answers to the concerns you have raised over the past months.

The appropriate manner which the General Council Bylaws outlines for handling charges against a minister is that they be dealt with first on a district level. Since you yourself have not placed formal charges against Rollin Carlson, nor has the district leadership felt any evidence existed to place those charges, the matter has not been formally dealt with on the district level.

I state the above because you quoted from General Council Bylaws Article X, Section 4,d. It would be our understanding here that the district has failed to take action because it has yet to have receive (sic) information which would give it probable cause to initiate disciplinary action against Rollin Carlson. The intervention of the General Council Credentials Committee only occurs when, in the opinion of the General Council Credentials Committee, the district has filed (sic) to take action. Further, it is the understanding of the General Council Credentials Committee that Article X, Section 4,d, relates to a matter in which the General Council Credentials Committee itself has requested the district to take action. If it so requests the district to take action, and the district does not take action within 90 days, then the General Council Credentials Committee reserves to itself the right to see that action is initiated.

I would join with the encouragement of your district superintendent to you in meeting with him and the other principal parties involved personally in an attempt to resolve this issue. I would further encourage you to limit your communication on this matter to your district superintendent and presbytery. In reviewing your letter I note that outside governmental agencies have been contacted by you -- and, to date, perhaps this contact has not been of a nature to compromise the ability of the church to deal with the problem itself. However, communication to third parties, including governmental entities and the press is not appropriate when there is every attempt to resolve this matter within the church itself.

We do pray that this matter will be resolved in a way that will bring glory and honor to the Lord and result in the building up of His church.

Sincerely yours in Christ,
George O. Wood
General Secretary

GW:jw
cc: Warren Bullock

****

4. June 3, 1994 letter of rebuttal to George Wood from Albert and Aimee Anderson

****

Albert E. and Aimee Anderson
— — — Avenue
Ellensburg, WA 98926

June 3, 1994

Rev. George O. Wood
General Secretary
The General Council of the Assemblies of God
1445 Boonville Avenue
Springfield, MO 65802-1894

Dear Bro. Wood:

    We have received your letter in response to the petition we sent, asking the General Council to fully investigate the manner in which the Northwest District Council of the Assemblies of God Presbytery and the Northwest District Council Credentials Committee handled information given them regarding Care-Net Outreach and the Kittitas Assembly of God. Your letter reflects several areas of gross misunderstanding.
    First of all, when Bro. Bullock called us on May 14, 1994, he asked Albert if he would come to Kirkland and speak with him, Les Welk, Elmer Kirschman and Rollin Carlson about Care-Net. Albert asked if Aimee could accompany him. Bro. Bullock said he would have to think about the request since Albert was the one who held the credentials. Later, Albert called Bro. Bullock and told him, "Since my wife has had more people and more information come to her, I think she should be there." At that time Bro. Bullock said he would set the ground rules, and that he would think about letting Aimee attend the meeting and would get back to Albert. Albert told him he and Aimee would plan on being there.

WHITED SEPULCHRES

On the morning of May 17, 1994, the following message was left on our answering machine: "Morning. This is Ann calling in behalf of Warren Bullock at the District Office, and we are just confirming whether Rev. and Mrs. Anderson will be at the District Office on Wednesday, May 18, at 1:30; and if there is any change in that, please let us know. Our number is 206-827-3013." Bro. Bullock had never called back saying whether or not Aimee would be allowed to attend the meeting.

On May 18, Albert phoned the Northwest District and talked to Warren Bullock's secretary. He asked if Bro. Bullock had received a copy of the petition sent to the General Council. She said she couldn't find it. He told her the original had been sent to General Council and a copy sent to the Northwest District by registered mail, return receipt. Albert had called General Council and was told by your secretary that Bro. Trask and you were out of town and that you would have the complaint on your desk the first thing in the morning. We had already received the return receipt from Springfield. Albert told Bro. Bullock's secretary he thought he and Aimee should wait until they had a response from General Council. Bro. Bullock's secretary said she would have to check with her boss.

It was our feeling that since the original "invitation" to meet with Bros. Bullock, Kirschman, Carlson and Welk had been made to discuss Care-Net, it was important that the Northwest District had at least received the complaint and had time to review it. Up until this time no acknowledgement had been made that they had received it.

On May 20, we checked with the Kirkland Post Office whether the registered package we sent the Northwest District had been delivered. The Postal clerk told us that the Northwest District office had received notice about the package on May 12; however, no one claimed it until May 19, 1994. We received the return receipt on May 21. Why did the Northwest District wait a whole week before picking up the registered package?

The second item in your letter that we take exception to is the statement: "It is also my understanding that you have never formally placed charges with the district against Rollin Carlson. You have brought certain documents and verbal statements and letters to the district regarding feelings you have on the Rollin Carlson matter — but you have not explicitly laid before the district charges against Rollin Carlson as a minister." If you will re-read our petition, you will note that on several occasions we have talked with Rev. Frank Cole, Rev. Warren Bullock, Rev. Don Strong, Rev. Dale Carpenter, Rev. Elmer Kirschman, and to Rev. Rollin Carlson about our concerns about Care-Net and the situation at Kittitas Assembly of God. In addition, documentation to support these charges and concerns were given or mailed to these men. It is our understanding that where there are reports or complaints made about a minister, it is the duty of the Northwest District to fully investigate the reports and complaints by interviewing all people concerned. According to the information given us, this has never been done. Why weren't Myron and Jean Rachinski ever contacted by the District? What was Rollin Carlson's interest in the Kittitas Assembly court hearing? Why have the people who have filed complaints with the Northwest District about Rev. Gary Jeffery of Kittitas Assembly never been contacted by the Northwest District? **Why has the Northwest District threatened Assembly of God ministers who are trying to get to the truth of the matter in both Care-Net and Kittitas Assembly? Why does the Northwest District continue to back ministers such as Rev. Rollin Carlson and Rev. Gary Jeffery who have time after time violated Scriptural principals and district bylaws?**

According to two of the deacons of Ellensburg First Assembly of God, Rev. Don Strong encouraged them to circulate a petition asking Rev. Albert Anderson to resign as pastor of the church. Apparently, there were no charges against us, but the reasons given for this action were "the church is not growing," and "the Andersons have been there too long." These two men, **Paul Bennett and Dale Ball, told Albert in a board meeting that Don Strong told them to tell their pastor to resign.**

The third item in your letter that we take exception to is the statement: "On the district's part, they have felt they have provided you satisfactory answers to the concerns you have raised over the past months." Again, re-read our petition. **Our questions and concerns were either ignored or followed by threats to our ministry.** Refer to Page 6, beginning with Line 18; Page 7, Line 5 and following; Page 9, Line 27 and following.

Fourthly, we have attempted to file what we thought were formal charges about Rev. Carlson's actions, but we have been blocked at every turn by officials of the Northwest District, up to and including the Superintendent of the Northwest District, Frank Cole, and now Warren Bullock. We thought our letters and documentation to the Northwest District constituted formal charges and that it was the duty of the district to fully investigate all reports and complaints, according to its bylaws, Article X, Section 4. Furthermore, your letter states that the district feels it "has yet to have received information which would give it probable cause to initiate disciplinary action against Rollin Carlson." The Northwest District has received all the documentation you received in our petition to General Council. In addition, much of the information they needed is contained in public records of the Kittitas County Courthouse in Ellensburg.

Fifthly, your letter states: "However, communication to third parties, including governmental entities and the press is not appropriate when there is every attempt to resolve this matter within the church itself." We have made every attempt to resolve this matter within the church itself, yet the information we have provided has been ignored and we have been threatened with disciplinary action. **There are criminal activities taking place within the Northwest District under the guise of**

Christianity, yet there have been no attempts by the district officials that we are aware of, to root out the evil. Instead, our ministry has been threatened by innuendos and by threats of disciplinary action against us by the district presbytery. Our board and congregation have been approached by at least one district official in an attempt to undermine our ministry.

Since the Northwest District contends that it has never received formal charges against Rollin Carlson from us, we have formally brought these charges against Rollin Carlson, in writing to the Northwest District Credentials Committee and to the General Council Credentials Committee. Also, we have brought charges against various other officials of the Northwest District Council of the Assemblies of God of ignoring and inappropriately responding to reports and complaints about Rollin Carlson, Care-Net, and Gary Jeffery of Kittitas Assembly. A copy of these charges is enclosed.

In our forty-plus years in ministry in the Assemblies of God, we are grieved about what is happening here in the Northwest District. We find it hard to believe that men of God are willing to engage in illegal activities under the guise of Christianity, yet this is what is happening. It is further hard for us to believe that other men of God continue to attempt to cover up these illegal activities by threatening disciplinary action against those who try to expose it, or by disallowing the information given them by quoting technical mumble-jumble.

Respectfully yours in Christ,

Albert E. Anderson,
Pastor, Ellensburg First Assembly

Aimee Anderson, Wife of Albert E. Anderson

cc: Rev. Thomas E. Trask
    Rev. Warren Bullock
    Northwest District Council Credentials Committee
    General Council Credentials Committee

5. Exhibit A, The Care-Net Outreach's CERTIFICATE of AFFILIATION as a Home Mission Assembly with the Northwest District Council and flip side a Brochure promoting the Care-Net ranch at Kittitas, Washington

****

Exhibit A

MEET THE PEOPLE

RANCH DIRECTOR -- Vicki & Randy Bale
Daniel, Hosanna, Isaac, Mary, Joshua, Sarah, Josiah

The Bale's ministry involves developing "Therapy Projects," livestock and crop planning and involvement in resident's spiritual/physical growth.

QUOTE:...
"Help provide 100 beef stock cows for the Care-Net Ranch in Kittitas, WA. Each year, the offspring from this herd of cows will create a perpetual source of funds for the Care-Net ministry to needy Men-In-Transition. The contribution needed is $700 per cow. Come to the Men's Retreat with your check filled out. Your church will receive World Ministries Credit, and your participation says, 'WE CARE ENOUGH TO GIVE NEEDY MEN A SECOND CHANCE.'" --Jerry Sandeno, Care-Net Board

QUOTES:...
"...as Christians, we need to minister, both individually and collectively, to the needs of a frustrated world ...–
Vern Reeves, Care-Net Board
"...God's love and care for the poor are central to Divine providence. Through Care-Net we show men

that God cares and we care..." -—Gaylord Pearson, Care-Net Board.

COUNSELLING & SCHEDULE COORDINATION - Jean & Myron Rachinski.

The Rachinskis minister to the residents in the area of food service, schedule planning, spiritual/physical growth, prayer and counseling.

QUOTES:...
"...One of the finest investments any Christian man can make; helping another man who is in need..."—Bill Handley, Care-Net Board.

"...God is honoring people who are willing to reach out to people in need. Care-Net is indeed, an Outreach Ministry..."

...Frank Anderson, Care-Net Board

NEWEST RESIDENT — Ed Morgan

Ed was alone, living in his vehicle and in need. He said, "Care-Net was there when I needed help. God has changed my life through Care-Net."

****

6. **Exhibit B, September 18, 1991, Minutes of Kittitas County Board of Adjustment**

****

EXHIBIT B

MINUTES OF KITTITAS COUNTY BOARD OF ADJUSTMENT

September 18, 1991

A public hearing was held concerning the Conditional Use C-91-06 - Care-Net. According to the official minutes of the Kittitas County Board of Adjustment, the board had received "40 letters from the public and a petition of 200 names, all in opposition to the application."

Further, the minutes state that Rollin Carlson, "... stressed the guest ranch wording of his application and said a rehabilitation center was of secondary importance as these men are not alcohol/drug users but are "homeless, hurting, and hungry." He cited Care-Net's work in Snohomish Co. and an $11,000.00 grant from the City of Everett. He said men considered must complete an application and are accepted on a trial basis. Nine men have lived at the current site in the past 27 months and all have returned to society. He explained that money has been raised for three bunkhouses and the service center initially. He stated that, regardless of the outcome, Care-Net will remain in Kittitas Co. even if on a limited basis. He emphasized this is not a group home or an institution."

Attorney Cole, "asked when the property was purchased and was told it was acquired one year ago. He said this conditional use would violate the intent and identity of Ag 20 zoning, and Care-Net knew the zoning when the property was purchased."

Hanson said, "if Care-Net chose to re-apply, it was her opinion the entire process will begin over including the SEPA process and that citizens should contact the Planning Dept. if they suspected any zoning infractions meanwhile."

Rollin Carlson, "agreed this was a complete withdrawal and said that he would start the process from the beginning including new fees."

Where is all the money Rollin said he raised for the three bunkhouses and the service center?

****

7. Exhibit C, September 25, 1991 Ellensburg newspaper article, "Rehab ranch plans put on hold by organizers" concerning Care-Net and letter to the Editor from Rollin Carlson

****

EXHIBIT C

September 25, 1991, Joseph Rose, staff writer for the *Ellensburg Daily Record*, reported:

Rehab Ranch Plans Put On Hold By Organizers... After hearing an earful of opposition from a roomful of concerned neighbors at a Kittitas County Board of Adjustment public hearing last night, the Care-Net Outreach organization of Everett pulled its application for a proposed guest ranch and rehabilitation center on land zoned Agricultural 20.

Care-Net, affiliated with the Northwest Council of Assemblies of God, requested a conditional use permit to allow a guest ranch and rehabilitation center on 160 acres of its property located in the Ag zone land off Vantage Highway.

Proposed was the construction of 20 12-by 24-foot bunkhouses and a central community service center with bathrooms, shower facilities, a laundry and storage area. Also planned was a community room addition to a farmhouse. ...

The stated goal of the Care-Net organization is to provide "transitional" and emergency housing for 30 days to a year, and counseling and job skills training for the homeless and unemployed. ...

"I'm not arguing against its (ranch and center's) purpose, but it can be carried out in another setting where it's allowed," said Rich Cole, speaking on behalf of some concerned residents who own land in the zone. "When the property was bought it was on Agricultural 20 land

and they (Care-Net) knew it. It's (ranch and center) should not be permitted there." ...

Cole told the board of adjustment there "was no way, legally the activity could be allowed to happen in the zone." After an attempt to renegotiate the application with the board and being told that it couldn't be done at a public hearing, Carlson decided to withdraw the original application and reapply.

"I'll have to find some way to approach this on a different basis," said Carlson. "I'm prepared to withdraw this application because I don't believe everyone is focusing on what we've been told to focus on. I'm confused, but I'm committed to this program and it will be in the county regardless."

In the same issue of the *Daily Record*, a letter Rollin Carlson wrote to the editor was printed and read as follows:

On behalf of several thousand dedicated Christians, I would like to express thanks to The Record for its fair reporting; the county officials who are helping clarify what is appropriate land use according to the county ordinance; to neighbors; supporters; local businesses and congregations.

The Care-Net Ranch voluntarily withdrew its conditional use application September 18, because of the need to clarify its purpose in construction and land use. Our intent is to be committed to the current (county) Ag-20 Zoning.

Care-Net has been operating in Kittitas and Snohomish Counties since November of 1988. We definitely intend to continue pursuing the challenge of President Bush's "1,000 Points of Light!" Care-Net is making a difference in the lives of homeless, hungry and hurting people. In the process we are serving over 2,000 meals annually plus spending $100,000.00 for goods, services, products and appropriate taxes in Kittitas County.

As we withdraw the current application, we reaffirm to all of our friends that Care-Net will continue what it has been doing for several years here by utilizing owned and rented facilities on whatever basis is commensurate with meeting the need of this present challenge and operating within zoning requirements.

Rollin J. Carlson,
Pastor/President
The Care-Net Outreach

****

8. **Exhibit D, September 20, 1992 letter To Whom it May Concern, from Myron Rachinski**

****

Exhibit D

Sept. 20, 1992

To Whom It May Concern:
 In response to the questions asked me I am writing this letter.
 In Dec. of 1991 Jean and I were making plans to move to W.VA. Pastor Carlson wanted us to stay. He wanted me to oversee the moving of the mobile home to Kittitas and said he had the leading of the Lord to use us with Care-Net.
 The next few weeks we talked about it and started making plans to work with him. He told us that he wasn't sure how he could work out our pay and was going to have a board meeting and let us know what he could do. His plan was to match our offer in W. VA. of $2000 dollars per mth. as soon as he could.
 What we accepted was $200 per week and by June, he hoped to meet the above proposed salary. Jean wasn't supposed to have to prepare meals until the multi-purpose room was complete and I in turn was only going to be at Care-Net a few days a week and the rest of the week be allowed to contract other work to help our income.
 Jan. 1992 we came to Kittitas and a week or so later so did a resident. So now, the job was full time for both Jean and I and our home became the multi-purpose room. The meals, showers, etc. took place there, and most nights ended 9, 10 o'clock. I'm not complaining because it was all done as ministry.
 Now I'm not sure how long after that we were there that I heard that the board members voted in favor of us being there. I asked one board member, "You mean Pastor Carlson hired us without

consulting the board first?" He told me the board members have given him the "ok" to make decisions without them, that they trust him. Here I thought he had discussed with them about us and our pay and job description. At this time I still thought that Care-Net was paying us the cash of $200 per week because I was signing a piece of paper with a photocopy of the money and date that it was for.

The fact is that the money was coming from Pastor Carlson and as he told me "an offering."

Pastor Carlson called me and told me that the Insur. Co was going to pay him back the money he had given me because of his car accident he had in '91 in which the doctor told him not to work because of the injury to his wrist or something like that and he related to the Insur. Co. that is why he had to hire me to work at the ranch. He also said that the receipts I have been signing were for the church record and the Insur. Co. didn't need to know anything about them. He told me that the Insur. Co was going to call me and confirm the fact that I have been working and for how much.

The agent asked me what I did at the ranch, what I received for payment, when did I start, did Pastor Carlson work at the ranch, and did I have any record of what I had been paid.

I remember in Pastor Carlson's office after all this was done and I was getting my next wks. pay, he asked me if I had a problem with that. I told him no. In my heart I didn't feel good about it and told my wife that there are probably some facts that we weren't aware of and him being our pastor we passed it off as being ok.

When Jean and I quit, I gave Pastor Carlson and Randy Bale (the ranch director) a 45 day notice in writing. Pastor Carlson tried to smooth things out for us to stay and in so doing never submitted our notice. A couple of weeks later he asked me to draft another letter of our notice because our position had not changed. I am enclosing my rough draft of that letter.

Before we left, about two weeks, I called the church to ask if they would take the freezer we had instead of the $200 for the mths. rent. Because we were using our freezer along with the ranch's they no longer had to rent freezer space at the locker in Ellensburg, so I thought that might be a workable deal. I didn't hear from the church until the day we were leaving and loading our furniture from out of storage. Pastor Carlson came by and said he didn't want the freezer, that he could get them for free. I asked him then if he could wait until the 15th because I was going to receive a check then from CWU but he had too many bills to pay on the first and really needed the money now, so I paid him.

The question about the cattle. All I can tell you is that all the receipts at the sale yard that I had ever seen were purchased in Rollin Carlson's name. We branded the cattle with the Care-Net Brand, but I don't know if the brand is registered to Care-Net or Rollin Carlson.

Sincerely yours,

Myron G. Rachinski

****

9. Exhibit E, November 26, 1993 Daily Record article concerning "Church squabble erupted into altercation at Sunday service."

****

Exhibit E

DAILY RECORD
Ellensburg, Washington, Friday, Nov. 26, 1993
35 Cents   Vol. 92, No. 282

CHURCH SQUABBLE ERUPTED INTO ALTERCATION AT Sunday service
By Mike Johnston
City Editor

A five-month long church dispute spilled into the public arena when City of Kittitas police were called to the Assembly of God Church shortly before noon on Nov. 14. The visit was in response to a fight reported during the Sunday morning worship service.

As a follow up to that incident, two city officers were instructed to standby at the city police station last Sunday in case there was another disturbance, but the worship service concluded without incident, according to Kittitas Mayor Mel Wilson.

Officer Vernon Rosa said that when he and Reserve Officer Gary Moore arrived at the church Nov. 14 the altercation was over. Rosa took statements from 12 people and said there were no injuries.

Rosa said he was later contacted by the church's pastor, Gary Jeffery, who told him he had been assaulted and threatened, but wanted to check with his attorney before deciding whether to pursue assault charges. After speaking with an attorney for the region's Assembly of God churches, Jeffery decided not to pursue charges.

"I'm into peace and restoring people," Jeffery said. "I want peace and harmony in the church.

It's too bad that some (people) created an environment of fear and violence."

But others believe it's the pastor and board's past action that is the root of the problem.

A group of about 17 former church members and others came to services that morning at the church on Main Street in Kittitas, intending to read letters to the congregation.

The letters had been sent from Jeffery and church board members to former board member Jerry Marchel and his wife, Phyllis. They state that their church memberships had been revoked by the board due to their disagreement with church leadership.

One letter alleges that actions by Jerry Marchel were having an adverse effect on the church: "What you have chosen to do is to malign and degrade the ministry here." Marchel denies the allegation.

Jerry Marchel, 58, said he and others disagree with the way the pastor and church board excluded two women, Pairlee Treat and her daughter Wanda Cotton, who were not members, from attending the church. Marchel said the women never knew who was accusing them of misconduct.

Treat, 71, said she has attended the church for 14 years. Cotton, 52, has attended for four years.

According to Jeffery, church rules were followed and efforts to meet with the two women privately have not been successful.

"All we want is a fair hearing before both members and non-members for the people who have been accused," said Anita Kazee, a former member who called police from the church during the Nov. 14 service. "We have not had due process of law. We want a chance to have the people hear the accusers face the accused."

"We just wanted to let others know the truth about what's been going on," said Jerry Marchel. "A lot of people didn't know what had happened to me and my wife. We're not in rebellion, we just don't agree with kicking a widow and her daughter out of the church. But I really don't believe anyone wanted what happened after we tried to read the letters in an orderly way."

Others, including Pastor Jeffery and board members, saw the actions at the Sunday service as a disruption to the service. Jeffery said he told those who wanted to read the letters from the board to Marchel, that they were out of order. When they insisted the letters be read, he declared the service over and asked people to join him in prayer.

There are different versions as to what occurred at the service, but most reported there was shouting and some brief grappling, pushing and shoving. People on both sides claim they were physically assaulted, though not seriously.

Jim Boswell, Marchel's son-in-law from Snohomish, said the pastor kneeled in prayer after dismissing the service and he bent down to talk to him. He said the only time he touched the pastor was when he put a finger under his chin and lifted his face up so the two could see eye to eye.

"That touching him wasn't an assault," Boswell said. "If he calls it an assault he's wrong." He also denies that he verbally threatened Jeffery.

Boswell also claims that he was assaulted by someone, though he has not pressed an assault complaint either.

Jeffery declined to comment on why the two women were not allowed to attend services or why the Marchels' church membership was taken away. He said it was a confidential church matter.

Marchel claims he and his wife were removed from membership because they disagreed with the pastor and the board's action. One former church member said attempts are being made to call in district or national Assembly of God leaders to mediate the situation.

"It's an internal church difficulty created by some disgruntled people who don't like me as a pastor," said Jeffery. "The whole thing is very sad, very sad." Jeffery, 39, has been the pastor at the church for a year and eight months. He has been an Assembly of God Church minister since 1974.

ALBERT & AIMEE ANDERSON

10. Exhibit F, December 09, 1993 letter to Warren Bullock from Albert and Aimee Anderson, concerning Kittitas Assembly of God church problems and the Care-Net ranch

****

Exhibit F

FIRST ASSEMBLY OF God
Capitol Avenue and Walnut Street
Ellensburg, Washington 98926

Albert E. Anderson, Pastor
December 09, 1993

Northwest District Council
of the Assemblies of God
Rev. Warren D. Bullock
Assistant Superintendent
Box 699
Kirkland, WA 98083

Dear Brother Bullock:

Sincere Christian Greetings!
Enclosed please find copies from the *Ellensburg Daily Record*, relative to the Kittitas Assembly of God situation. Presumably, the *Yakima Herald* newspaper is also planning on articles on this issue (none have appeared thus far).
My concerns are:

1. Obviously, just the unwanted publicity is enough to give cause for concern.
2. The question of civil legal action pertaining to church/spiritual problems seems to me to be unscriptural.

Relative to the other issue we discussed briefly in our phone conversation; namely, CARE-

NET, my concern is simply that all business conducted by CARE-NET will be of such a nature that it will never be called into question. (Enclosed also find the letters from Myron Rachinski.)

Thank you for the opportunity to speak with you by phone and also write about the issues addressed above.

Sincerely in our Lord,

Albert E. Anderson,
Pastor

****

11. Exhibit G, December 1993 Care-Net promotional brochure.

****

Exhibit G

The December 1993 Care-Net Outreach brochure states the following:

"Together, we're equipped to meet the needs of the homeless, the hungry and the hurting.

CARE-NET...Caring enough to act!

The problems people face are many, so the opportunities to care for others are many. No one person, church, organization or agency can do it all alone.

Care-Net networks concerned individuals, churches, businesses and organizations to respond to the homeless, the hungry, and the hurting. Collectively, a difference is being made.

The plight of homeless, abused and hurting people is growing more serious each day. Simply recognizing the problem is not enough. CARING enough to act will bring new hope and help! CARING enough to feed, clothe, and house is making an impact! CARING enough to give a second chance is infusing meaningful direction in human life!

THANK YOU FOR CARING ENOUGH TO ACT!

"Men are arriving and receiving supports and accountability in a loving ranch environment. It's been thrilling to see God change men's lives through His word, His counsel and by working in God's beautiful creation at Care-Net in Kittitas. Guys are helped from all walks of life and at any age."

Randy Bale
Ranch Director

"Care-Net is an exciting ministry that touches body and spirit. It is recognized by the Northwest

District as a Home Missions endeavor. It has truly been life changing for those to whom it has ministered."
Dr. Warren Bullock, Asst. Supt.
N.W. District of the Assemblies of God

"I believe in the ministry of Care-Net. It's a ministry that has been neglected for too long and it's time we do something about it. Care-Net is one way to do something."
Irwin Kruger, Construction Coordinator
N.W. District of the Assemblies of God

****

OCTOBER REPORT

1,202	Meals served
333	Overnight housing opportunities
2,210	Miles traveled
50	Bible studies/Worship services
73	Counseling/Interview sessions
331	Therapy Project units tended

****

THERAPY PROJECT

What is a "THERAPY PROJECT?" Good question! The initial plan for providing land, buildings and equipment for Care-Net is to seek donated livestock, hay and grain. Several hours are programmed in the resident's daily schedule for outside fresh air and ranch involvement. The acquired animals are cared for and grown in the therapy project until a combination of body weight and price per pound yield the desired cash return. Therapy project revenue is designated to provide the long-term debt service and ranch operational budget. Stock cows, feeder cattle, and horses have been donated to date.

****

PERSONNEL

In addition to CareNet residents, we appreciate the following personnel support: Randy and Vickie Bale, Ranch Director; Jason Ringe, Counseling and Schedule Coordinator; Vi Lien, Secretary; Sharon Redford, CPA; John and Jan Mustered, MAPS Volunteers; and Robbie Mitchell, former resident/volunteer. Also many construction volunteers, Pastors and congregations are supporting this exciting ministry for which Care-Net is blessed.

****

THE FIRST NOEL

We pray that the Peace of God, about which the angels sang so long ago, will be yours as we celebrate once again the birth of the Saviour.

Thank you for your faithful support to the Care-Net Outreach Ministry during 1993.

All of the World Ministries contributions are necessary and deeply appreciated, whether a one-time gift or a monthly support pledge.

The heart of Christmas is "giving" and the very heart of Care-Net Ministry is "giving." YOUR caring, giving hearts make the on-going work of Care-Net possible. We are truly laborers together as we become willing to be "His Hand extended" in reaching out to hurting men, women and children for whom Christ died.

Care-Net Residents,
Board of Directors
and Staff

****

THE FINANCIAL PLAN OF CARE-NET

I. Long Term Debt Service and Ranch Budget
   Therapy Project Revenue
II. Staff Salaries
   A net-work of Volunteers, MAPS personnel and trainees
III. Residence Ministry Budget
   $21 per day per resident

****

SACRIFICIAL PARTICIPATION

NAME_____

ADDRESS_____

CITY_____

STATE_____ZIP_____

FAX_____

HOME
CHURCH_____

For World Ministries Credit
By God's help I/we will provide $21 for_____day(s) each month, commencing_____
_____/_____93.

MAIL TO:
Care-Net Outreach
2715 Everett Avenue
Everett, WA 98201

****

12. Exhibit H, December 14, 1993 letter to Frank Cole from Albert and Aimee Anderson relative to the Kittitas A/G situation and the Care-Net ranch

****

EXHIBIT H

FIRST ASSEMBLY OF GOD
Capitol Avenue and Walnut Street
Ellensburg, Washington 98926

Albert E. Anderson, Pastor

December 14, 1993

Rev. Frank Cole
Northwest District Council
of the Assemblies of God
Box 699
Kirkland, WA 98083

Dear Brother Cole:

Sincere Christian Greetings!

    We want to thank you again for the opportunity to talk with you on the telephone today; we deeply appreciate it.
    Enclosed please find copies of newspaper articles relative to the Kittitas A/G situation from the Ellensburg and Yakima newspapers. Also, we decided to send you copies of the other material that was sent to Brother Bullock.
    We have been and will continue to pray about the concerns expressed in our phone conversations

today. Only God can ultimately sort out all the details and extenuating circumstances, and for this we pray.

We trust that Jean is feeling much better and back to her usual strength and ability.

May God bless you especially at this joyous season of the year!

Sincerely in our Lord,

Albert & Aimee Anderson

     ****

13. Exhibit I, December 22, 1993 letter to Albert and Aimee from Frank Cole in response to their December 14, 1993 letter

****

Exhibit I

NORTHWEST DISTRICT COUNCIL
OF THE ASSEMBLIES OF GOD
Frank E. Cole
District Superintendent

December 22, 1993

Rev. Albert Anderson
— — Ave.
Ellensburg, WA 98926

Dear Albert and Aimee:

Thank you for the newspaper articles and the materials you sent. I am sorry that these issues have become so publicized by the newspapers. Usually, we are able to settle church problems within the framework of the membership and it becomes doubly hard when the media is involved.
I attended service at Kittitas last Sunday, and I had dinner with Pastor Gary Jeffery. Things are much quieter and we continue to be in prayer that the matter will be settled soon.
May the Lord richly bless you as you continue to serve Him.

Sincerely,

Frank E. Cole
District Superintendent

****

14. **Exhibit J, July 18, 1991 County of Kittitas Board of Adjustment Conditional Use Permit Application**

****

EXHIBIT J

On July 18, 1991, Rollin Carlson filed a Conditional Use Permit Application with the Kittitas County Board of Adjustment, along with two other pages of proposal, analysis and recommendation. These documents state: "The applicant has presented this use as continuing on a permanent year-round basis. ...The facilities proposed consist of 20 "bunkhouses," each of which would house up to four men. These bunkhouses would have no plumbing or kitchen facilities and would measure 288 square feet in area, for a total of 5760 square feet... There is proposed a central "service center" which would provide a shower, toilet, laundry, and storage facilities. This is proposed to be 864 square feet in area... The existing farmhouse would have an addition of a "community room," which would provide a bathroom, storage, kitchen, and a community area. This is proposed to be 936 square feet in area... The total for all of the proposed structures is 7,560 square feet."

Rollin Carlson failed to get the permit for the bunkhouses, service center and/or the community room. Yet, Rollin Carlson went ahead with building the community room, providing a bathroom, storage, kitchen, and a community area, by applying for it under the word "residence." This was the same community room that Myron and Jean Rachinski used to cook and serve meals and counsel the few men that came to the Care-Net Ranch for rehabilitation.

****

15. Exhibit K, September 25, 1991 letter to Mr. Bruce Eggleston, Assistant County Planner, from Rollin Carlson, assuring him that "The AG/20 Zoning is clear and certainly meets the expectation of everything the Care-Net Ranch plans to accomplish

****

Exhibit K

CARE NET
2715 Everett Avenue
Everett, WA 98201-3795
(206) 339-3303

September 25, 1991

Mr. Bruce Eggleston, Assistant County Planner
Kittitas County Planning Office
Room 182 - Court House
Ellensburg, WA 98926

Dear Bruce,

   I am taking this opportunity to thank you and your office personnel for helping us through the current permit application process. I believe we are on track and things look in order for accomplishing what needs to be done prior to the change of weather.
   The AG/20 Zoning is clear and certainly meets the expectation of everything the Care-Net Ranch plans to accomplish.
   I look forward to a continuing meaningful relationship with all of you.

Very sincerely,

Rollin J. Carlson
PASTOR/PRESIDENT

RJC/sp

16. Exhibit L, April 4, 1994 letter to Robert Cousart from Frank Cole warning him to stay out of the Kittitas Assembly of God situation, with a Copy of his letter mailed to Albert Anderson warning him to stay Out of the situation as well

****

Exhibit L

April 4, 1994

Reverend Robert E. Cousart
Box 930
Kittitas, WA 98934

Dear Brother Cousart:

Re: Your March 14, 1994 letter addressed to Don Strong

Brother Cousart, your letter was completely out of line. I take exception to your statement concerning wrongs that were done by the District Officials in relationship to the Kittitas situation.

Your second paragraph was that we never tried to hear the other side of the story. That is incorrect. A letter to me from Jeff Slothower, attorney asked that we sit down with his clients and listen to their grievances. My letter to him dated February 10th, asked that he set a meeting with his clients, giving us dates that would accommodate the District Officials schedules. I received a subsequent letter from Mr. Slothower, dated February 15th, questioning my authority to conduct such a hearing. Subsequently, I sent a letter dated February 17th, which is enclosed.

In this instance, the District officials followed the Bylaws of the local church and the District Council. Brother Cousart, nonmembers of Assemblies of God churches do not have voice or vote in any business meeting. That ruling has prevailed for as long as the Assemblies of God has been organized. That position has not changed.

The fact that you have taken sides with a dissident group has placed your position as a credentialed minister of the Assemblies of God in jeopardy. The Bylaws state on page 47 (b), that it is the duties of the Ministerial Relations Committee to, "Review all disciplinary matters and take appropriate action." This was done in regard to Kittitas. The Bylaws on page 74.i., (1), (a) also states that, "All discourteous conduct is disapproved, and Assemblies of God ministers are advised against interfering with pastors in charge of assemblies, whether it be by infringing upon their work without consent or by communication with members of the assembly that will hurt the influence of the leader."

Also, (c) states, "Any Assemblies of God minister who so offends shall be subject to scriptural discipline by the Northwest District Credentials Committee. Such discourtesy shall seriously affect the minister's credential status and may be the basis of discipline." Item f. on page 73 also applies to your situation: "Assemblies of God ministers shall refrain from taking any attitude toward disciplined members that would tend to nullify the action of the Credentials Committee. Non-compliance with the forgoing shall be cause for appropriate discipline. Any minister who violates this principle shall be subject to censure or charge which may necessitate the recall of his/her credential."

I am hereby notifying you that unless you withdraw from participation in this conflict, whether by meeting, phone or letter, it will be necessary for you to meet with the Ministerial Relations Committee.

If you have any questions, please advise me by letter.

Sincerely,

Frank E. Cole District Superintendent
gu

Enclosure:

cc: Dale Carpenter
    Warren Bullock
    Elmer Kirschman
    Rollin Carlson
    Al Anderson
    Don Strong

             ****

17. Exhibit M, a copy of the April, 1994 "Northwest District Council of the Assemblies of God Emergency Resolution of the Northwest District Council."

****

EXHIBIT M

NORTHWEST DISTRICT COUNCIL OF THE ASSEMBLIES OF GOD

EMERGENCY RESOLUTION OF THE NORTHWEST DISTRICT COUNCIL

Whereas the financial restructuring of the Northwest District is an immediate necessity; therefore be it resolved that:

The District Presbytery is hereby authorized and directed to take any and all action necessary to resolve the problems with the Revolving Fund Promissory Notes ("Loan Fund") of the Northwest District of the Assemblies of God (the "District"). This authorization and direction includes, but is not limited to, the authority to do any or all of the following:

1. reorganize the District into two separate corporate entities and separate the church administrative function from the Loan Fund;

2. obtain financial assistance, if needed, for both corporations;

3. provide appropriate names for the corporations, including but not limited to, using the name "Northwest District Loan Fund" for the Loan Fund and using the District's current name for the District's other programs and administrative functions;

4. divide the assets and liabilities of the District between the two corporations;

5. obtain financial guarantees and other financial assistance from the General Council of the Assemblies of God, and provide appropriate security for those guarantees and assistance; and

6. any and all other action the District Presbytery deems appropriate.

In dealing with this matter, the District Presbytery may delegate its authority to the Executive Presbytery or to its Executive Officers, as it deems appropriate.

The undersigned, being the Superintendent and Secretary of the Northwest District Council, hereby certify that the _____ day of April, 1994, the above emergency resolution was properly submitted to the Northwest District Council at its annual session and properly approved by a majority vote of all the ballots cast on this issue. A quorum was present.

Date:_____   _____
                          It's Superintendent

Date:_____   _____
                          It's Secretary

This emergency resolution specifically authorizes and directs the District Presbytery to take all appropriate action to resolve problems with the District's Loan Fund. According to the 1993 audited financial statements for the District, the District has a DEFICIT in net assets of $3,481,324. The District Presbytery with the advice of its attorneys, accountants and financial advisors will attempt to resolve this and other problems encountered by the District with respect to its Loan Fund.

The plan also calls for the District to be reorganized into two separate corporations. The corporation handling the loan fund functions would have a net worth of approximately 0. The new corporation handling the church and other ministry functions would have a DEFICIT of approximately $3.8 million.

****

18. Exhibit N, Great Commission full page advertisement in *Mountain Movers*, a Foreign Missions magazine of the Assemblies of God

****

EXHIBIT N

"DO YOU WANT TO MULTIPLY YOUR ABILITY TO HELP FULFILL THE GREAT COMMISSION?" ... ...
... (This document reads in part)... ...
"The Great Commission Partners program is for you. Great Commission Partners is a unique way to join hands with others interested in fulfilling Christ's command. You can invest in our next generation WHILE providing current support for Assemblies of God ministries.

Great Commission Partners is a three-way stewardship program: DONORS - RANCHERS - MINISTRIES.

The Assemblies of God Foundation, through donors, provides the resources to purchase livestock to be raised by ranchers or farmers. ... ... YES! I'm interested in multiplying my ability to help fulfill the Great Commission as a: DONOR RANCHER/FARMER ASSEMBLIES OF GOD MINISTRY RECIPIENT."

****

19. Letter from Kittitas group — to Rev. Elmer Kirschman & Rev. Tom Trask, appealing for help concerning the problems in the Kittitas Assembly of God

****

Even though this letter did not have an exhibit letter, it was included in the charge packet. Please refer back to Section 1, Church Brawl, Page 68, for the full text of this letter.

ALBERT & AIMEE ANDERSON

20. Extra Exhibit List
****

June 6, 1994

TO: NORTHWEST DISTRICT COUNCIL CREDENTIALS COMMITTEE AND GENERAL COUNCIL CREDENTIALS COMMITTEE

CREDENTIALS COMMITTEE—COPIES ...

    1. Rev. Warren Bullock   (OTHER COPIES:)
    2. Rev. Les Welk
    3. Rev. Elmer Kirschman   1. Rev. Frank Cole
    4. Rev. Rollin Carlson   2. Rev. Don Strong
    5. Rev. Allen Baunsgard
    6. Rev. Gregory Austin
    7. Rev. Dale Carpenter
    8. Rev. Julius Jepson

EXTRA EXHIBITS ENCLOSED ...

1. James Brown
2. Kennon Forester
3. Kittitas County Building Department
4. $350,000.00 — Deed of Trust — Northwest District
5. May 22, 1994 — Letter from George O. Wood, General Secretary (To: Albert & Aimee Anderson)
6. June 03, 1994 — Letter to George O. Wood, General Secretary (From: Albert & Aimee)
7. Joe & Bev Laub — Letter to KITTITAS COUNTY PLANNING COMMISSION, September 15, 1991
8. John & Christy McGrath — Letter to: KITTITAS COUNTY BOARD OF ADJUSTMENT, September 18, 1991
9. $135,000.00 DEED OF TRUST — Northwest District THE CARE-NET Ranch

       10. Delinquent Tax Statement
       11. November 19, 1993 letter from the Kittitas group

21. James Brown "To Whom it May Concern Letter"

****

6/3/94

TO WHOM IT MAY CONCERN:

   I, James Brown, was contacted by Care-Net out in Kittitas to build bunkhouses for both men and women.
   The bunkhouses were to be put on pier blocks; this is when I refused to go any farther with wanting to build a bunkhouse for this group, as it is illegal in this area. I own a small construction company and don't want to get involved with an illegal building.
   This all happened right after a men's retreat in 1992. Randy Barton never called back. This has always bothered me why he never called back as he said. The next thing I know, Maltby Assembly of God men came. My dad goes to this church. They were on their way to go to the Care-Net ranch to build bunkhouses.

Sincerely yours,

James Brown

****

22. Kennon Forester's, "To Whom it May Concern Letter"

****

Kennon Forester
17669 Rd. 9 SW
Royal City, WA 99357

TO WHOM IT MAY CONCERN,

 In the winter of 91-92 I sold Rollin Carlson 175 tons of hay for the Care-Net operation. The hay cost was $75/ton delivered, $15 of the cost was for the delivery of the product.
 When the hay was all delivered, I set up an appointment with Rollin and met with him at the Ellensburg Livestock Auction to settle the account for the hay delivered. He stated that he needed two separate bills, one for the hay and one for the freight. When I presented my bills to him, he stated that they would not work. He then produced a set of bills that he had worked up that totaled the same as mine, however he had devalued the cost of the hay and increased the cost of the freight. He then presented me with two checks that were for the respected amounts. The Banks were unfamiliar to me that they were drawn from. I accepted them and took them to be cashed, they were from a Bank back east and I did have quite a bit of trouble getting my Bank to cash them. After several tries they did go through.
 A month or so later I received a phone call from an Insurance Firm that stated that because Rollin had been in a car accident he had required my services to do the hay hauling. They were confirming the billing amounts that Rollin had given them. The bill that was given them was the inflated one that Rollin had produced for me. I informed them that the rate they received from him was much higher than I charged for freight into the Ellensburg area. I suggested there might be

some fraud involved. There were no further communications from the Insurance Firm.

Sincerely,

Kennon Forester

****

23. Kittitas Planning Department letter

****

KITTITAS COUNTY PLANNING DEPARTMENT
Room 182, Courthouse, Ellensburg, WA 98926
509-962-7506

June 3, 1994

To Whom It May Concern,

An application for Conditional Use permit was submitted by Care-Net July 18, 1991 for "Bunk Houses/Service Center constructed in AG/20 Zoning for Agricultural Housing." The application (file C-91-06) was initiated after a building permit application was submitted to the Kittitas County Building Dept. for "10 bunkhouses and 1 service center" on a site east of the City of Kittitas. The building permit application was placed on hold pending granting of the Conditional Use permit as the proposed use of the structures was ruled requiring a Conditional Use permit. The application site was and remains designated under the Agriculture-20 zoning district. The application did not identify which specific, explicitly listed Conditional Use was applied for, however, the file jacket and applicant's public hearing testimony both state the use as "guest ranch."

A public hearing was held before the Kittitas County Board of Adjustment on Sept. 18, 1991 for the application. The question of appropriateness of the requested use under Agriculture-20 zoning was discussed during the public hearing and the applicant made aware by County staff that the proposed use may not be considered appropriate. In order to grant a Conditional Use permit, the Board of Adjustment must make a finding that the proposed use is either explicitly listed and/or otherwise an appropriate use within the zoning district.

The Board was unable to rule on the appropriateness of the proposed use because the applicant withdrew the application during the Sept. 18, hearing. To date, no re-submittal of the Building or Conditional Use applications have occurred. The only Kittitas County applications submitted for the site since September, 1991 have been three building permits, for a single-family residence, for an addition to an existing single-family residence, and for a work shed/garage. If the use of the site (present or future) were to be similar to that applied for in the 1991 applications a Conditional Use permit would, as in 1991, be necessary.

Sincerely,

KITTITAS COUNTY PLANNING DEPARTMENT
Debbie Randall, Assistant Planner

cc: Mark Carey, Planning Director

****

24. April 1, 1993 Deed of Trust between The Care-Net Outreach and The Northwest District Council of the Assemblies of God for $350,000.00

****

This document reads in part as follows:

File #558269	KITTITAS COUNTY
CHICAGO TITLE INSURANCE	AUDITOR, FILED
COMPANY	REQUEST OF KCTC
	93 APR-1 PM 4:49

WHEN RECORDED RETURN TO

Name - Ruth Gangwish, Northwest District Council of the A/G
Address - P.O. Box 699
City, State, Zip - Kirkland, WA 98083

DEED OF TRUST

THIS DEED OF TRUST, made this 1st day of April 1993, between THE CARE-NET OUTREACH —— a Washington Non-profit Corporation ——, GRANTOR, whose address is 2715 Everett Avenue, Everett, WA 98201 and CHICAGO TITLE INSURANCE COMPANY, a corporation, TRUSTEE, whose address is 1300 Columbia Center, 701 Fifth Avenue, Seattle, Washington 98104 and THE NORTHWEST DISTRICT COUNCIL OF THE ASSEMBLIES OF God —— BENEFICIARY, whose address is P.O. Box 699, Kirkland, WA 98083 WITNESSETH: Grantor hereby bargains, sells and conveys to Trustee in Trust, with power of sale, the following described real property in Kittitas County, Washington:
    Parcel 1: Tract A and Tract B
    Parcel 2:
    PER EXHIBIT A ATTACHED AND INCORPORATED
    HEREIN BY REFERENCE.
Which real property is not used principally for agricultural or farming purposes, together with all the tenements, hereditaments, and

appurtenances now or hereafter thereunto belonging or in any wise appertaining, and the rents, issues and profits thereof.

This deed is for the purpose of securing performance of each agreement; of grantor herein contained, and payment of the sum of ($350,000.00 ———) Three Hundred Fifty Thousand
And no/100 ——— Dollars
   Signed by: THE CARE-NET OUTREACH
         Rollin J. Carlson, President
         William R. Handley, Secretary

(Meneva Patteson, Notary Public)

    ****

25. September 15, 1991 letter to the Kittitas County Planning Commission from Joe and Bev Laub

****

September, 1991

Kittitas County Planning Commission
County Building Dept.
Kittitas County Courthouse Room 182
Ellensburg, Washington 98926

Re: Care-Net

Dear Sir:

    We have lived in our country home on the Old Vantage Highway just below this so-called "Care-Net" project for 24 years. We moved here to get away from the city and all the things that city life brings. Now it appears the city is trying to come to us. We have always felt safe in our homes and want to continue to feel that way.

    We are in an agricultural area. We understand Care-Net is planning to put up bunkhouses with as many as 80 men there at one time. We understand there will only be men housed at the facility. This does not sound like an agriculture venture to us. The picture that is on the Care-Net Brochure is of our property and also our neighbors Kenny Jenks. This is deceiving.

    It seems as though they have already started this project with out the OK. They have started some building, sent out brochures asking for donations, and have brought in one man that I know of. He stayed there a month, living in a trailer with no running water, electricity, or sewer.

Sincerely,

Joe & Bev Laub

26. **September 18, 1991 letter to the Kittitas County Board of Adjustment from John and Christy McGrath**

****

September 18, 1991

Kittitas County Board of Adjustment

RE: Care-Net Outreach conditional use request

We would like to express our opposition to the proposed Care-Net guest ranch/rehab center east of Ellensburg on the old Vantage highway for the following reasons:

1. The potential safety of women and children would be placed in jeopardy!
2. A very poor effort, if any, was made on the part of the Care-Net organization to inform neighborhood residents of the true scope of the proposed project and disclosure of subsequent details. Furthermore, the few details that were disclosed have varied greatly and have therefore undermined neighborhood confidence in the nature and credibility of the project as a whole.
3. We have been told personally, by Care-Net personnel, that funding was originally secured for five units; now we are told for three. The conditional use application requests approval for ten units and one service center. Plans submitted to county planners discloses a twenty-unit complex. No one in the entire neighborhood was told that there was a request for ten units, nor plans for twenty units, until these details were made available on public record at the courthouse in compliance with conditional use application

procedures. With four men per bunkhouse, this could potentially become a sizable community of its own, and consequently, be a detriment to the entire neighborhood.

4. Inadequate criteria have been disclosed as to how these individuals would be screened, monitored, cared for, kept busy, etc.

5. Long-term health effects and disease control.

6. Cabin fever!

7. The presence of a state correctional facility, the Park Creek Group Home, within 2 miles of the proposed site that has repeated and recent difficulty with occupants escaping to return home.

For the reasons stated, we hereby ask that the conditional use permit requested by the Care-Net organization be denied.

Respectfully,

John and Christy McGrath

****

27. **May 20, 1991 Deed of Trust between The Care-Net Outreach and The Northwest District Council of the Assemblies of God for $135,000.00**

****

CHICAGO TITLE   54027
INSURANCE COMPANY

Kittitas County Auditor
Filed Request of:
NW Dist. Council of the A/G
1991 Jun 20 PM 4:14

When Recorded Return to
Name: Gail Nelson,
The Northwest District Council of the Assemblies of God
Address: P.O. Box 699
City, State, Zip: Kirkland, WA 98083-0699

DEED OF TRUST
(For Use in the State of Washington Only)

THIS DEED OF TRUST, made this 20th day of May, 1991, between The Care-Net Outreach, Grantor, whose address is 2715 Everett Ave., Everett, WA 98201 and CHICAGO TITLE INSURANCE COMPANY, a corporation, TRUSTEE, whose address is 1800 Columbia Center, 701 Fifth Avenue, Seattle, Washington 98104 and The Northwest District Council of the Assemblies of God, BENEFICIARY, whose address is 5710 108th Ave. N.E., Kirkland, WA 98033

WITNESSETH: Grantor hereby bargains, sells and conveys to Trustee in Trust, with power of sale, the following described real property in Kittitas County, Washington:

ALBERT & AIMEE ANDERSON

See Attached Sheet which real property is not used principally for agricultural or farming purposes, together with all the tenements, hereditaments, and appurtenances now or hereafter thereunto belonging or in any wise appertaining, and the rents, issues and profits thereof.

This deed is for the purpose of securing performance of each agreement of grantor herein contained, and payment of the sum of $135,000.00.

One Hundred and Thirty Five Thousand and No/100—Dollars with interest, in accordance with the terms of a promissory note of even date herewith, payable to Beneficiary or order, and made by Grantor, and all renewals, modifications and extensions thereof, and also such further sums as my be advanced or loaned by Beneficiary to Grantor, or any of their successors or assigns, together with interest thereon at such rate as shall be agreed upon.

****

28. The Care-Net Outreach's Delinquent Tax statement

****

DELINQUENT TAXES

as of 6/03/94

QCD #534005 - 10/08/90   CARE-NET OUTREACH   RANCH

  WD #558268 - 04/01/93   KITTITAS, WA
   '93 - 2nd 1/2   '94

17-20-0400-0006/00	$ 96.02	$ 172.55
17-20-0400-0014/00	369.20	976.78
17-20-0500-0010/00	63.90	196.74
17-20-0500-0011/00	492.44	1697.55
17-20-0500-0013/00	88.93	287.83
17-20-0500-0015/00	19.51	236.17
17-20-0500-0016/00	34.05	87.99
17-20-0500-0017/00	138.56	249.63
17-20-0500-0018/00	44.53	102.94
70-11-0000-1236/00 (Pers. Prop.)		138.65
	$ 1347.14	$ 4146.83

COMBINED TOTAL.........................$ 5493.97
AS OF: 06/03/94

****

ALBERT & AIMEE ANDERSON

Because the Andersons received no response to the June 7, 1994 Formal Charges from either the Northwest District or the General Council, they wrote the following letter:

****

DATE: September 16, 1994

FROM: Albert E. and Aimee Anderson
          — — — Avenue
          Ellensburg, WA 98926

TO: Rev. Thomas E. Trask, General Superintendent;
          Rev. George Wood, General Secretary; and General Council Credentials Committee
          The General Council of the Assemblies of God
          1445 Boonville Avenue
          Springfield, MO 65802-1894

RE: Formal Charges of Unchristian Conduct of Assemblies of God Ministers in the Northwest District Council

Dear Bros. Trask, Wood, and Members of the Credentials Committee:

We are writing to you in regard to the matter noted above, which material was dated June 3, 1994 and mailed to you June 6, 1994.

We met with the Executive Officers and Executive Presbytery at the Northwest District Office on June 7, 1994, at which time a copy of the formal charges, including exhibits — which you also received in the materials mailed to you — was given to each one present.

According to the General Council Bylaws, Article X, Sections 4.d. through Section 5.a, which read as follows:

        Section 4, d: Responsibility of General Council Credentials

Committee. In the event a district fails to take action within 90 days after a matter has been referred to it, it shall be the responsibility of the General Council Credentials Committee to see that action is initiated.

Section 5: Investigation of Reports or Complaints of Alleged Violations or Confessions of Violations of Assemblies of God Principles.

    a. Within the Districts of the General Council of the Assemblies of God. Reports or complaints of alleged violations of Assemblies of God principles (Article X, A, Section 3) or confessions of such by a Minister shall be investigated. The Superintendent of the district in which the alleged offense is reported to have occurred, and/or an appointed representative(s) shall conduct the investigation to determine their source and validity. It is the responsibility of the district superintendent to safeguard the church, the minister, the district, and the Fellowship. In the event such reports or complaints against a minister are filed with the General Council Credentials Committee, they shall be referred to the district in which the offense occurred for investigations. A copy shall be sent to the

> district with which the minister is affiliated.
>
> (1) Interview with complainant(s). The persons involved shall be interviewed in order to ascertain the facts in the case and the reasons underlying the persistence of the reports or complaints.

It is now over a week past the 90-day deadline for the Northwest District to interview complainants, and we have not received any official communication from the Northwest District Office regarding this matter. We were interrogated by Warren Bullock and Rollin Carlson at the Executive Presbyter meeting June 7, 1994. Moreover, we know that a number of the people mentioned in or referred to in our formal charges as "complainants" have not been interviewed. The names of those people are as follows:

> Myron and Jean Rachinski, Care-Net counselors and workers (contacted in the evening of September 15, 1994)
> Jim Brown, Building Contractor
> Rev. Robert and Anna Mae Cousart, Assembly of God Ministers
> Pairlee Treat*
> Wanda Cotton*
> Jerry and Phyllis Marchel*#
> Bonnie Clement*#
> Del and Anita Kazee*
> Jim and Sherry Boswell*
> Jim Scones*
> Chris Marchel*
> Bill Peterson*
> Laurie Brune#

*Denotes those against whom Gary Jeffery filed anti-harassment papers.

WHITED SEPULCHRES

#Denotes those who had their memberships in Kittitas Assembly of God taken from them by Gary Jeffery because they did not agree with him.

Rev. Don Strong encouraged two of our deacons at First Assembly of God in Ellensburg, and another man, a member of our church, to ask Albert to resign as pastor. He also encouraged them to circulate a petition asking for his resignation, even though there were no charges against Albert. Several members of our congregation, including family members of a dying woman, two recently widowed women, and an elderly man just home from the hospital, were approached by these board members to sign the petition asking for Albert's resignation.

The threats and pressure put on us from District Officials and the two deacons adversely affected our health and hurt several members of our congregation. To spare our congregation any further hurt, Albert formally resigned as pastor of First Assembly of God in Ellensburg on June 19, 1994, Father's Day.

We implore you, in the name of our Lord and Savior, Jesus Christ, to investigate fully the charges we have brought against members of the Northwest District Council of the Assemblies of God. What has taken place in the name of Christianity is an affront to God, and is extremely damaging to the witness of the Assemblies of God and of the Church as a whole. This is no longer a matter that is "in house" only. The mishandling of funds in the Northwest District has already made front-page news in the Seattle Post-Intelligencer July 27, 1994. Before that, the situation at the Kittitas Assembly of God made front-page headlines in both Ellensburg and Yakima, and was covered by television news reporting. How bad does the situation have to get before something is done?

Sincerely in Christ,

Albert Anderson

Aimee Anderson

Enclosed: Formal Charges dated June 3, 1994
   Summary of Formal Charges
   November 19, 1993 letter from Kittitas Assembly

cc: Rev. Warren Bullock, District Superintendent and
   Northwest District Council Credentials Committee
   Northwest District Council of the Assemblies of God
   P. O. Box 699
   Kirkland, WA 98083-0699

****

Following is the response the Andersons received from the General Council in Springfield:

****

THE GENERAL COUNCIL OF THE ASSEMBLIES OF GOD
1445 Boonville Avenue
Springfield, Missouri 65802-1894

George O. Wood
General Secretary

September 19, 1994

Rev. & Mrs. Albert E. Anderson
— — — Avenue
Ellensburg, WA 98926

Dear Brother and Sister Anderson:
   Greetings in the Lord!
   My office is in receipt of your letter of September 16 in which you request the General Council Credentials Committee to assume responsibility for making an investigation of named ministers against whom you have proffered charges.
   The General Council Credentials Committee meets again on November 14-16.
   I am requesting the Northwest District superintendent, Warren Bullock, to respond in writing to the General Council Credentials Committee regarding the matters you have articulated.
   We will be in prayer about these matters and pray that the Lord will give everyone concerned great wisdom — and the end result will be the glorification of His name and the edification of His Church.

Sincerely yours in Christ,

George O. Wood
General Secretary

GW:jw

cc: Warren Bullock

The Andersons replied as follows:

****

Albert and Aimee Anderson
— — — Avenue
Ellensburg, WA 98926

September 28, 1994

Rev. George Wood
General Council of the Assemblies of God
1445 Booneville Avenue
Springfield, MO 65802-1894

Dear Bro. Wood:

Sincere Christian greetings!

    We wish to thank you for your immediate response to our letter with enclosures received by you September 19. We are encouraged to know that the General Council Credentials Committee is assuming responsibility for making an investigation of certain Northwest District officials against whom charges have been brought. It is our understanding that the Northwest District must respond to the charges filed with specific statements and documented results of interviews conducted. We believe each one of the many charges listed is significant and important; therefore, we will continue in much prayer that each issue will receive careful study and appraisal.

    May God give you and the General Council Credentials Committee great wisdom as you deal with this entire matter.

    Again, thanks for your quick response to our communicated concerns.

Sincerely,

Albert E. Anderson & Aimee D. Anderson

cc: Rev. Thomas E. Trask, Superintendent

The General Council Credentials Committee
NORTHWEST DISTRICT COUNCIL
of the Assemblies of God
October 14, 1994

Rev. & Mrs. Albert Anderson
— — — Avenue
Ellensburg, WA 98926

Dear Brother and Sister Anderson,

 As you know, a specially appointed committee was formed by the District Presbytery to review the accusations that you submitted to the Executive Presbytery on June 7, 1994. While the investigation was not completed within ninety days, it was initiated immediately and has been ongoing in compliance with Northwest District by-laws. A report of findings was formulated and forwarded to the District Presbytery during the course of their regular meetings on October 10-12. At that point, the report became the ownership of the District Presbytery.

 The report was reviewed and decisions were made concerning each accusation. Since you have forwarded the matter to the General Council Executive Officers and the General Council Credentials Committee, the Northwest District Presbytery took action to submit their final report to the same.

 We will all await the response to the Northwest District Presbytery report and any subsequent recommendations that may arise from the executive officers and/or the General Council Credentials Committee. I trust that you will receive the conclusion of the Northwest District Presbytery and the General Council as a final disposition of these matters.

Respectfully yours,

Leslie E. Welk
Assistant Superintendent/Special Committee Chairman

cc: Rev. Thomas Trask

Rev. George Wood
Rev. Warren Bullock

THE GENERAL COUNCIL OF THE ASSEMBLIES OF GOD
1445 Boonville Avenue
Springfield, Missouri 65802-1894

George O. Wood   Phone: (417) 862-2781
General Secretary   Fax: (417) 863-6614

November 22, 1994

Rev. and Mrs. Albert E. Anderson
— — — Avenue
Ellensburg, WA 98926

Dear Brother and Sister Anderson:

Greetings in the Lord!
At the recent meeting of the General Council Executive Presbytery, a careful review was made of the information and report from the Northwest District Presbytery's special committee investigating the ministerial conduct accusations you made against certain ministers credentialed through the Northwest District.
That body has taken the following actions:

> "A motion prevailed that the General Council Credentials Committee receive the report of the Northwest District's examination of charges made by Rev. and Mrs. Albert Anderson against certain ministers credentialed through the Northwest District.

> "A motion further prevailed to accept the investigation as complete, and totally exonerative of the individuals charged, and that no basis exists for further action by the General Council Credentials Committee."

May the Lord bless you abundantly.

Sincerely yours in Christ,

George O. Wood
General Secretary

GW:jw
cc: Leslie Welk

****

ALBERT & AIMEE ANDERSON

THE GENERAL COUNCIL OF THE ASSEMBLIES OF God
1445 Boonville Avenue
Springfield, Missouri 65802-1894

February 7, 1995

George O. Wood   Phone: (417) 862-2781
General Secretary   Fax: (417) 863-6614

Reverend Albert E. Anderson
— — — Avenue
Ellensburg, WA 98926

Dear Brother Anderson:

Greetings in the Lord!

You have now reached the age of sixty-five and we wish to express our deep appreciation to you for your dedication, ministry, and labor through the years! We also rejoice with you in anticipation of the rewards for faithful service!

"In respect and honor to those ministers who have given years of service to the Fellowship, senior status shall automatically be given to all credential holders who have reached the age of 65, whether they continue in full-time ministry or not" (Bylaws Article VII, Section 7).

Since you have reached this age, we are listing you as a senior-active minister. Senior ministers who are not fully active may file a request with their district to be listed in one of the other two following categories:

1. Senior-active: Those who continue to serve ¾ to full time in the ministry.
2. Senior-semiretired: Those who continue to be active, but half time or less.
3. Senior-retired: Those who have ceased to engage in any regular appointed ministry.

WHITED SEPULCHRES

All senior ministers are still required to renew annually. Senior-active and senior-semiretired are required to designate $10.00 monthly to the support of the General Council. Senior-retired ministers have no further financial obligation.

We pray that God shall yet give you good health and strength so that you may be able to continue your ministry as He opens doors of service.

Sincerely yours in Christ,

George O. Wood
General Secretary

GOW: lr
cc: Elmer E. Kirschman

****

ALBERT & AIMEE ANDERSON

NORTHWEST DISTRICT COUNCIL OF
THE ASSEMBLIES OF GOD

Warren D. Bullock, Superintendent
Leslie E. Welk. Assistant Superintendent
Elmer E. Kirschman, Secretary-Treasurer
7001 220th Street SW, Suite 101
Mountlake Terrace, WA 98043-2164
Telephone (206) 640-0222   Fax (206) 640-0333

March 23, 1995

Rev. Albert E. Anderson
— — — Ave.
Ellensburg, WA 98926

Dear Bro. Anderson:

Greetings in Jesus' Name!

It is indeed unfortunate that you have found it necessary, in your opinion, to engage in certain personal investigations which have led you to bring accusations and charges against District leadership. It is further unfortunate that after repeated efforts by we, your brethren, to bring resolve and closure to these matters it appears that our efforts have not to date reached this desired goal. The Executive Presbytery believes the time has come to bring closure to the matters which have continued over many months.

In their March 6, 1995 meeting, a motion prevailed unanimously that you, Bro. Anderson, be requested to meet with the Executive Presbytery at their April 4, 1995 meeting at the Northwest District office in Mountlake Terrace at 2:00 p.m. This is an urgent request and will be in the best interest of us all that you plan to be present.

Please check the response portion of this letter and return it to me as soon as possible.

Sincerely,

E.E. Kirschman

EEK:tt

RESPONSE FORM

Al Anderson

( ) Yes, I will attend the Executive Presbytery meeting on April 4, 1995 at 2:00 P.M.

( ) No, I choose not to comply with the request to attend.

_____Signed

****

Albert replied that he did not choose to comply because of a prior commitment. He signed the form and returned it to the Northwest District. This response was enclosed with the following March 30, 1995 letter.

****

DATE: March 30, 1995

FROM: Albert E. and Aimee D. Anderson
        — — — Avenue
        Ellensburg, WA 98926

TO: Rev. Thomas E. Trask, General Superintendent
        Rev. Charles T. Crabtree, Assistant General Superintendent
        Rev. George O. Wood, General Secretary
        Rev. James K. Bridges, General Treasurer, and
        The General Council Credentials Committee of The Assemblies of God
        1445 Boonville Avenue
        Springfield, MO 65802-1894

RE: Formal Charges of Unchristian Conduct of Assemblies of God Ministers in the Northwest District Council
        and
        Appeal of decision concerning the Formal Charges

Dear Brothers Trask, Crabtree, Wood, Bridges, and all the Members of the General Council Credentials Committee:

We are writing to you in regard to the matter noted above, which material was dated June 3, 1994 and mailed to you June 6, 1994.

We met with the Executive Officers and Executive Presbytery at the Northwest District Office on June 7, 1994, at which time a copy of the formal charges — including exhibits, which you also received in the materials mailed to you — was given to each one present. The Executive Presbyters present were forbidden by Warren Bullock to open their individual packets containing the formal charges, neither were Albert and Aimee permitted to go over the individual charges with the officials present at that meeting.

Sometime after the June 7 meeting, Executive Presbyter Julius Jepson said to the Andersons, "Les Welk told the whole committee that he would be contacting Albert and Aimee Anderson to arrange a time for them to meet for the purpose of going over each of the charges, point by point." We were reassured of this several different times. We still are waiting for this to take place.

We have not received any official communication from the Northwest District concerning the formal charges, except the October 14, 1994 brief letter from Les Welk. In this letter he says, "The report was reviewed and decisions were made concerning each accusation. Since you have forwarded the matter to the General Council Executive Officers and the General Council Credentials Committee, the Northwest District Presbytery took action to submit their final report to the same." No mention was made of going over any charges with Albert and Aimee Anderson.

In a phone conversation with Brother Crabtree after the November 1994 General Council Executive Presbyters meeting, Brother Crabtree told Aimee that you will be hearing from the Northwest District concerning the charges and if you don't hear from them, let us know." To this date, Brother Leslie Welk has not gone over the formal charges, one by one with us as he told the Northwest District investigative sub-committee he would do, nor have Albert and Aimee Anderson received any official word from the Northwest District concerning the formal charges, as Brother Crabtree said we would.

We received the November 22, 1994 letter from George O. Wood, General Secretary, which contains the following statements: "A motion further prevailed to accept the investigation as complete, and totally exonerative of the individuals charged, and that no basis exists for further action by the General Council Credentials Committee." Les Welk emphatically says, "exonerative" is the General Presbytery's word and not the District's.

How can the individuals charged be totally exonerated of the formal charges, when Executive Presbyter Julius Jepson, Les Welk, and Elmer Kirschman in personal conversations have indicated to the Andersons that Rollin Carlson was not totally exonerated and in fact was strongly admonished concerning the charges in some areas?

March 27, 1995, Albert E. Anderson received a certified letter from Elmer Kirschman requesting Albert E. Anderson to meet April 4, 1995 with the Executive Presbytery to "bring resolve and closure to these matters."

March 28, 1995 in a phone conversation, Elmer Kirschman told Albert and Aimee Anderson that the charges were "dead and gone" and "it's now become a credentials matter." He also told Aimee, "you are unreasonable." Aimee responded, "Why, because I want sin and corruption exposed?" In an earlier phone conversation with Les Welk, he said, "If you choose to pursue this, the ramification will be felt." Aimee asked, "Is that a threat?" Les responded, "That's just the way it is."

In a phone conversation on March 29, 1995, Aimee asked Brother James Bridges if he knew about the formal charges brought against Rollin Carlson, Care-Net and other District Officials. He said, "I don't know what you are talking about." She asked if he had seen the charges, he said, "No, maybe it will be coming up at our next meeting." Aimee asked if he was part of the Executive Presbytery and he said, "Yes." Aimee said, "We sent a letter to you, the Executive Presbytery; and you did not receive it or know anything about it?" Brother Bridges further indicated he did not know anything about the charges or what she was talking about and said he would have Brother Crabtree phone Aimee.

The Care-Net Outreach has several boards. One of these boards is the Northwest District Presbytery, thus each and every one of the Northwest District Officers and Northwest District Presbyters should be disqualified from being on the investigative sub-committee chosen to investigate the formal charges brought against Rollin Carlson, the Care-Net Outreach and other district officials named in the June 7, 1994 formal charges. Please check the Northwest District and General Council Bylaws concerning conflict of interest. Also, Glen Cole is related to Frank Cole, again a conflict of interest for him to be part of the General Council Executive Presbytery decision-making process in regards to the formal charges.

Brother Crabtree not only told Aimee to let them know if Albert and Aimee Anderson did not receive any official response from the Northwest District concerning the formal charges, he also told Aimee that they could appeal the decision. Thus, this letter is our formal appeal of the decision exonerating the individuals charged. Some changes have and are presently being made in response to the formal charges Albert and Aimee Anderson brought against certain Northwest District Officials and in response to our bringing some of these issues to the attention of the District Officials and General Council Officials several months ago. Some of those changes are as follows:

> 1. Tom Mahon, Care-Net Ranch director, (quitting as of April 1, 1995) says he is being paid a salary with the withholding of federal taxes and the paying of Social Security taxes. (See charge No. 11.)
>
> 2. The delinquent taxes on the Care-Net Ranch were paid. (See charge No. 14.)

3. According to Tom and Jeanne Mahon, no men for rehabilitation or transitional housing purposes have been at the ranch since last August or September 1994. Yet, no notice has been mailed to the ministers and churches stating that the Care-Net Outreach ranch is not a transitional housing for men nor a rehabilitation ranch for men. It only has a residence permit, which is for a related family or five unrelated people on a personal basis, but not as an organized church ministry. According to the County, Rollin Carlson and the Northwest District do not have a permit for the type of ministry they have been soliciting funds for. The County spokeswoman says, they (Rollin and Care-Net) have nothing in writing from us that would allow them to do this. Fact is, the Care-Net Outreach received a violation notice from the Kittitas County Building Department in February, 1994. In spite of this violation notice, Rollin Carlson and the Care-Net Outreach, including other Northwest District officials named in the formal charges, as well as Leslie Welk, have continued on with this deception that the Care-Net Outreach ranch can legally be used as a shelter for homeless men, including a counselor.

4. The large amounts of food commodities to feed the needy men at the transitional housing Care-Net ranch at Kittitas, Washington, have stopped coming to the ranch.

This whitewash job of investigating the charges and then Leslie Welk, Elmer Kirschman and other district officials threatening Albert and Aimee Anderson by saying, "It's now become a credentials matter," as well as other threatening statements, is indeed, a tragedy. Hasn't there been enough damage done to the innocent parties trying to do what is right? Isn't it enough that Albert Anderson was pressured into resigning as pastor of the First Assembly of God church in Ellensburg, Washington, on Father's day, 1994, after ten years of faithful service, the longest term of any pastor to that Assembly?

Again, we appeal the decision to exonerate the individuals charged and again appeal to the General Council Credentials Committee to form a new sub-committee — with no conflict of interest — to investigate the formal charges of unchristian conduct on the part of Rollin Carlson mainly, and of Don Strong, Frank Cole, Elmer Kirschman, Dale Carpenter, Warren Bullock and now Leslie Welk in varying lesser degrees.

Albert E. Anderson
Senior-active Assemblies of God minister

Aimee D. Anderson
Wife of Albert E. Anderson

cc: Warren Bullock
   The Northwest District Council Executive Presbytery
   E. E. Kirschman

Enclosure: Copy of March 23, 1995 letter from E. E. Kirschman to Rev. Albert E. Anderson

****

ALBERT & AIMEE ANDERSON

THE GENERAL COUNCIL OF THE ASSEMBLIES OF GOD
1445 Boonville Avenue
Springfield, Missouri 65802-1894

April 7, 1995

George O. Wood   Phone: (417) 862-2781
General Secretary   Fax: (417) 863-6614

Rev. and Mrs. Albert E. Anderson
— — — Avenue
Ellensburg, WA 98926

Dear Brother and Sister Anderson:

Greetings in the Lord!

This is to acknowledge receipt of your March 30, 1995, letter appealing the decision concerning the formal charges you placed against certain ministers of the Northwest District.

I will see that this matter is placed on the agenda for the May 31 to June 1, 1995, meeting of the Executive Presbytery. I will also see that all members of the Executive Presbytery receive copies of this correspondence as well as the original charges.

May the Lord bless you abundantly.

Sincerely yours in Christ,

George O. Wood
General Secretary

GW:jw
cc: Warren Bullock

****

DATE: April 12, 1995

FROM: Albert E. and Aimee D. Anderson
         — — — Avenue
         Ellensburg, WA 98926

TO: Rev. Robert L. Brandt, Regional Executive
         Presbyter
         1601 Judd Circle
         Billings, Montana 59102

TO: Rev. Charles E. Hackett, Executive
         Presbyter
         3954 East Washita
         Springfield, Missouri 65809

RE: Formal Charges of Unchristian Conduct of
         Assemblies of God Ministers in the
         Northwest District Council
                      And
         Appeal of decision concerning the Formal
         Charges

Dear Brothers Brandt and Hackett:

On May 10, 1994, we mailed a "Petition for investigation of certain Northwest District Officials" to the General Council of the Assemblies of God Credentials Committee.

Brother George Wood responded with his May 22, 1994 letter to Brother and Sister Anderson, indicating that Albert and Aimee had not filed formal charges against Rollin Carlson.

On June 3, 1994, Albert and Aimee Anderson, by certified mail, sent to the Northwest District Council Credentials Committee and the General Council Credentials Committee the following (On June 7, 1994, the Andersons hand-delivered these documents to the Northwest District Executive Presbytery):

    1. Fourteen pages of Formal Charges
    2. Summary of Formal Charges

3. Letter to Brother Wood and the General Council of the Assemblies of God (with copies to Rev. Thomas E. Trask, Rev. Warren Bullock, Northwest District Council Credentials Committee, and General Council Credentials Committee)
4. Pages of other exhibits and documentation

On September 16, 1994, Albert E. and Aimee Anderson, mailed a letter addressed to Brothers Trask and Wood, and to members of the Credentials Committee. (With copies mailed to Rev. Warren Bullock, District Superintendent, and Northwest District Council Credentials Committee.)

September 19, 1994, George Wood responded to Albert and Aimee Anderson's September 16, 1994 letter. The following are quotes from the September 19, letter: "The General Council Credentials Committee meets again on November 14-16. I am requesting the Northwest District Superintendent, Warren Bullock, to respond in writing to the General Council Credentials Committee regarding the matters you have articulated."

September 28, 1994, Albert E. and Aimee D. Anderson mailed a letter to Brother Wood, expressing appreciation. The following are quotes from that letter: "We are encouraged to know that the General Council Credentials Committee is assuming responsibility for making an investigation of certain Northwest District officials against whom charges have been brought... May God give you and the General Council Credentials Committee great wisdom as you deal with this entire matter."

Albert and Aimee Anderson received a letter dated October 14, 1994, from Leslie E. Welk, Assistant Superintendent/Special Committee Chairman. (With copies to Rev. Thomas Trask, Rev. George Wood, and Rev. Warren Bullock.)

Albert and Aimee Anderson received a letter dated November 22, 1994, from George Wood, General Secretary. (Copy to Leslie Welk) The following are quotes from that letter: "At the recent meeting of the General Council Executive Presbytery a careful review was made of the information and report from the Northwest District Presbytery's special committee investigating the ministerial conduct accusations you made against certain ministers credentialed through the Northwest District... That body has taken the following actions: 'A motion prevailed that the General Council Credentials Committee receive the report of the Northwest district's examination of charges made by Rev. and Mrs. Albert Anderson against certain ministers credentialed through the Northwest District.' 'A motion further prevailed to accept the investigation as complete, and totally exonerative of the individuals charged, and that no basis exists for further action by the General Council Credentials Committee.'"

Elmer Kirschman mailed a certified letter to Albert Anderson, dated March 23, 1995, requesting him to meet with the Executive Presbytery at their April 4, 1995 meeting... "to bring closure to the matters which have continued over many months."

On March 30, 1995, Albert E. and Aimee D. Anderson mailed certified letters Appealing the decision concerning the Formal Charges to Rev. Thomas E. Trask, Rev. Charles Crabtree, Rev. George Wood, Rev. Bridges, and to The General Council Credentials Committee of The Assemblies of God. (With copies to Warren Bullock, The Northwest District Council Executive Presbytery and Elmer Kirschman.) A copy was also sent by certified mail to Loren Triplett and enclosed with Brother Triplett's letter was the fourteen pages of charges. Included with this letter of Appeal, was a copy of the March 23, 1995 letter from E. E. Kirschman to Rev. Albert E. Anderson with Albert's response, "No, I choose not to comply with the request to attend, due to a prior commitment."

During these past months, now almost one year, we have been led to believe that the whole General Council of the Assemblies of God Credentials Committee, each and every member, were prayerfully and seriously looking into the formal charges brought against Rollin Carlson, Care-Net, and other Northwest District Council Officials named in the Formal Charges. Much to our deep dismay, we so recently found out that this is not so. Apparently, only those we addressed by name on the envelopes, Rev. Trask, Rev. Crabtree, and Rev. Wood, received a copy of the charges.

We have not contacted all of the individual General Council Credential Committee members yet, but the four, Rev. Bridges, Rev. Triplett, Rev. Brandt, and Rev. Hackett, we have phoned and asked, "Do you know about the formal charges brought against Rollin Carlson, Care-Net and other Northwest District Officials?", have all responded the same way, "No, I don't know what you are talking about. I have not seen the charges."

Rev. Triplett said he did not attend the November 1994 Presbyters meeting, but seemed very concerned about the fact that he had no knowledge of all the communication directed to the Credentials Committee. Rev. Bridges, Rev. Brandt, and Rev. Hackett, all said they attended the November 1994 Presbyters meeting at which time Brother Wood said the Formal Charges were taken care of. Yet, all three of these men present at that meeting said they had no knowledge of the Formal Charges. It appears as though something is seriously wrong.

Again, we trust and pray that the Assemblies of God General Council Credentials Committee will fully investigate the charges we have brought against members of the Northwest District Council of the Assemblies of God.

We express appreciation to both of you for your help.

Albert E. Anderson
Senior-active Assemblies of God minister

Aimee D. Anderson
Wife of Albert E. Anderson

Enclosures:

February 1992 seven-page mailing to all
Northwest District Pastors from Rollin Carlson
Violation notice from County of Kittitas
Letters dated 9/16/94, 9/19/94, 9/28/94, and
10/14/94
Letter dated November 22, 1994
June 3, 1994 Formal Charges of Unchristian
Conduct, together with all exhibits
March 30, 1995 Appeal of decision concerning
   the Formal Charges, together with letter from
   Rev. Elmer Kirschman dated March 23, 1995

cc: Rev. Thomas E. Trask
     Rev. Charles T. Crabtree
     Rev. George O. Wood and General Council
         Credentials Committee
     Rev. James K. Bridges
     Rev. Loren Triplett
     Rev. Warren D. Bullock
     Rev. Elmer E. Kirschman and Northwest
         District Presbytery
     Rev. Leslie E. Welk
     Rev. Julius W. Jepson
     Rev. Glen D. Cole
     Rev. David W. Argue
     Rev. Almon Bartholomew
     Rev. Ronald F. McManus
     Rev. Armon Newburn
     Rev. Robert Schmidgall
     Rev. Philip Wannenmacher

               ****

ALBERT & AIMEE ANDERSON

THE GENERAL COUNCIL OF THE ASSEMBLIES OF GOD
1445 Boonville Avenue
Springfield, Missouri 65802-1894

George O. Wood   Phone: (417) 862-2781
General Secretary   Fax: (417) 863-6614

April 21, 1995

Rev. and Mrs. Albert E. Anderson
— — — Avenue
Ellensburg, WA 98926

Dear Brother and Sister Anderson:

Greetings in the Lord!

I am in receipt of a copy of your letter of April 12 to Rev. Robert Brandt and Charles Hackett.

We have provided copies of your correspondence to the General Council Credentials Committee.

May the Lord bless you abundantly.

Sincerely yours in Christ,

George O. Wood
General Secretary

GW:jw
cc: General Council Credentials Committee

****

WHITED SEPULCHRES

THE GENERAL COUNCIL OF THE ASSEMBLIES OF GOD
1445 Boonville Avenue
Springfield, Missouri 65802-1894

George O. Wood　　　　　　Phone: (417) 862-2781
General Secretary　　　　　　Fax:　 (417) 863-6614

June 1, 1995

Rev. and Mrs. Albert E. Anderson
— — — Avenue
Ellensburg, WA 98926

Dear Brother and Sister Anderson:

Greetings in the Lord!

At the meeting of the General Council Executive Presbytery held yesterday and today, your appeal for reconsideration of the charges you have filed against certain ministers of the Northwest District was given thorough review by that body.

Following a time of careful study of the entire file and the charges filed by you, the following action was taken:

> Rev. and Mrs. Albert Anderson have Appealed the decision of the General Council Credentials Committee regarding Formal charges they placed against certain ministers of the Northwest District. The General Council Credentials Committee took note that no specific right of appeal is conferred by the General Council Bylaws to one who makes an accusation; the right of appeal is given to the accused. The General Council Credentials Committee also took note of General

Council Bylaws Article X. A., Section 4.d.:

> d. Responsibility of General Council Credentials Committee. In the event a district fails to take action within 90 days after a matter has been referred to it, it shall be the responsibility of the General Council Credentials Committee to see that action is initiated.
>
> A motion prevailed to inform Rev. and Mrs. Anderson that the General Council Credentials Committee affirms that the district did indeed take action within 90 days following the Andersons' accusations and determined that no charges should be filed against the ministers accused; and, that the General Council Credentials Committee concurs with the district action and regards the matter closed.

It is the hope of the executive Presbytery that this action will bring a close to this matter.

May the Lord bless you richly!

Sincerely yours in Christ,

George O. Wood
General Secretary

GW:jw

With all the documentation -- including the Care-Net video, legal documents, personal letters, and quotes from newspaper articles and brochures — to this point no one has explained to Albert and Aimee Anderson how the Northwest District Council Officials and the General Council Officials could determine, "That no charges should be filed against the ministers accused; and, that the General Council Credentials Committee concurs with the district action and regards the matter closed."

With four boards including: The Everett Bethany Assembly Church Board, The Care-Net Outreach Board, The Northwest District Home Missions Board, and The Northwest District Presbytery Board, backing Rollin Carlson and The Care-Net Outreach, the following offenses should not have taken place:

1. The **Washington State Food** programs are for the purpose of providing food for qualified needy people. It is a shame when this program is abused and **government commodities are received through deception for other than rightful causes.** The forms filled out and filed for The Care-Net Outreach Ranch at Kittitas, Washington, state the following: "Transitional Housing, for 10+ needy served, 3 meals, 7 days each week;" then it was changed to "20 needy, 3 meals, 7 days each week;" then changed to "45 needy served, 3 meals, 7 days each week," up to "135 meals each day." From every source of our information there were never more than (5) five or (6) six, if that, needy men there at one time. Obviously, this food was not used for the stated number of needy men applied for, nor was it used for a legal rehab ranch.

2. The Care-Net Outreach received a **Violation Notice** from the Kittitas County Building Department in February, 1994. **In spite of**

this Violation Notice, Rollin Carlson and The Care-Net Outreach have continued deceiving the Kittitas County people and the Kittitas County Building Department, as well as Ministers and laity, by word of mouth and by written word.

In September, 1991, Rollin gave the same message, in two different letters (that he is going to abide by the Kittitas County AG/20 Zoning): one Letter to the Editor is recorded in the Ellensburg Daily Record and the other letter is to the Kittitas County Building Department. Carlson and The Care-Net Outreach continued to portray a different message to the ministers and laity: "The Care-Net Outreach ranch is for homeless men, for rehabilitation/transitional housing purposes."

Also, Rollin Carlson continued to solicit funding for the Care-Net Ranch as a rehabilitation/transitional housing for men, without the proper land use permits, and in so doing he violated the Kittitas County Zoning laws.

3. The **United States Postal Service** is a real blessing to Americans and it is unlawful to abuse it by **soliciting donations or contributions through deception**, especially for something that is **illegal and dishonest**, as well as **crossing state lines**.

In the September 18, 1991 Minutes of the Kittitas County Board of Adjustment, Rollin Carlson states, "A rehabilitation center was of secondary importance as these men are not alcohol/drug users... He emphasized this is not a group home or an institution... Carlson agreed this was a complete withdrawal and said that he would start the process from the beginning including new fees." Then seven days later, September 25, 1991, Rollin Carlson wrote a Letter to the Editor, in which he makes the following statement, "Our intent is to be committed to the current (county) Ag/20 Zoning." Also, September

25, 1991, Rollin Carlson wrote a letter to Mr. Bruce Eggleston, Assistant County Planner. In that letter, he made the following statement, "The AG/20 Zoning is clear and certainly meets the expectation of everything the Care-Net Ranch plans to accomplish."

In spite of all this, in February, 1992, Rollin Carlson sent a seven (7) page mailing to all the Northwest District Pastors, (Assembly of God) soliciting funds through the United States mail for The Care-Net Outreach Ranch. In his letter he stated, "Care-Net Ranch near Kittitas, Washington... This ministry provides a transitional housing program for homeless men and can serve all churches in the Northwest District... Care-Net is a ministry... All for the single purpose of bringing change to the lives of high risk men who are in need... We are not interested in being in the cattle business primarily... Care-Net pays no administrative salaries." In this same mailing Rollin Carlson also states, "Care-Net is helping homeless men put their lives back together through its Transitional Housing Program at Care-Net Ranch. This 100 acre ranch is located near Kittitas, Washington and is providing 24-hour per day housing, meals, ministry of love and instruction in God's Word and spiritual training... Care-Net is a Washington State Non-Profit Corporation." In this 1992 letter to Northwest Assembly of God ministers, Rollin indicated that the cattle business was secondary, yet, in the September 18, 1991 Minutes of the Kittitas County Board of Adjustment, Rollin, indicated that the Rehabilitation center was secondary. **When Rollin is talking to the Kittitas County the Care-Net ranch is one thing and when he is talking to the ministers and churches the Care-Net ranch is for something entirely different.**

Then again, in December 1993, Rollin Carlson sent through the United States mail another brochure soliciting funds for the Care-Net Ranch. In that brochure Randy Bale states, "Men are arriving and receiving supports and accountability in a loving ranch environment... God's beautiful creation at Care-Net in Kittitas. Guys are helped from all walks of life and at any age."

Then again, in November 1994, months after Rollin Carlson and The Care-Net Outreach ranch had received the violation notice from the Kittitas County Building Department, The Executive Newsletter was mailed from the Northwest District office to all of the Northwest District Assembly of God ministers. Leslie Welk, The Northwest District Home Missions Director and Assistant Superintendent solicited funding and volunteer construction help for the Care-Net Home Missions Work (meaning The Care-Net Ranch) at Kittitas even though, apparently there had not been any men for rehabilitation/transitional housing at the ranch since August or September 1994. (Evidently Rollin Carlson stopped sending men to the ranch for rehabilitation purposes, about (6) six months after he and The Care-Net Outreach received the Violation Notice in 1994.

4. **Illicit solicitation of funds** for the Lord's work is a serious thing. Thus, it is a serious matter when there was **illicit solicitation of funds** for The Care-Net Outreach by the following means:

   a. Rollin Carlson's February 1992 Care-Net seven (7) page promotional mailing.
   b. The December 1993 Care-Net promotional brochure.
   c. The November 1994 mailing from the Northwest District Office containing Leslie Welk's appeal for Home Missions Volunteer Workers and Funding for different Home Missions works. One included and named was, the Care-Net Ranch at Kittitas, Washington.

d. The public meeting of over 2000 men including the Ministers, from around the Northwest District, during which time the Care-Net promotional video was shown and big appeal was made for contributions to be given to the Care-Net Outreach Ranch Ministry.
e. Around the Northwest District, the Care-Net Outreach ranch has been promoted and used as a means of illicit solicitation for funds and volunteer labor.
f. The September 18, 1991 Minutes of Kittitas County Board of Adjustment, reads as follows:
"Rollin Carlson, Everett, the applicant... He explained that money has been raised for three bunkhouses and the service center initially." Also, Rollin was quoted as saying in the Ellensburg September 25, 1991 Daily Record article the following, "We have money for three bunk houses and one service center." If indeed, Rollin Carlson and/or someone else raised enough money for three bunkhouses, where has all this money gone? And do all the generous people who have given the money to build the three bunkhouses and service center know that there are no bunkhouses (except the

small existing one that the volunteer laborers worked on, shortly after the ranch was purchased) and/or no service center on The Care-Net Ranch?

g. Listing the Care-Net Outreach Ranch as a "satellite church" and soliciting money for the Care-Net Outreach Ranch as a Home Missions church is deceitful. Is the Care-Net Outreach Ranch at Kittitas really a Home Missions church? The "1994 Church Giving Report" listed the Everett Care-Net Outreach giving $21,192.00 to World Missions and $300.00 to Foreign Missions in 1994. Was it possible for needy people in Everett, who are fed government food, to give this money, or did the Care-Net Outreach Ranch, listed as a church, give this money, while at the same time people were giving charitable contributions to this same Care-Net Outreach rehabilitation ranch?

5. **Insurance companies** are supposed to be there to help when someone has a rightful and honest claim. In 1992, Rollin Carlson used Myron Rachinski, Kennon Forester and The Care-Net Ranch to **gain money**, apparently in a **deceptive** way, from All State Insurance Company. It appears Rollin Carlson tried to make the insurance company think he had to hire Rachinskis to work on the ranch while he was unable to do the farm work because of an

injury sustained in a vehicular accident. Also, it was very **deceptive and wrong** for Rollin Carlson to personally collect money from the insurance company by presenting them with an **inflated hay-hauling bill**, especially when his job was not hauling hay but pastoring the Bethany Christian Assembly in Everett, Washington, which is approximately 140 miles across the State of Washington from the Care-Net ranch.

6. With four boards backing The Care-Net Outreach Ranch, we wonder how all of **the misrepresentations and false statements** in documents, letters, brochures, and the Care-Net promotional Video, could possibly have occurred in the following:

    a. USDA Food Commodity Forms, stating 10+, then it goes to 20, then changes to 45 needy served 3 meals each day, 7 days each week.
    b. Building Applications for permits and other legal documents, that state, The Care-Net Outreach is a Non-Profit Corporation licensed in the State of Washington, leaving a false impression that the Care-Net Outreach Ranch is a valid, legal Home Missions church/ministry.
    c. On the Application for Permit in Kittitas County, Rollin Carlson stated that he is applying for a building permit for a residence (meaning a private family). This was for the benefit of the Kittitas County, but the Assembly of God ministers

and other church people were told bunkhouses were being built on the Care-Net ranch at Kittitas, Washington, for men in rehabilitation to live in.
d. The February 23, 1993 Building Application for Permit states, The Care-Net Outreach is the Owner of Record, when Melvin and Winnie Chapman were still the owners of Record.
e. In the September 18, 1991 Minutes of the Kittitas County Board of Adjustment, Rollin Carlson stated, "these men are not alcohol/drug users but are homeless, hurting, and hungry." Apparently this was not always true concerning the few men they did have at the ranch, as Jeff, one of the residents living at the ranch in 1994, told Aimee in a phone conversation, that he was there for rehabilitation because he had a drinking problem.
f. The Care-Net Outreach brochures, that have been used to solicit funds for the Care-Net Outreach Ranch contain several false Statements.
g. How could Rollin Carlson and Northwest District officials show the deceptive Video, which states, "Care-Net is a non-profit Corporation licensed in the State of

Washington?" How could they show this deceptive Video in March, 1992, to about 2000 men promoting The Care-Net Outreach as a rehabilitation and/or a transitional housing ranch for needy men? How could they promote it as a home missions work without the proper land use permits outside the law of Kittitas County and deceive the public into giving money to this phony rehab ranch?

****

ELLENSBURG FIRST ASSEMBLY OF GOD

PASTOR ALBERT and AIMEE ANDERSON

ALBERT & AIMEE ANDERSON

KITTITAS ASSEMBLY OF GOD

WHITED SEPULCHRES

CARE-NET ranch house where, Randy and Vicki Bale and Tom and Jeanne Mahon lived. Also, the former residential garage/addition -- the "community room," that, Myron and Jean used for the men.

Back side of ranch house, with entrance to the "community room" (former residential garage)

Driveway to the Care-Net ranch house and
"community room"
(former residential garage)

Hay barn back of the ranch house and "community room"

WHITED SEPULCHRES

Residential daylight basement house, which was called the
"bunkhouse, for nine to ten men." The "loafing shed"
behind the garage cannot be seen.

DAYLIGHT BASEMENT HOUSE in the distance, behind the trees.

WHITED SEPULCHRES

The original small existing bunkhouse and steel granary across the driveway from the daylight basement house

Steel Granary and Hay Barn/storage
across the road from the
daylight basement house

Section 3.

BLENDED INTRIGUE

(We have taken the liberty to change three different Bible quotes in "Wolves Among the Flocks" — from the NIV Version to the King James Version of the Bible.)

****

Wolves Among the Flocks
(Two Parables)
by Bonnie Clement

"So when they had dined, Jesus saith to Simon Peter, Simon, son of Jonas, lovest thou me more than these? He saith unto him, Yea, Lord; thou knowest that I love thee. He saith unto him, Feed my lambs.

"He saith to him again the second time, Simon, son of Jonas, lovest thou me? He saith unto him, Yea, Lord; thou knowest that I love thee. He saith unto him, Feed my sheep.

"He saith unto him the third time, Simon, son of Jonas, lovest thou me? Peter was grieved because he said unto him the third time, Lovest thou me? And he said unto him, Lord, thou knowest all things; thou knowest that I love thee. Jesus saith unto him, Feed my sheep." (John 21:15-17)

I.

There was a flock in the Kingdom that for many years lived in harmony. New sheep who came to the flock immediately felt the love the sheep had for one another, and they knew the shepherd cared for them and did his best to lead them according to the directions of the Chief Shepherd. A few sheep, who disagreed with the leading of the shepherd, left and went to other flocks. Some of these sheep had actually been wolves in sheep's clothing and the shepherd knew it. He refused to let them become leaders in the flock.

One day the shepherd left to take care of another flock, and a new shepherd came in his place. At first, the shepherd appeared to love the sheep and his leading of them appeared to be in accordance with the instructions of the Chief Shepherd. However, some of the sheep began to be uneasy about some of the paths on which the shepherd led the flock. One ram asked the shepherd about the direction the flock was going and was firmly told to either submit and obey or leave the flock. Meekly, the ram tried to do as he was told, but he still felt something was wrong. Some of the sheep who had left when the other shepherd led them, began returning. Some of the wolves returned also, and were welcomed by the shepherd and put into positions of leadership. One day a ewe fell seriously ill and was unable to keep up with the flock. The shepherd ignored her, and when he was asked by another ewe why he didn't do something to help, he grew angry at her and told her to find another flock. Later he accused the ewe and her mother of serious misconduct and forbid them to return to the flock. Other sheep became alarmed at this callous treatment of one of their members, and asked the shepherd to reconsider. One by one, he told them to leave the flock and never come back. One old ram had grown up in that flock, and it was not easy for him to leave what had been his home and family for so many years. This ram refused to leave, even after the shepherd turned the remaining members of the flock against him.

> "Feed the flock of God which
> is among you, taking the oversight
> thereof, not by constraint, but
> willingly; not for filthy lucre,
> but of a ready mind;

"Neither as being lords over God's heritage, but being examples to the flock.

"And when the chief Shepherd shall appear, ye shall receive a crown of glory that fadeth not away."

(I Peter 5:2-4)

II.

There was a shepherd in the Kingdom who truly looked out for his sheep. He made mistakes from time to time, but he was always ready to ask forgiveness and tried not to repeat the same mistake again. Sheep who visited the shepherd's flock felt the love he had for all the sheep belonging to the Chief Shepherd. One day a small band of battered and torn sheep came to him. Their shepherd had attacked them viciously and had run them out of the flock. Concerned by what he saw, the shepherd contacted the leader shepherds who were in charge of the district in which he was located. He was told the matter did not concern him.

For several months, different sheep came to this shepherd, all of whom had been abused by their shepherds. Again and again, the shepherd tried to get the leader shepherds to do something about the abusive shepherds; but they ignored his reports and warned him to leave the matter alone. He was threatened with removal from his position as shepherd if he did not cease caring for troublemaker sheep. The shepherd was greatly saddened by what was happening, and he refused to ignore the wounded sheep who came to him for help.

One evening the shepherd was ambushed and attacked by two of the leader sheep of his flock. They let him know they no longer wanted him as their shepherd. A leader shepherd had told them to make him leave. A few days later the shepherd was called to a meeting of the leader shepherds.

Several of them attacked him; and during the battle, their disguises fell off and he recognized them as wolves.

   Battered and torn as the sheep to whom he had ministered, the shepherd sought the help of the Chief Shepherd. The chief Shepherd told him many wolves had infiltrated the flocks of the Kingdom, disguised as sheep and as shepherds. The Chief Shepherd assured him that the wolves would be defeated one day. Meanwhile, He was calling all those who were still loyal to Him to come away from those flocks to minister to those who had been wounded by wolves and to warn the sheep and shepherds of the Kingdom about the danger in their midst.

> *"Take heed therefore unto yourselves, and to all the flock, over the which the Holy Ghost hath made you overseers, to feed the church of God, which he hath purchased with his own blood.*
>
> *"For I know this, that after my departing shall grievous wolves enter in among you, not sparing the flock*
>
> *"Also of your own selves shall men arise, speaking perverse things, to draw away disciples after them."* (Acts 20:28-30)

****

This section contains the chronology of events, which reveals the connection between the turmoil at the Kittitas Assembly of God Church, the deceptive activities at the Assemblies of God Care-Net ranch located near Kittitas, Washington, and the involvement of the Executive leadership of the Northwest District Council and the General Council of the Assemblies of God.

****

June 29, 1983

1. A Real Estate Excise Tax form was filed. Sellers/Grantors, David and Barbara Carlson — Buyer/Grantee, U. S. A., date of sale 12/21/82 (Kittitas County Treasurer #16687). David Carlson is Rollin Carlson's brother. This property was sold to the Care-Net Outreach in 1990.

May 30, 1990

2. A Real Estate Excise Tax form, file #030715, dated May 30, 1990, and filed on October 08, 1990, showed a gross sale price of $93,236.00 for approximately 120.28 acres including the ranch home and other out buildings. Randy and Vicki Bale, and later Tom and Jeanne Mahon, lived in the ranch house when they were managers of the ranch. The parcels were listed in the deed as #172005000016, #172005000011, #172005000013, #172005000010, #172005000018, and #172005000015. The Seller/Grantor was The United States of America, acting through the Administrator of the Farmers Home Administration, U.S. Department of Agriculture. * * * * Buyer/Grantee, Care-Net Outreach, a Washington non-profit corporation.

QUESTION: Where are the records to prove the "non-profit corporation" status with "letter of intent," which apparently is required to legally solicit charitable contributions? (This is the same property referred to in the preceding number 1.)

September 28, 1990

3. A Deed of Trust, file #534553, was signed between Frontier Bank, Arlington, Washington, and The Care-Net Outreach, in the amount of $60,720.93. This document was signed by Rollin J. Carlson, Borrower; and William R. Handley, Borrower. It states on this document that The Care-Net Outreach is "a Washington non-profit corporation." Again, where are the records to prove the "non-profit corporation" status license to solicit charitable contributions for the Care-Net ranch at Kittitas?

October 08, 1990

4. A quitclaim Deed, file #534005, states: the United States of America, acting through the Administrator of the Farmers Home Administration, United States Department of Agriculture, Conveys and Quitclaims to Care-Net Outreach, a Washington non-profit corporation. (This is the property referred to in the preceding number 1.)

December 1, 1990

5. Rollin Carlson signed a food commodity form to obtain food supplies for the Transitional Housing at the Care-Net Outreach Ranch. This form, file #70052-200, indicates ten+ needy would be fed three meals per day, seven days a week. **Where is the proof that ten men were fed all this government surplus food?** According to Mark Severn, with the USDA food commodities, the transitional housing referred to here is at the Care-Net Ranch at Kittitas.

The USDA file number for the transitional housing at the Care-Net Ranch at Kittitas, Washington, is 70052-200. The file number for the homeless feeding in Everett, Washington, is 70052-000.

Information disseminated by Rollin states, "Care-Net also offers thirty days to one year rehabilitative support programs. The first facility for such programs is a 100-acre ranch near Kittitas. Care-Net provides long term housing, all meals, spiritual training, counseling, job therapy, plus the time to find meaningful direction in life free from pressures of the past." (This quote is from the Kittitas County Board of Adjustment Conditional Use Permit Application that was signed and filed 7/18/91.)

December 18, 1990

6. Northwest District Superintendent, Frank E. Cole, and Elmer Kirschman, Secretary/Treasurer, signed a Certificate of Affiliation designating the Care-Net Outreach Ranch as a Home Missions Assembly under the direction of the Northwest District Council of the Assemblies of God. The certificate reads: "This is to certify that The Care-Net Outreach of Everett, State of Washington, has entered into fellowship with the Northwest District Council of the Assemblies of God, with right to proper representation in district affairs so long as maintaining a scriptural standard in teaching and doctrine."

January 28, 1991

7. Appointment of Successor Trustee and Full Reconveyance was signed 1/28/91. Grantor, The Care-Net Outreach, a Washington non-profit Corporation, and Trustee, Chicago Title Insurance Company, filed 1/30/91, #536765, Volume #319, page #771.

February 25, 1991

8. Special Warranty Deed, file #537551, for purchase of approximately 223.03 acres of farm

land east of Kittitas, Washington, was signed and then filed on 3/5/91. Grantor Farm Credit Bank of Spokane, a Federal corporation, to Melvin L. Chapman and Winnie Chapman, husband and wife. The purchase price was listed in the real estate excise tax form as $105,000.00.

February 25, 1991

9. Real Estate Excise Tax form, file #031500, dated 2/25/91, was filed on 3/5/91, Buyer/Grantee, Melvin L. Chapman and Winnie Chapman, address 2715 Everett Avenue, Everett, Washington. The address used as Chapmans' permanent address in Everett is the same as that for Bethany Christian Assembly, the Assemblies of God church where Rollin Carlson was senior pastor. The parcels were listed in the deed as: #17-20-0400-0006, #17-20-0500-0017, and #17-20-0400-0014 and adjoins the property purchased by Care-Net on October 8, 1990. The gross sale price was shown as $105,000.00.

May 20, 1991

10. A deed of trust was filed in the Kittitas County Courthouse showing that the Northwest District Council of the Assemblies of God loaned $135,000.00 to The Care-Net Outreach. The property to which this deed of trust refers is the same as that purchased on May 30, 1990 by Care-Net for $93,236.00.

May 29, 1991

11. Rollin Carlson signed an application for food commodities for Snohomish County Transitional Housing at an address of 2715 Everett Avenue, Everett, Washington, for the feeding of 10+ needy, for 3 meals each day for 7 days per week. According to Mark Severn of the Food Commodities this file #70052-200, refers to the Care-Net Ranch at Kittitas, Washington.

Summer of 1991

12. Ruth Townley was approached to be the cook for men at the Care-Net ranch. In 1994, Ruth Townley gave the following written and notarized letter to Aimee Anderson:

****

October 05, 1994
To Whom It May Concern:

My name is Ruth G. Townley. I live in Kittitas, Wash. I am a retired Chef 43 years.

In the summer of 1991, I was approached at the Kittitas Assembly of God Church by a Mr. Bale. He asked if I would consider cooking and supervising a facility out on Vantage Highway that he and his wife were running, for a program named "Care-Net". I was told that they help people who were underprivileged with food, clothes and a place to stay.

The next day I met with him and we went thru the kitchen to check out procedures and the food. He said at that time there were only 3 men there but, there would be more later. He said these 3 were Mexicans. We walked through the kitchen and he opened 2 large chest type freezers that were full of frozen food, chicken, hamburger, packages of vegetables, etc. On shelves were over stocked amounts of government powdered milk, cheese, cans of pork, butter, corn meal, peanut butter and canned fruit.

We talked and he asked what type wages I would accept for 3 hours a day and I told him $5.00 an hour was as low as I could go. But for what he wanted I could see 3 hours a day would not be enough time to do all he wanted done. With a possibility of more people coming to eat and stay there, the whole plan was just not possible. At that time he asked me to think about it and get

back to him. I would see him at church, after that he would say hello but nothing about the job. So I assumed that he had changed his mind. No more was said and nothing was done.
Mrs. Ruth Townley
P.O. Box 534
Kittitas, Wash. 98934

IN WITNESS WHEREOF, I have here unto set my hand and affixed my official seal on this date I have signed below.

NOTARY PUBLIC FOR THE
STATE OF WASHINGTON

Residing at: Cle Elum, Wash.
My commission expires: 8/8/96

****

June 3, 1991

13. Satisfaction of Mortgage, for $75,000.00 paid U. S. Bank by the Care-Net Outreach, a Washington corporation (This time it is listed only as a Washington corporation). It was filed as #540272, Volume #322, Page 1626.

June 27, 1991

14. Rollin Carlson submitted an application for a building permit to build ten bunkhouses and one service center at the Care-Net Outreach Ranch, on acreage located at Rt. 3, Box 1060, Ellensburg, Washington 98926. He signed this document as President of Care-Net.

1991 Care-Net brochure

15. The Care-Net Outreach distributed a brochure, which was filed in the Kittitas County records, soliciting funds and help for the: "Care-Net Transitional Housing and Rehabilitation programs ... The first facility for such programs is a 100 acre ranch near Kittitas, Washington."

NOTE: There seems to be a "mixing" of the feeding program in Everett by Everett Bethany Christian Assembly, with the Care-Net Outreach rehabilitation/transitional ranch. Yet, the above mentioned brochure was filed in the Kittitas County courthouse, thus making it pertinent to the local Care-Net Outreach ranch.

July 18, 1991

16. Rollin Carlson filed a Conditional Use Permit Application with the Kittitas County Board of Adjustment, along with two other pages of proposal, analysis and recommendation. These documents state: "The applicant has presented this use as continuing on a permanent year-round basis...The facilities proposed consist of 20 'bunkhouses,' each of which would house up to four men. These bunkhouses would have no plumbing or kitchen facilities and would measure 288 square feet in area, for a total of 5760 square feet...There is proposed a central 'service center' which would provide a shower, toilet, laundry, and storage facilities. This is proposed to be 864 square feet in area... The existing farmhouse would have an addition of a 'community room,' which would provide a bathroom, storage, kitchen, and a community area. This is proposed to be 936 square feet in area... The total for all of the proposed structures is 7,560 square feet."

Rollin Carlson failed to get the permit for the bunkhouses, service center and/or the community room. Yet, Rollin Carlson went ahead with building the community room, providing a bathroom, storage, kitchen, and a community area, by applying for it under the word "residence." This was the same community room that Myron and Jean Rachinski used to prepare and serve meals and counsel the few men that came to the Care-Net Ranch for rehabilitation. Also, it was the same "community room" with bathroom/shower etc. used by the men.

This same Conditional Use Permit Application, also gives Melvin L. Chapman's address as, 2715 Everett Avenue, Everett, WA 98201, (this is Everett Bethany Christian Assembly's address, the church where Rollin Carlson was the senior pastor). Right below Chapman's name and address is the following: "I, THE UNDERSIGNED, understand that this application must be complete and accurate ..." This document was signed by Rollin Carlson, President.

August 30, 1991

17. An order for food commodities for Snohomish County Homeless Feeding at 2715 Everett Avenue, Everett, Washington for feeding 100+ needy, 1 meal, 1 day per week. File #70052-000. (Dorothy Deweber, an Assemblies of God minister's

wife, who attends Everett Bethany Assembly, told Aimee Anderson that the feeding program was one meal every other week, and not every week. Her husband's name is Hubert Deweber).

September 14, 1991

18. An Affidavit of Publication was placed in the Daily Record, Ellensburg's local newspaper, which read: "Notice of Determination of Non-Significance. The proponent, The Care-Net Outreach organization, is planning a transitional housing and rehabilitation center for the homeless and unemployed located on a farm in the Agricultural 20 zone."

September 15, 1991

19. Joe and Bev Laub wrote a letter to the Kittitas County Planning Commission. In that letter they stated: "The picture that is on the Care-Net Brochure is of our property and also our neighbors Kenny Jenks. This is deceiving.

It seems as though they have already started this project without the OK. They have started some building, sent out brochures asking for donations, and have brought in one man that I know of. He stayed a month, living in a trailer with no running water, electricity, or sewer."

September 17, 1991

20. Kenneth and Ilene Jenks wrote to the Kittitas County Planning Department. In that letter they stated: "Also we believe you should seriously consider the reputation of Mr. Carlson who we understand will head the center."

September 18, 1991

21. A list of at least 137 or more signatures of people opposed to the "Guest ranch-rehab

center" was submitted to the Kittitas County Planning Office according to the Kittitas County records.

September 18, 1991

22. Another letter was written to the Kittitas County Board of Adjustment about the Care-Net Outreach Conditional Use request. This letter, from John and Christy McGrath, says in part: "A very poor effort, if any, was made on the part of the Care-Net organization to inform neighborhood residences of the true scope of the proposed project and disclosure of subsequent details. Furthermore, the few details that were disclosed have varied greatly and have therefore undermined neighborhood confidence in the nature and credibility of the project as a whole.

We have been told personally, by Care-Net personnel, that funding was originally secured for five units; now we are told for three."

September 18, 1991

23. A public hearing was held concerning the Conditional Use C-91-06 Care-Net. According to the official minutes of the Kittitas County Board of Adjustment, the board had received, "40 letters from the public and a petition of 200 names, all in opposition to the application."

Further, the minutes state that "Rollin Carlson, Everett, the applicant, stressed the guest ranch wording of his application and said a rehabilitation center was of secondary importance as these men are not alcohol/drug users but are 'homeless, hurting, and hungry.' He cited Care-Net's work in Snohomish Co. and a $11,000.00 grant from the City of Everett. He said men considered must complete an application and are accepted on a trial basis. Nine men have lived at the current site in the past 27 months and all have returned to society. He explained that money has been raised for three bunkhouses and the service center initially. He stated that, regardless of the outcome, Care-Net will remain in Kittitas Co. even if on a limited basis. He emphasized this is not a group home or an institution."

NOTE: According to DOC. #534005, dated 10/08/90 - Quit Claim Deed; and Real Estate Excise Tax form #030715, dated 05/30/90, THE CARE-NET OUTREACH did not hold title to the property in question 27 months prior to September 18, 1991.

Attorney Cole, "asked when the property was purchased and was told it was acquired one year ago. He said this conditional use would violate the intent and identity of Ag/20 zoning, and Care-Net knew the zoning when the property was purchased."

Hanson said, "If Care-Net chose to re-apply, it was her opinion the entire process will begin over including the SEPA process and that citizens should contact the Planning Dept. if they suspected any zoning infractions meanwhile."

Rollin Carlson, "agreed this was a complete withdrawal and said that he would start the process from the beginning including new fees."

QUESTIONS: Where is all the money Rollin said he raised for the three bunkhouses and the service center? Were these donations channeled into other areas without the donors knowledge? Three bunkhouses and the service center were never built.

September 23, 1991

24. Rollin Carlson filed an application for permit with the Kittitas County Building Department to "complete existing residence/carport area, complete existing area which is partially enclosed now." County Code indicates this is intended for a grandma or other family member.

This addition to the existing farmhouse was really the forbidden "community room" that was originally applied for in, The Application For Conditional Use Permit, and then withdrawn by Rollin Carlson, at the September 18, 1991 County meeting. The Application for Conditional Use permit states, "Community Room, which would provide a bathroom, storage, kitchen, and a community area. This is proposed to be 936 square feet in area..."

The addition applied for under, "Complete existing residence/carport area" was furnished and used, not as stated in the permit, but as a room where men living on the ranch for rehabilitation were served meals and were given counseling, actually as the forbidden "community room," even though it was used on a very limited basis. (See #16 above)

Ministers and laity have been told on more than one occasion, up to February 1995, "they are almost done with another bunkhouse that will house nine or ten men." Then for the Kittitas County records, it is listed as only a "residence" for a family.

According to the code number 17.08.230, "Family" means a number of related individuals or not more than five unrelated individuals living together as a single housekeeping unit, and doing their cooking on the premises exclusively as one household. (Res. 83-10, 1983) According to Debbie Randall, with the Kittitas County Planning Department, the "five unrelated individuals" does not mean an "organized" activity or ministry.

After the Andersons started bringing attention to the alleged illegal activities relative to The Care-Net Outreach ranch, a Violation Notice was sent by Certified mail to The Care-Net Outreach ranch in February 1994. Some months after this violation notice, apparently Rollin Carlson stopped sending men to the ranch for rehabilitation/transitional housing purposes.

It's too bad Rollin Carlson waited until he and the Care-Net Outreach Ranch at Kittitas, Washington received the "Violation Notice" to stop sending men to said ranch.

The Care-Net Outreach never received the Conditional Use Permit for a Rehab ranch. The alleged illegal activity at the ranch was finally exposed. Rollin Carlson did receive a permit to build but not the right permit to build "Bunkhouses and Community Room."

Could it be that the statement, "they are almost done with another bunkhouse," (meaning the 4 bedroom daylight basement house) that will house nine or ten men, has kept the Ministers and churches satisfied that the money given for three bunkhouses and service center, apparently was being used for the purpose it was given for? Moreover, according to the ranch managers Tom and Jeanne, the February 1994 violation notice was disregarded until August or September 1994 when rehab men finally were no longer sent to the ranch.

NOTE: When the Care-Net Outreach ranch was originally bought, a very small bunkhouse was on the property. It contained no bathroom or kitchen. Volunteer church laborers helped sheetrock and paint it.

September 23, 1991

25. Rollin Carlson submitted an Application for Permit for a "Machine Shed/Barn/Equipment Storage" 864 square feet. (This is the same square footage as the Service Center he applied for, but for which he did not receive the permit.) Hopefully, this is used as a Service Center for the cattle. (See #16 above)

ALBERT & AIMEE ANDERSON

September 25, 1991

****

26. The **Ellensburg *Daily Record*,** reported: "Rehab Ranch Plans Put On Hold By Organizers... After hearing an earful of opposition from a roomful of concerned neighbors at a Kittitas County Board of Adjustment public hearing last night, the Care-Net Outreach organization of Everett pulled its application for a proposed guest ranch and rehabilitation center on land zoned Agricultural 20.

"Care-Net, affiliated with the Northwest Council of Assemblies of God, requested a conditional use permit to allow a guest ranch and rehabilitation center on 160 acres of its property located in the Ag zone land off Vantage Highway.

"Proposed was the construction of 20 12-by 24-foot bunkhouses and a central community service center with bathrooms, shower facilities, a laundry and storage area. Also planned was a community room addition to a farmhouse...

"The stated goal of the Care-Net organization is to provide 'transitional' and emergency housing for 30 days to a year, and counseling and job skills training for the homeless and unemployed ...

"'I'm not arguing against its (ranch and center's) purpose, but it can be carried out in another setting where it's allowed,' said Rich Cole, speaking on behalf of some concerned residents who own land in the zone. 'When the property was bought it was on Agricultural 20 land and they (Care-Net) knew it. It's (ranch and center) should not be permitted there.' ...

"Cole told the board of adjustment there 'was no way, legally, the activity could be allowed to happen in the zone'...

"Carlson stated, 'We have money for three bunkhouses and one service center right now.'...

"After an attempt to renegotiate the application with the board and being told that it couldn't be done at a public hearing, Carlson decided to withdraw the original application and reapply.

"'I'll have to find some way to approach this on a different basis,' said Carlson. 'I'm prepared to withdraw this application because I don't believe everyone is focusing on what we've been told to focus on. I'm confused, but I'm committed to this program and it will be in the county regardless.'"

****

QUESTION: Is Rollin Carlson publicly declaring his intention to have the Care-Net Outreach ranch in Kittitas County even if done illegally?

September 25, 1991

27. In the same issue of the **Ellensburg** *Daily Record*, a letter Rollin Carlson wrote to the editor was printed and read as follows:

****

"On behalf of several thousand dedicated Christians, I would like to express thanks to *The Record* for its fair reporting; the county officials who are helping clarify what is appropriate land use according to the county ordinance; to neighbors; supporters; local businesses and congregations.

"The Care-Net Ranch voluntarily withdrew its conditional use application September 18, because of the need to clarify its purpose in construction and land use. Our intent is to be committed to the current (county) Ag/20 Zoning.

"Care-Net has been operating in Kittitas and Snohomish Counties since November of 1988. We definitely intend to continue pursuing the challenge of President Bush's '1,000 Points of Light!' Care-Net is making a difference in the lives of homeless, hungry and hurting people. In the process we are serving over 2,000 meals annually plus spending $100,000.00 for goods, services, products and appropriate taxes in Kittitas County.

"As we withdraw the current application, we reaffirm to all of our friends that Care-Net will continue what it has been doing for several years here by utilizing owned and rented facilities on whatever basis is commensurate with meeting the need of this present challenge and operating within zoning requirements. Rollin J. Carlson, Pastor/President The Care-Net Outreach."

****

NOTE: Rollin makes it sound like $100,000.00 is being spent each year in Kittitas County by the

Care-Net Outreach ranch operation. Moreover, how could the Care-Net Ranch have been in operation since November 1988, when the first land purchase at Kittitas, Washington, by the Care-Net Outreach was October 08, 1990?

September 25, 1991

28. Rollin Carlson wrote another letter on this same day to Bruce Eggleston, Assistant County Planner, **Kittitas County Planning Office**:

****

Dear Bruce,

I am taking this opportunity to thank you and your office personnel for helping us through the current permit application process. I believe we are on track and things look in order for accomplishing what needs to be done prior to the change of weather.
The AG/20 Zoning is clear and certainly meets the expectation of everything the Care-Net Ranch plans to accomplish.
I look forward to a continuing meaningful relationship with all of you.

Very sincerely,

Rollin J. Carlson
Pastor/President

****

QUESTION: Is the September 25, 1991 letter to the Editor and the September 25, 1991 letter to Bruce, full of double talk? Does the AG/20 Zoning really meet the expectation of everything the Care-Net Ranch planned to accomplish? And did Rollin Carlson intend to be committed to the current (county) AG/20 Zoning for the Care-Net Outreach ranch?

Rollin Carlson withdrew his conditional use application, September 18, 1991, because of the strong opposition to the Rehabilitation/Transitional Housing, that was being proposed for the Care-Net Ranch and as Rich Cole stated, "... only things related to agriculture are allowed on the property ... there 'was no way, legally the activity could be allowed to happen in the zone.'"

QUESTION: In his letter to Bruce Eggleston, why did Rollin Carlson thank him and his office, "for helping us through the current permit application process?"

Is he thanking them for helping him get the permit, that the Kittitas County rejected in the September 18, 1991 Kittitas County Board of Adjustment public meeting when he "agreed this was a complete withdrawal and said that he would start the process from the beginning including new fees?" Or is he thanking them for helping him file new applications on September 23, 1991, to "Complete Existing Residence/Area/Carport, complete existing area which is partially enclosed now — 936 square feet" and another application for a, "Machine Shed/Barn/Equipment/Storage, construct new building for machine shed/barn equipment storage 864 square feet?"

The 936 square feet addition to the existing residence was the forbidden "community room." This addition to the existing house was actually used as the "community room" for the men at the Ranch, for eating, counseling, cleaning up, etc. even though it was forbidden by Kittitas County.

Did Rollin Carlson forget about the June 27, 1991 original application for, "10 Bunkhouses and 1 Service Center?" Was it possible for him to get his desired "community room" by calling it "an addition to an existing residence" and also, go ahead with the (same square feet) original "service center" by calling it a "Machine Shed/Barn?" Apparently, he did not feel he could go ahead with the 10 Bunkhouses even though both the 10 bunkhouses and the service center were on the same original application form.

October 03, 15, 16, 1991

29. Building inspections for Residential Addition/Garage by building Dept. (B.B.).

November 28, 1991

30. Surplus Food Commodity Order Form was filed for, "10+ needy, served 3 meals, 7 days a week."

QUESTIONS: Did Rollin Carlson forget he did not obtain a Conditional Use Permit for Rehabilitation/Transitional Housing for the Care-Net Ranch? Again, who cooked all these meals for the 10+ men supposedly at the ranch?

February, 1992

31. Rollin Carlson sent through the United States mail, a seven-page packet to "All Northwest District Pastors." (The Northwest District, includes all of the State of Washington and part of Idaho). This mailing solicited funds for The Care-Net Outreach Ranch, asking the Ministers and men of the Assemblies of God churches throughout the Northwest District, Washington and part of Idaho, to bring large contributions for the Care-Net ranch to the Men's Retreat in Yakima. (He asked for $700.00 per cow and for 100 cows, a total of at least $70,000.00.) Milton Lewis, a member of Ellensburg First Assembly of God, remembers Rollin Carlson asking for the $70,00.00 at the Men's retreat.

****

ALBERT & AIMEE ANDERSON

Albert E. Anderson was Pastor of the Ellensburg First Assembly of God when he received the following **seven page promotional mailing** at the church's address, 701 East Capitol Avenue, Ellensburg, Washington 98926:

****

BETHANY CHRISTIAN ASSEMBLY
2715 Everett Avenue
Everett, WA 98201-3795
(206) 339-3303

February, 1992

TO: All Northwest District Pastors
SUBJECT: 1992 MEN'S RETREAT "SPECIAL PROJECT"

GREETINGS, IN JESUS' NAME!

Last month, District Men's Ministries Director, Bob Unruh, wrote to all of us announcing the exciting news for our District Men's Retreat March 6 & 7 in Yakima. Many exciting events are planned for our district men again this year. My purpose in writing to you today is two-fold.

First, I encourage every pastor to make a special effort to attend this year's retreat with your men. I have found, personally, it is "good" for me to be present with the "Men of Bethany." It becomes a special time of togetherness, opens opportunity for one-on-one communication and lets my men see me function and worship God with them, side-by-side. It is a lot of fun, too!

Second, I encourage every pastor to prayerfully consider participating in the "Special Project." The final paragraph of Bob Unruh's letter said "...a project approved by the District Presbytery and myself, for the men of the Northwest District to become involved in..." This "Special Project" is sponsoring/providing 100 bred beef stock cows as a "therapy project" basis for the Care-Net

Ranch near Kittitas, Washington. This ministry provides a transitional housing program for homeless men and can serve all churches in the Northwest District. An informative video will be presented at the Retreat, a booth will be staffed by members of the Care-Net Board of Directors/Staff and a descriptive hand-out will be distributed to assist in communicating the creative ministry of this newly District Presbytery appointed District Home Mission Outreach.

Brother Bob's letter challenged us all "...to come to the Retreat ready to become involved." In the Care-Net Ranch program I see a "joint effort, resulting in joint success." Care-Net is a ministry blessed of God, endorsed by the District Presbytery, the Men's Department, the Home Missions Department, Pastors, Congregations and the Care-Net Board/Staff. All for the single purpose of bringing change to the lives of high risk men who are in need.

This "Special Project" can happen by calling the CareNet Ranch Director, Randy Bale, telling him to "come pick up a cow or cows." His phone number is (509) 968-4543 or you can fill out the enclosed response form for whatever amount your Congregation/Missions Board or Men's group can invest. The important thing is that we all ask God what He would have us do — then do it! Your one-time contribution will bless the lives of men-in-need, perpetually.

Finally, please consider this thought. A vehicle or printing press assists our missionaries as a "tool for ministry." That identical dynamic is at work in this "special in-District project for men."

We are not interested in being in the cattle business primarily. We are focused on Ministry — seeking God's help to see lives changed. This "therapy project" concept is included in the Apostle Paul's appeal, "Win them by all means." Hence, God has ordained the livestock "Therapy Project."

In Yakima you will meet changed lives, as a result of the Care-Net Ranch. Also, from the "Therapy Project," $15,000 annually is dedicated to the Decade of Harvest for New Church Planting in the Northwest District. The residents have a self-worth awareness of being able to return something in response to what they are receiving.

Please Care Enough to Give Men a Second Chance! Let's get excited about a "joint effort, which will result in joint success" for men and to God's glory!

SEE YOU IN YAKIMA!

The CareNet Outreach,

Rollin J. Carlson,
PASTOR/EXECUTIVE PRESBYTER

RJC/sp

PS: Please call me if you have any questions or ideas! Care-Net pays no administrative salaries. If this ministry ceases to function, for any reason, the assets ultimately revert to the Home Missions Department of the Northwest District.

****

NOTE: In the above February 1992 letter to All the Northwest District Pastors, **Rollin Carlson states, "We are not interested in being in the cattle business primarily."** Then a quote taken from the September 18, 1991 official minutes of the Kittitas County Board of Adjustment reads as follows: "**Rollin Carlson**, Everett, the applicant, **stressed the guest ranch wording of his application and said a rehabilitation center was of secondary importance…**"

QUESTION: How can both the cattle business and the rehabilitation center be of secondary importance? To the Ministers and churches Rollin Carlson apparently tries to make the cattle business of secondary importance and then to the Kittitas County he makes the rehabilitation center of secondary importance.

****

MEET THE PEOPLE

RANCH DIRECTOR - Vicki & Randy Bale
Daniel, Hosanna, Isaac, Mary, Joshua, Sarah, Josiah

The Bale's ministry involves developing "Therapy Projects," livestock and crop planning and involvement in resident's spiritual/physical growth.
   QUOTE: ..."Help provide 100 beef stock cows for the Care-Net Ranch in Kittitas, WA. Each year, the offspring from this herd of cows will create a perpetual source of funds for the Care-Net ministry to needy Men-In-Transition. The contribution needed is $700 per cow. Come to the Men's Retreat with your check filled out. Your church will receive World Ministries Credit, and your participation says, 'WE CARE ENOUGH TO GIVE NEEDY MEN A SECOND CHANGE.'" —Jerry Sandeno, Care-Net Board
   QUOTES: ...
   "...as Christians, we need to minister, both individually and collectively, to the needs of a frustrated world."—Vern Reeves, Care-Net Board
   "...God's love and care for the poor are central to Divine providence. Through Care-Net we show men that God cares and we care..." —Gaylord Pearson, Care-Net Board

   COUNSELlING & SCHEDULE COORDINATION — Jean & Myron Rachinski
   The Rachinski's minister to the residents in the area of food service, schedule planning, spiritual/physical growth, prayer and counselling.
   QUOTES: ...

"...One of the finest investments any Christian man can make; helping another man who is in need..." —Bill Handley, Care-Net Board

"...God is honoring people who are willing to reach out to people in need. Care-Net is indeed, an Outreach Ministry..." —Frank Anderson, Care-Net Board

NEWEST RESIDENT - Ed Morgan

Ed was alone, living in his vehicle and in need. He said, "Care-Net was there when I needed help. God has changed my life through Care-Net."

****

On the other side of this Care-Net brochure is the following:

****

CERTIFICATE OF AFFILIATION
as a
Home Missions Assembly
with the
Northwest District Council of the Assemblies of God

THIS IS TO CERTIFY that THE CARENET OUTREACH of Everett, State of Washington, has entered into fellowship with the NORTHWEST DISTRICT COUNCIL OF THE ASSEMBLIES OF GOD, with right to proper representation in district affairs so long as maintaining a scriptural standard in teaching and doctrine.

Given this Eighteenth day of December, 1990

Frank E. Cole   E. E. Kirschman
Superintendent   Secretary

****

PERPETUAL MINISTRY OPPORTUNITY

Care-Net is helping homeless men put their lives back together through its Transitional Housing Program at Care-Net Ranch. This 100 acre ranch is located near Kittitas, Washington and is providing 24-hour per day housing, meals, ministry of love and instruction in God's Word and spiritual training. Counseling and job therapy is putting meaningful direction back into the lives of men.

Care-Net is funded by contributions of individuals and churches. Care-Net also has the unique potential of self funding through it's THERAPY PROJECTS revenue. One of those Therapy Projects is the livestock operation. Animals are provided by interested contributors, cared for by Care-Net Ranch residents and marketed for cash.

ALBERT & AIMEE ANDERSON

The livestock feed is produced on the ranch, labor is provided by the residents and supported by our MAPS ministers who reside at the ranch facilities.

Care-Net needs "support tools" for this ministry. The District Presbytery and Men's Director Bob Unruh have approved a 1992 project whereby the Men-of-the-Northwest can provide an important "support tool."

The Project: **OPERATION CARING COWS**

OPERATION CARING COWS will provide 100 bred beef stock cows for the Care-Net Ranch. Each year, the offspring from this herd of cows will create a perpetual source of cash flow to fund the Outreach Ministry to needy Men-in-Transition. The contribution needed is $700 per cow. Your participation says, "WE CARE ENOUGH TO GIVE NEEDY MEN A SECOND CHANCE."

Come to the Men's Retreat with your participation response completed and your check filled out. We're believing God to complete this project at the Retreat. Your church will receive World Ministries Credit.

YOUR ONE TIME GIFT WILL CONTINUE MINISTERING TO NEEDY MEN YEAR AFTER YEAR.

___I will give $700 to fund the purchase of one beef cow
___One time gift attached
___One time gift by_____(date)
___Seven monthly installments of $100 per month
___Other_____

Name_____

Address_____City_____State____Zip

Church Name_____City_____State
Care-Net is a Washington State Non-Profit Corporation.

CareNet assets revert to the Northwest District Council of the Assemblies of God should the corporation cease to function as a ministry.

OUR HOME MISSION
   The CareNet Outreach of the Assemblies of God in The Northwest District ..."...CARING IS CONTAGIOUS ...!" Together we can make a difference in ministering to The Homeless, The Hungry, and The Hurting.
   ( ) Church Pledge   ( ) Personal Pledge

Donor's Name: _____

Donor's Address: _____

We promise to invest each month as the Lord enables $_____.

We promise to invest a one time gift as the Lord enables $_____.

For the support of The CareNet Outreach of the Assemblies of God.

World Ministries Credit will be granted to your church.
Please name church_____

Pastor or Individual_____

Phone number_____District_____Date_____

****

ALBERT & AIMEE ANDERSON

NORTHWEST DISTRICT COUNCIL OF
THE ASSEMBLIES OF GOD

March 19, 1990

Rev. Rollin Carlson
2715 Everett Avenue
Everett, WA 98201

Dear Brother Carlson:

This is to confirm to you and the Care-Net Ministries that the District Presbytery in their recent meeting unanimously approved Care-Net for World Missions credit for contributing churches. I wanted you to have it in writing to accompany the minutes of the presbytery action.

Congratulations and may God continue to bless this needed outreach ministry. Thank you for your continued faithfulness to the work of the Northwest District. God bless you in your ministry.

In His service,

E. E. Kirschman

EEK/ct

****

NOTE: This letter dated March 19, 1990, was written months before the Care-Net ranch was purchased at Kittitas.

****

February 9, 1992

32. Myron and Jean Rachinski first attended the Ellensburg First Assembly of God in the morning. Jean gave Aimee The Care-Net Outreach blue brochure with a picture of Myron and Jean Rachinski as, "Counselling & Schedule Coordination ... The Rachinskis minister to the residents in the area of food service, schedule planning, spiritual/physical growth, prayer and counselling."

For other quotes from this Care-Net Outreach brochure, see number (31) above, under MEET THE PEOPLE. Included was a picture of Randy Bale as Ranch Director, with his wife Vicki and family.

QUESTION: Why does Rollin Carlson keep mixing the feeding of the needy in Everett, Washington, with the Care-Net ranch at Kittitas, Washington? It certainly does cloud the issue and makes you wonder sometimes who he is referring to. Is this a good way to get funds for the illegal transitional/rehabilitation ranch at Kittitas?

Undated Care-Net Bookmark

33. There is an undated bookmark advertising the Bale family and Care-Net at their "Home Address, c/o Care-Net, P.O. Box 775, Kittitas, WA 98934" indicating they are under MAPS (the Assemblies of God home missions organization), and requesting people to "Make all checks payable to: MAPS Office 1445 Boonville Avenue, Springfield, MO 65502

1991-1992

34. Kennon Forester states in his "To Whom It May Concern" letter, "In the winter of '91-'92 I sold Rollin Carlson 175 tons of hay for the Care-Net operation." Furthermore, the letter tells how Rollin asked Ken to increase the cost of the hauling since he was going to collect that amount from the insurance company.

February 27, 1992

   35. A Surplus Food Commodity Order Form was signed by Rollin Carlson, for 10+ needy, 3 meals, 7 days a week. File or ID #700522.

March 6, 1992

   36. Pastor Albert Anderson and several other men from Ellensburg First Assembly of God, attended the Men's Retreat in Yakima where over 2,000 men from the Northwest district gathered. Rollin Carlson, Randy Bale and Myron Rachinski were all on the platform promoting the Care-Net Outreach ranch as a viable legitimate ministry for needy men located at Kittitas, Washington. In this service, the promotional video about Care-Net was shown, stating The Care-Net Outreach to be a Non-profit Corporation licensed in the State of Washington.

   NOTE: Rollin Carlson did apply to the Washington Secretary of State for non-profit corporation status but did not answer all required questions. The application was returned to Rollin indicating all questions must be answered.

   QUESTION: How was it possible that Rollin Carlson could publicly withdraw his Conditional Use permit on September 18, 1991 -- because of failure to meet requirements in the Ag/20 zoning -- and then less than six months later present the Care-Net Outreach to about 2000 men, as though every requirement had been met? **Is this the quality of integrity in leadership ministers and laity are exhorted to follow?**

   While the Biblical standard of righteousness is for all believers, it is also true that those in spiritual leadership must adhere even more closely to that standard because of the position of trust and influence. Paul declared: **"Giving no offence in anything, that the ministry be not blamed."** (II Corinthians 6:3)

April 6, 1992

37. Rollin Carlson attended the evening service at Ellensburg Assembly. He took it upon himself to go to the platform and take an anniversary offering for the Andersons. It surprised them, as this was not something visiting ministers or District Officials were in a habit of doing. At this time, the Andersons still had no knowledge of the rejection of Rollin Carlson's rehabilitation/transitional housing ranch by the Kittitas County, (Nor his public withdrawal of his application for Conditional Use permit at the public hearing in Ellensburg, September 18, 1991). To our knowledge, another application has never been submitted.

May 29, 1992

38. Rollin Carlson signed a Surplus Food Commodities Order Form.

June 11, 1992

39. Albert and Aimee had a 10:00 A.M. appointment at the Care-Net ranch with John Dudley, (one of the men there for rehabilitation) and Myron Rachinski, the ranch counselor. Albert helped Myron counsel John, while Aimee helped Jean prepare and serve the dinner for the two men who were there for rehabilitation. The Rachinskis and Andersons joined the two men for dinner. Jean gave Aimee a tour of the storage room where the stockpile of USDA government food was stored.

ALBERT & AIMEE ANDERSON

August 1, 1992

40. The Andersons and Rachinskis ate dinner at Larry and Deborah Chase's home (Deborah is Albert and Aimee Anderson's oldest daughter). The Rachinskis were getting ready to move to West Virginia because of all the problems involving Rollin Carlson and the Care-Net ranch. They expressed, "We can hardly wait to get out of the Northwest."

August 6, 1992

41. About noon, the Andersons had an appointment to meet with Don Strong -- presbyter of the Yakima/Tri-Cities section of the Northwest District -- at Vantage in order to discuss Care-Net. They had lunch and were together almost two hours. The Andersons shared their concerns about the way the Rachinskis were treated at the Care-Net ranch by Rollin Carlson, as well as other issues concerning the Care-Net ranch. (This was the first effort by the Andersons to bring notice of complaints or questions concerning Rollin Carlson and the Care-Net ranch to the Assemblies of God leadership.)

August 6, 1992

42. This evening around 9:30 P.M., Rollin Carlson returned Albert's August 3rd phone call. They talked about Care-Net for approximately one hour. Albert had several concerns about the Care-Net ranch and asked a number of questions. Rollin made the phone call to Albert, from his brother, Joe Carlson's home in Ellensburg.

August 27, 1992

43. A Surplus Food Commodity Order Form was submitted with *Rollin J. Carlson, Pastor*, printed on the form. The number was changed from 10+ to 20

needy, being fed 3 meals per day, **(60 meals each day)** 7 days a week.

September 14, 1992

44. Rollin Carlson unexpectedly stopped by the Andersons' home. (The Andersons believe the August 6th phone conversation Albert had with Rollin, while he was at his brother Joe's place, caused Carlson such great concern, he decided to make a personal visit to the Andersons' home.) The Andersons asked Rollin Carlson a number of questions during the course of the visit, such as; "How were the Rachinskis paid?" He answered, "My wife and I talked it over and decided to give Myron a gift of $200.00 a week."

Aimee asked Rollin Carlson this question because Jean Rachinski had told her that Rollin would make a copy of two $100.00 bills on a sheet of paper; then Myron would sign it for Rollin to use as a receipt for that week's services. The Andersons understood it was for the Church records.

Aimee asked about the insurance claim. Rollin responded, "I told the insurance company all about it and they said it was okay." Apparently, Rollin Carlson was reimbursed for the weekly $200.00 paid to Myron by the insurance company. (At this time, the Andersons did not know the name of the insurance company.)

Myron Rachinski was paid approximately $5,200.00 for the 26 weeks work plus board and room.

Aimee asked Rollin, "Did you tell Myron not to tell the Insurance Company about the $200.00 cash receipts that you received from Myron?"

Rollin answered, "No! Do you believe me?"

Aimee answered, "I'm trying!"

As Rollin's story goes, his wrist was hurt in a car accident sometime late in 1991, thus he was supposedly not able to do his job at the ranch, so he had to hire Myron to do his work for him.

ALBERT & AIMEE ANDERSON

At this time, the Andersons had no knowledge of Rollin Carlson's hay dealings with Kennon Forester and Rollin Carlson's insurance claim for the inflated freight bill from Kennon.

QUESTION: Who really hired Myron? Rollin Carlson, Care-Net, or did Myron receive only gifts for his six months service at the ranch?

Apparently, it was convenient to call the $200.00 paid per week to Myron Rachinski by Rollin Carlson for all his work at the Care-Net ranch, a gift or gifts, in order not to have to comply with Federal (IRS) payroll deductions, for January through June 1992.
(Also, it veils the fact that they were breaking County statutes).
Second, it was very convenient, in order to collect insurance money under a false claim, to make the insurance company believe Rollin Carlson had to hire Myron Rachinski for the special purpose of doing Rollin's work on the ranch because of the injury to his wrist due to the car accident he was involved in.
Third, the Care-Net video and brochure promoted Myron Rachinski as a staff member. How were staff members supposed to receive their salaries?

QUESTION: Could all of these stories be true, a gift and/or hire because of the car accident, when the fact is, Myron Rachinski is in the Care-Net Ranch Video and both Myron and his wife, Jean, are shown in the Care-Net Brochure as part of the Care-Net Outreach staff?

Apparently, this would make it appear more credible when soliciting funding for all the staff workers (including Myron and Jean Rachinski) at the Care-Net ranch.
The "Meet The People" brochure states, "The Rachinskis minister to the residents in the area of food service, schedule planning, spiritual/physical growth, prayer and counseling." If Rollin Carlson either gave the $200.00 per week

WHITED SEPULCHRES

to Myron as a gift or had to hire him to do his work at the ranch because of an injury to his wrist, then why is Myron's wife Jean's picture shown in the Care-Net Brochure as part of the staff? Jean definitely did, "minister to the residents in the area of food service," even though there were only a few there at one time. Myron also did a lot of the carpenter work, as this is his trade.

QUESTION: Is this really why Rollin hired Myron in the first place, because he was a carpenter **(which would be very helpful in his illegal building schemes)**, and not a qualified counselor?

During the March 6, 1992 Men's Retreat in Yakima, where over 2,000 men from the Northwest district gathered, Myron Rachinski was on the platform in the Friday evening service helping to promote the Care-Net ranch. Also, the Care-Net video was shown promoting the Care-Net ranch.

Aimee asked Rollin Carlson, "Do you have any of your personal cattle out at the Care-Net ranch?" Rollin answered, "No." Later in the evening Rollin informed the Andersons that he or his son had one, or two or possibly more head of stock out at the Care-Net ranch.

One of the last things spoken to Rollin Carlson by Albert was, **"I don't want Care-Net to be doing or be involved in any thing which would be questionable or be a reproach to the Gospel."** The Andersons do not remember Rollin making any response to this statement.

When Rollin left he put his arm around Albert's shoulder and said, "We're buddies, remember!"

September 20, 1992

45. Myron Rachinski mailed a "To Whom It May Concern" letter to Albert and Aimee Anderson wherein he told about the manner in which he was paid and what Rollin told him to tell the insurance company if they should call.

September 20, 1992

46. Myron also enclosed with his September 20, 1992, "To Whom It May Concern" letter, a copy of a rough draft of a hand written resignation letter he had written to Carlson and the Board Members, which reads as follows:

****

CARE-NET OUTREACH

Pastor Carlson & Board Members:

Jean and I have some urgent financial needs and obligations that have to be addressed. We are looking for employment in the Kittitas area, so we still can be involved with the Care-Net ministry on a volunteer basis.

Because of the full time schedule of the ranch I have not been able to supplement my income with outside work and we have reached a point to where we have to find work elsewhere to meet our needs. We thank you so much for your faithfulness both financially and with housing. It is very much appreciated.

Jean & I don't have the money to move to another location right now and would like you to consider renting this mobile home to us for at least the month of July and possibly August.

I would like to still be involved with counseling and discipling with the residency but it would have to be either before or after work, whatever the case may be. I would like to do this and give my time to help. As for Jean she is looking for different avenues to help us financially and cannot commit her day to the food preparation and the needs of the residents in this area.

Thank you for your consideration and prayers.

Sincerely,

Myron & Jean Rachinski

September 28, 1992

47. Don Strong visited the Andersons in their home. They gave him Myron Rachinski's "To Whom It May Concern" letter and a copy of his hand written resignation letter. Don promised to give the letters to the District Officials at the up-coming Presbyters meeting. **Don told the Andersons, "this could be a big stink;"** also he said, **"Rollin is known as a 'Wheeler Dealer.'"** He expressed his concerns as his church had contributed several thousand dollars to the Care-Net ranch.

October 15, 1992

48. After several tries to reach Don Strong by phone, Albert and Aimee Anderson gained an audience with him following a Minister's meeting. Don told the Andersons that he did not have time to present Myron's letter at the Presbyter's meeting. He said he talked to Rollin about it and also made reference to another letter, which seemed to negate the "To Whom It May Concern" letter. We did not realize at the time that the "another letter" Don referred to, was the other handwritten letter that the Rachinskis had given to us as well and we in turn had given a copy of it to Don to deliver to the District Officials (Refer to #46). Moreover, Don said, "If you do anything about it, I will not back you and you will look questionable." **This was the beginning of a series of threats.** What power did Rollin Carlson have over Don Strong to keep him from presenting Rachinski's letter to the Presbytery? The Andersons thought Don Strong appeared uneasy.

January 21, 1993

49. A food commodities form was submitted for pick up for the Transitional Housing, for 20 needy served, 3 meals each day, 7 days each week.

February 23, 1993

50. Rollin Carlson submitted an Application for Permit to the Kittitas County Building Department — "To construct and landscape a 4 bedroom residence" on Tax Parcel No. 17-20-0500-0017 Permit #K-93-409. This property was deeded 2/25/91 from Farm Credit Bank of Spokane, a Federal corporation, to Melvin L. Chapman and Winnie Chapman, husband and wife. (Included with this February 23, 1993, application are the following: Attachment B, BUILDING RECORD in which the proposed building is to be a single family dwelling; Kittitas County Construction Permits, giving building details for a single family dwelling [Permit #K-93-409 and Permit #K-93-410, which covered the daylight basement for this house], And the Kittitas County Health Department certificate for this house where the term "group home" is used, dated 04/09/93.)

On this February 23, 1993, application it states that, "The Owner of Record, is The Care-Net Outreach, 2715 Everett Ave., Everett, WA 98201." This application is signed by Rollin Carlson. Who really is the owner of this property, Chapmans or Care-Net? (At a later date) Winnie Chapman told Aimee over the phone, **"we were willing for our name to be used"** when referring to the **Care-Net ranch**. Two days after this document, another one was filed stating that Mel Chapman is the owner of record.

QUESTION: Is Rollin Carlson trying to hide something? Is Rollin applying for a four bedroom residence before Care-Net owns the property or does The Care-Net Outreach, Rollin Carlson, or someone else actually own this property while at the same time using Mel and Winnie Chapman's name as a go between?

February 25, 1993

51. Two strange letters on the same page are filed in the Kittitas County records. One is a letter by Rollin Carlson to The Kittitas County Building Department stating that Mel Chapman had agreed to the terms of sale of the property to Care-Net, and the other letter by Mel Chapman to the Building Department, stating that he is "totally in agreement with the vision of the Care-Net Outreach." May we ask again, who is the real owner of this property at this time? February 23, 1993 Rollin filed an Application for Permit (Permit Number K-93-409) stating that the Care-Net Outreach is the "Owner of Record." Then two days later on February 25, the page containing two short letters reads as follows:

****

ALBERT & AIMEE ANDERSON

Care-Net
2715 Everett Avenue
Everett, WA 98201-3795
(206) 339-3303

February 25, 1993

The Kittitas County Building Department
507 Nanum Room 2
Ellensburg, Washington 98926

Dear Sir:

The following statement is provided for Care-Net to present to you from the present owner of record, Mel Chapman. Mr. Chapman has agreed to the terms of sale, transferring the property from himself to the Care-Net Outreach. That closing is scheduled for April 2nd, at which time the property will be transferred by record. It is our request to proceed with the application process, so that we can commence construction immediately after closing. I have discussed this desire with Billy Barrett, and together we agreed it would be appropriate for Mr. Chapman to give you this attached statement.

Sincerely,

Rollin J. Carlson,
President, the Care-Net Outreach

RJC/vl

****

WHITED SEPULCHRES

To Whom it May Concern:

   I have agreed to the sale of my property off Kauffman Road to the Care-Net Outreach. The sale will be closed on April 2, 1993. I hereby grant permission to the Care-Net Outreach to commence site preparation and application for a building permit. I am totally in agreement with the vision of the Care-Net Outreach.

Sincerely,

Mel Chapman

              ****

   TWO QUESTIONS: Did Mel Chapman really own this property? Would Rollin Carlson actually help someone make a profit of $155,000.00 on a sale to Care-Net and in order to do so, use The Northwest District of the Assemblies of God, Church Loan Fund money (while he was Chairman of the Northwest District Finances)?

              ****

April 1, 1993

52. A Statutory Warranty Deed states that "Melvin and Winnie Chapman, as Grantors conveyed to The Care-Net Outreach, a Washington non-profit corporation," the property that the daylight basement house was built on. (This is the same property that Rollin submitted an Application for Permit on February 23, 1993, stating that The Care-Net Outreach was the Owner of Record. On this County Application For Permit Rollin Carlson states that the Use of Structure is "Residence". Yet, time after time it is told to the Ministers and laity, "The day light basement house is a bunkhouse to house 9 to 10 men.") The Statutory Warranty Deed is #558268 in Vol. 341, page 61 in the Kittitas County records. This document states that The Care-Net Outreach is a Washington non-profit corporation.

April 1, 1993

53. A Deed of Trust was filed in Vol. 341, page 65, #558269, stating that, The Northwest District Council of the Assemblies of God loaned $350,000.00 to The Care-Net Outreach, A Washington Non-profit Corporation. (Where is the "Letter of Intent" qualifying the ranch for charitable contributions?)

The Northwest District Council of the Assemblies of God loaned The Care-Net Outreach on April 1, 1993, $90,000.00 more than The Care-Net Outreach paid for the property that they bought on April 1, 1993. The $350,000.00 loan to the Care-Net Outreach ranch almost covered the full amount of both the May 30, 1990 $93,236.00 sale and the April 1, 1993 $260,000.00 sale, which added together comes to a total of $353,236.00.

This Deed of Trust dated April 1, 1993 declares that the Chapmans are the owner of this property. On February 23, 1993, Rollin Carlson filed an Application for Permit for a (4) four-bedroom house on this property, that states The Care-Net

Outreach is the owner of record. Who is the real owner before April 1, 1993? Is this what Winnie Chapman was talking about when she told Aimee, "we were willing for our names to be used?"

NOTE: Significantly, this Deed of Trust for the Care-Net Ranch declares "...which real property is not used principally for agricultural or farming purposes..." Apparently, this is the standard form used by the Northwest District council in its acquisition of property for Home Missions churches. But the Care-Net Ranch property is clearly used for agricultural purposes and thus it is illegal to use it for a church rehabilitation/transitional ministry. **Is it not possible to do God's work honestly and legally? Yet, our District and National leaders have tried to cover up this deception.** Apparently, District and National officials were deeply involved in this ungodly/illegal mess. Yet, it would have been much better for all concerned to come clean. **Nothing is hidden from Almighty God.**

April 1, 1993

54. A Real Estate Excise Tax form was filed, which stated that Melvin L. Chapman and Winnie Chapman are the sellers and The Care-Net Outreach is the Buyer for $260,000.00. On paper, Chapmans bought this property February 25, 1991, for $105,000.00. This appears to be a profit of $155,000.00, either Chapmans, Rollin Carlson, or someone else made.

QUESTION: Did Rollin Carlson help Chapmans gain $155,000.00 at the Northwest District's expense by using Northwest District Church Loan Fund money?

The February 25, 1991, Real Estate Excise Tax form #031500, states that Melvin L. and Winnie Chapman's permanent address "for all property tax related correspondence," is 2715 Everett Avenue, Everett, WA 98201, which is the Everett Bethany Christian Assembly church's address. Now on this

Real Estate Excise Tax document, dated April 1, 1993, Chapmans permanent address is, P. O. Box 218, Arlington, Washington 98223.

This Real Estate Excise Tax form also states that The Care-Net Outreach is a Washington non-profit corporation.

April 1, 1993

55. Rollin Carlson and the Care-Net Outreach submitted an Application for Permit to build a daylight basement, an addition to the four bedroom, single-family dwelling.

This is the same property, which is referred to — #50, February 23, 1993, -- of the Care-Net chronology. It states The Care-Net Outreach to be the "Owner of Record."

This is the same property conveyed by Statutory Warranty Deed, to The Care-Net Outreach on April 1, 1993, by Chapmans. Attached to this document is a Construction Permit for a single Family residence, dated 04/14/93.

April, 1993

56. A food commodities form states a pick up date for 45 needy served at the Transitional Housing, 3 meals, 7 days each week. Also there is a note in the margin which says, "Transitional housing, 45 served daily — 3 meals per day, 70% Homeless." This is a total of 135 meals served each day. No one seems to know who was supposed to be doing all the cooking for the 45 needy men that were supposed to be served the 135 meals each day. Apparently, no one has met such a person, as it never took place. This is the second time in less than a year that the number of needy people served 3 meals each day, has been changed on the Food Commodities order form. On the August, 1991, form it was changed from 10+ needy to 20 needy and then in April, 1993, it was changed from 20 needy to 45 needy, served 3 meals each day.

Some of the Government Surplus Food Commodities brought to the Care-Net ranch, were used to feed the one, two, three, four, or possibly five men sent there for rehabilitation/transitional housing purposes. Some was used to feed the Assembly of God construction volunteer laborers who came to the ranch to work on the buildings, etc. and some was given to other people. What happened to the rest of all the Government Surplus Food given to the Care-Net Outreach ranch to feed the "45 needy, three meals each day?"

Moreover, what happened to the cases of Government Food that Jeanne Mahon said she saw the men load up in the truck and haul away before the Food Commodities man (Mark Severn) appeared at the ranch with Rollin Carlson for inspection in the spring of 1994?

May 20, 1993

57. Another Food Commodities order form was filed for the Transitional Housing, the average needy 45, 3 meals each day, for 7 days each week. A total of 135 meals supposedly served each day. This order had Rollin's secretary's name, Vi Lien, as the person who placed the order.

June 14, 1993

58. Rollin Carlson signed an Application for Permit to build a loafing shed. This loafing shed blew over in 1994. The poles apparently were buried in less than two feet of dirt instead of the four (4) feet of sand or cement that the County required.

July 19, 1993

59. Aimee tried for the second time to reach Elmer Kirschman by phone. (On July 9, she tried to phone him, but he was not available.) Again, he was not available but later he did phone back and

Aimee was given an opportunity to share with Elmer Kirschman some of the Andersons' concerns about Rollin Carlson and the Care-Net ranch. After telling about Myron Rachinski's "To Whom It May Concern" letter, she asked, "What shall we do with his letter?" **Elmer Kirschman answered, "Send it back to him, no need to get the Andersons' hands dirty."** Why would he make such a statement, unless he knew there was some wrong concerning Care-Net? Apparently, he did not show any interest in doing anything about it. The message Aimee received was very clear, don't get your **"hands dirty."**

August 30, 1993

60. A Food Commodities order form was filed for Transitional Housing, the average needy 45, 3 meals, 7 days each week, a grand total of meals served for the week comes to 945. This is a good way to receive free Government food to feed the construction volunteers, who came from the different churches throughout the District volunteering their labor for construction of buildings. (Jean Rachinski told Aimee that she used the Government Surplus Food Commodities in preparing the meals for the Northwest District church volunteer workers.)

November, 1993

61. The Kittitas Assembly of God troubles were brought into the public arena. The Daily Record and the Yakima Herald both ran a series of articles concerning the court trial of the (12) twelve people served with restraining orders.

November 30, 1993

62. Vi Lien, Rollin Carlson's secretary, signed a Food Commodities Form for Transitional Housing, the average needy 45, 3 meals each day, 7 days each week.

November/December, 1993

63. *The Northwest District Messenger*, a Northwest District Council of the Assemblies of God bi-monthly magazine sent to all the ministers and churches in its district, shows a promotional page with pictures of men working on buildings at the Care-Net ranch. That page reads in part: "Construction Volunteers working on the Care-Net Outreach Center in Kittitas. Volunteers are from several churches — Maltby Christian Assembly, South Whidbey Assembly of God and Everett Bethany Christian Assembly."

December 2, 1993

64. Albert and Aimee Anderson had a phone conversation with Warren Bullock, at the Northwest District office. The Andersons expressed their concerns about The Care-Net Outreach ranch and the trouble at the Kittitas Church. They told him about some of the wrongs concerning Rollin Carlson and The Care-Net ranch. Warren Bullock asked them to send the newspaper clippings and the "To Whom It May Concern" letter from Myron Rachinski. Albert said he would do so; however, no written response or thanks to the letter and enclosures was received by the Andersons.

December 11, 1993

65. The Andersons received, through the United States mail, another Care-Net Ranch Brochure soliciting funds for the Ministry at The Care-Net ranch. The impression given is that the Care-Net ranch is a rehabilitation facility servicing several people at a time.

December 14, 1993

66. Albert and Aimee talked with Frank Cole on the phone. They expressed their concerns about Rollin Carlson, The Care-Net Outreach ranch and the situation at the Kittitas Assembly of God.

December 22, 1993

67. Albert and Aimee received a letter from Frank Cole in response to their phone call and documentation mailed to him. No mention was made of the Care-Net ranch problems, only that the situation at Kittitas Assembly seemed improved. (See Exhibit I in Section 2, Formal Charges)

January 7, 8, and 10, 1994

68. Rollin Carlson attended the Kittitas County court hearing concerning the restraining order against the twelve people who were excommunicated from the Kittitas Assembly of God Church by Pastor Gary Jeffery. He told Aimee in the courtroom when sitting by the Andersons, "Frank Cole sent me to the hearing in his place since he (Frank) could be subpoenaed to Court." The Andersons could not understand why he would do such a thing after Albert had mailed him the documents concerning Rollin Carlson and the Care-Net Outreach ranch at Kittitas, Washington.

January 21, 1994

69. Albert and Aimee Anderson met with Kittitas County prosecutor David Pitts for one hour. They told him about Care-Net and Rollin Carlson receiving money apparently from a false insurance claim. One statement he made to the Andersons was, **"The way Rollin Carlson had it set up, it encouraged fraud."**

January 28, 1994

70. Aimee made an anonymous phone call to Mike Johnson, Ellensburg Daily Record, City Editor. She made the following statement to him, "I don't believe it was possible for the Northwest District Officials (themselves) to take care of the Kittitas Pastor properly, since Randy Bale was the deacon supporting Pastor Jeffery and Randy was the Care-Net Ranch director. Thus, Rollin Carlson was his Care-Net Pastor. This created a big "Conflict of Interest."

This bears repetition — Gary Jeffery was Randy Bale's pastor, and Rollin Carlson was Randy's Care-Net Pastor. Rollin signed legal documents as "President/Pastor" of the Care-Net Ranch. Also, see Section 2, Formal Charges, exhibit G — the December 1993 Care-Net brochure — promoting the Care-Net Outreach Ranch at Kittitas, Washington. It contains Rollin Carlson's picture with the caption, "Rollin Carlson, NWD Executive Presbyter, Care-Net Pastor."

January 30, 1994

71. In a phone conversation with Virgil Derek, manager of Columbia Cattle, at George, Washington, he said, "I gave several cattle to Care-Net when they were starting. Also, I get good hay buys for them. I know Rollin and last week I had Randy Bale and his family out to my place to dinner."

Some time earlier in the month, Aimee had received a phone call from a stranger (to her), who said he was Virgil Derek. He requested the Andersons to get in touch with a boy named Casey, to see if they could get him to go to church. He thought it was an Ellensburg number. After trying to reach the boy by phone, Aimee phoned Virgil Derek to tell him about her effort to contact the boy. Because Aimee wanted to know why he phoned the Andersons in the first place, she asked him several questions which led to the above statements.

February 5, 1994

72. For months, Aimee had been searching for the insurance company that Rollin filed his deceptive claim with concerning Myron Rachinski. Myron couldn't remember the name of the insurance company, except that it was well known. After many phone calls and questions, Aimee phoned one of State Farm's (800) numbers and a switch board operator answered and gave her Bethany Christian Assembly's claim number #472558139; the agent, Bob Kaine's phone number, (206) 774-8900, and Dave McKeeken, fraud agent's phone number, (800) 541-8636. Later, Aimee phoned the regional office in Salem, Oregon, and told them about the insurance claim from Rollin Carlson using Myron Rachinski as a means for receiving money deceptively. The person Aimee talked to was very helpful and told her she would be receiving a call from Gene Simpson, Regional Fraud Unit, (206) 882-5577. He said he found the claim number on the Ford Van, December, 1991, and everything else, except Rollin's personal claim. He had the files pulled and started an investigation. Aimee felt comfortable talking to him and thought it would be all right to send him the documents he asked for.

February 10, 1994

73. Two letters and two brochures with cover letter from the Andersons were mailed to Gene Simpson, STATE FARM INSURANCE, SIU, relative to Rollin Carlson's deceitful insurance claim.

February 17, 1994

74. Aimee phoned the Care-Net Outreach Ranch number early this morning. Jeff, from Whidbey Island, a resident at the ranch, told Aimee he had lived there about two months and expected to be there possibly up to a year. Aimee asked, "How do you get to live there?" Jeff answered, "You have

to talk to Rollin Carlson." In their conversation Jeff related to Aimee the following items:

1. He had an alcohol problem.
2. He was living in a bunkhouse that could house 4 or 5 men.
3. Care-Net had about 100 cattle at the ranch. He works with the cattle, feeding them, etc.
4. Someone takes him to town every day for classes.
5. He is helping them finish the new bunkhouse, now almost complete. Jeff said, "We are really excited, our new bunkhouse is almost done. It will house ten (10) men." (This is the house referred to earlier for which Rollin Carlson only received a residential building permit.)

February 17, 1994

75. In another phone conversation with Gene Simpson, Insurance Investigator for State Farm Insurance, he asked Aimee if they would be willing to be interviewed by an Investigative Reporter for the P.I. She said, "Yes." He said his name is Dick Clever and he would be sending him to the Andersons after he had received a few more facts.

February 17, 1994

76. Aimee phoned Anita Kazee at the County Commissioner's office and gave her the information that Jeff had given her over the phone. Anita, along with Patty Jo and Allison (employees at the Kittitas County Building Department) had already been doing some checking. A few days earlier, the Andersons loaned Anita the Care-Net ranch Video. Also, they gave her a copy of the December 1993 Care-Net brochure that had been mailed to Albert E. Anderson, at the Ellensburg First Assembly of God address. The Andersons started putting all the pieces together and discovered that Rollin Carlson and Care-Net did not receive a variance or permit

for the rehabilitation/transitional housing, that they had been promoting and receiving charitable contributions for. Thus, they were operating illegally.

February 18, 1994

77. Aimee Anderson phoned Prosecutor David Pitts and told him Rollin Carlson and The Care-Net Outreach ranch did not have a permit for a land-use variance.

February 22, 1994

78. The following conversation took place between Aimee and Mel and Winnie Chapman:
Aimee, "Are you Winnie, with Care-Net?"
Winnie, "Yes. We used to be affiliated with Care-Net but not any longer. We also used to be with MAPS."
Aimee, "Do you know if there is a Care-Net Ranch in Snohomish County?"
Winnie, "No, the only Care-Net Ranch is in Kittitas. The Care-Net feeding is in Everett; it is statewide. I have to hurry and go to work but you can phone Bethany at Everett."
They both said good-bye.

February 23, 1994

79. The Kittitas County Department of Building & Fire Safety sent a certified letter containing a violation notice, to Care-Net Outreach, Everett, WA, and one was sent by certified mail to the Care-Net ranch, from Code Enforcement Inspector, Patti McLean. Also, copies were sent to the Planning Department, and the Prosecuting Attorney's office.
Some documents contained in the building department file are the following:

(a) 02/17/94 — Kittitas County Verification of Violation;
(b) The complaint that produced the violation letter;
(c) Letter from the Kittitas County Planning Department, (Patti McLean, Code Enforcement Inspector);
(d) March 18, 1994, memo to Care-Net Outreach from Billie Barrett, Building, Inspector/Permit Tech., concerning final inspection of the machine shed;
(e) Certificate of Occupancy for Residence, for addition to existing building. (Actually this was the community room that the rehab men used for cleaning up, eating, counseling, etc.);
(f) March 2, 1994 letter from Patti McLean, Code Enforcement Inspector, to Care-Net Outreach, RE: Building Permits.

February 23, 1994

80. Aimee found out from the treasurer's office, that Care-Net is delinquent on property taxes. Also, that the **Northwest District Council, loaned $135,000.00 to The Care-Net Outreach.** The Deed of Trust, dated May 20, 1991, was executed almost two years before they made the April 1, 1993 loan of **$350,000.00** to the Care-Net Outreach. Together the two different loans total $485,000.00, apparently both from the Northwest District Church Loan Fund. (December 1995, the Andersons discovered another Deed of Trust for **$30,000.00**, dated July 1, 1993, **from the Northwest District Church Loan Fund to The Care-Net Outreach.**)

February 24, 1994

81. Patty Jo with the Kittitas County Department of Building and Fire Safety, told Aimee that she had mailed a letter yesterday, to both Rollin Carlson in Everett and Randy Bale at the

ranch, letting them know they would like to inspect their buildings. She also said, "They do not have a conditional use permit for a rehabilitation center in that zone. It's not a guest ranch. They can invite a guest in." Patty Jo did not tell Aimee that the Violation Notice had been sent by certified mail to both Care-Net Outreach, 2715 Everett Avenue, Everett, WA 98201 and to Care-Net Outreach, Route 3, Box 1060, Ellensburg, WA 98926.

February 25 and 28, 1994

82. Copies were obtained of certified receipts from the mailing of the violation notice.

February 25, 1994

83. Patti McLean, Code Enforcement Inspector sent a memorandum to Scott Staab, Prosecuting Attorney's office about the Care-Net Outreach.

February 25, 1994

84. Aimee tried to phone Frank Cole and then Warren Bullock at Central University in Ellensburg, where they were meeting for a Church growth seminar. Aimee finally reached him at the Best Western Motel. At that time, the following phone conversation took place:

Aimee, "Albert and I would like to talk to you. Would that be possible?"

Warren, "Well, you know how it is at these meetings. There's not much time. What's it about?"

Aimee, "It's serious. I don't know if I should say over the phone? Just a minute." Aimee then asked Albert, "What should I tell him, he wants to know what it's about?" Albert answered, "Care-Net." Aimee then answered Warren Bullock's question, "Rollin Carlson and Care-Net are operating illegally!"

WHITED SEPULCHRES

Warren, "That's pretty serious, you better be able to back it up with proof."

Aimee, "I can, we have documentation. I am the one who talked Albert into phoning you, even though Albert told me, 'Warren Bullock probably won't pay any attention to us' since he didn't pay any attention to us before, after we talked to both him and Frank Cole, as well as mailing them the documentation."

Warren, "If it's that serious then I think Frank Cole and Elmer Kirschman need to be with me."

Aimee, "When would that be?"

Warren, "About two or three days."

Aimee, "Then I guess you will just have to find out about it when it comes out. It is in the Prosecuting Attorney's hands now. Somebody from the Courthouse said, 'When this blows, it will blow big.'"

Warren, "How about 10:00 A.M.?"

Aimee, "We will plan on seeing you tomorrow morning at 10:00 A.M. at C.W.U."

February 26, 1994

85. At the conclusion of the Assemblies of God, church growth conference held at Central Washington University, Albert and Aimee had a personal conversation with Warren Bullock for almost 50 minutes, concerning The Care-Net Outreach ranch and Rollin Carlson.

The Andersons gave Warren Bullock the following documents:

1. Rollin Carlson's Conditional Use Permit Application.
2. Minutes of Kittitas County Board of Adjustment meeting on 09/18/91.
3. Newspaper clippings entitled, "Rehab Ranch Plans Put on Hold by Organizers."

4. Rollin Carlson's letter on behalf of Care-Net to the County Planner, Bruce Eggleston, and dated 09/25/91.

NOTE: Some statements Warren Bullock made during that conversation are as follows: **"Rollin has a way of being able to explain himself out of situations ... We have enough to be able to ask Rollin some very pointed questions ... This is different ... This is serious ... I passed information along to Frank Cole, up the chain of command** ... If it will make you feel better, I will tell you that Rollin asked to borrow money for Care-Net in 1993 and the District Presbytery turned him down ... District Officials are not given financial accounting from Care-Net."

Aimee asked Warren, "Why was Rollin sent over for the Court trial of the Kittitas people, in Frank Cole's place?" The Andersons are not sure if they received any real answer to that question. Albert told Warren, "In my understanding, it is mail fraud to solicit contributions for an illegal operation."

Albert and Aimee also briefly talked to Warren Bullock about the following pre-planned agenda:

1. They met the Rachinskis for the first time on February 9, 1992. Shortly thereafter, the Rachinskis started talking to the Andersons about some of their problems with Rollin and Care-Net.
2. The March 6-7, 1992 men's retreat in Yakima when the Care-Net video was shown and Rollin Carlson, Randy Bale and Myron Rachinski were on the platform as part of the big Care-Net promotion.
3. Rollin visiting (April 5, 1992) Ellensburg First Assembly of God and taking the liberty to receive an Anniversary offering for Pastor Albert and Aimee Anderson.
4. Albert and Aimee ate lunch (June 11, 1992) at the Care-Net ranch with Myron and Jean

Rachinski and the two resident rehab men. This was the time that Albert and Myron counseled one of the men.
5. The phone conversation (July, 1993) between Aimee and Elmer Kirschman, when he said, "Send the letter back, no need to get the Andersons' hands dirty!"
6. Albert and Aimee meeting (August, 1992) with Don Strong at Vantage, when they shared their concerns about Rollin Carlson, the treatment of Rachinskis by Carlson and the operation of the Care-Net ranch.
7. Rollin's visit (September 14, 1992) to the Andersons' home to talk about questions concerning the Care-Net ranch.
8. Don Strong's visit (September 28, 1992) to the Andersons' home and their conversation about Rollin Carlson and the Care-Net ranch.
9. The Andersons talking to Don Strong (October 15, 1992) in Yakima about his refusal to give Myron Rachinski's "To Whom It May Concern" letter to the District Officials as he had promised.
10. Albert and Aimee's phone conversation (December 2, 1993) with Warren Bullock about the Kittitas Assembly problems, Rollin Carlson and the Care-Net problems.
11. Albert and Aimee's separate phone conversations (December 14, 1993) with Frank Cole concerning the Kittitas Assembly problems, Rollin Carlson and the Care-Net ranch.
12. In his summation of the trial pertaining to the restraining orders on the twelve Kittitas Assembly adherents and members, Judge Thomas Haven said Pastor Jeffery fabricated. Perjury charges were filed with the police against Gary Jeffery in January, 1994, by eleven of the twelve pressed into court.
13. Zoning violations were to be investigated by the Prosecutor, David Pitts.
14. Don Strong's November 16, 1993 letter to the Northwest District Council Attorney, James Hansen, accusing Pairlee and the

excommunicated people from the Kittitas Assembly.
15. A lot of people have been expressing anger about the Kittitas church mess. This coupled with the Care-Net violations have made a lot of neighbors outraged.

February 28, 1994

86. Albert and Aimee Anderson went to the Fellowship meeting at Harrah. At the evening meal, Irwin Krueger came over to where the Andersons were sitting and sat two seats over from Aimee. During the evening dinner, the following conversation took place between Aimee and Irwin Krueger; while at the same time, Albert knowing what was taking place, made conversation with another individual:

Aimee, "Brother Krueger, are you still building?"

Krueger, "Yes."

Aimee, "Did you help build up at the Care-Net ranch?"

Krueger, "Yes, they are almost finished with another bunkhouse, that's going to house nine (9) to ten (10) men."

Aimee, "How do you get in there?"

Krueger, "You mean the process?"

Aimee, "Yes, the process."

Krueger, "O.K. the process is this: Rollin Carlson has a big feeding program over there. They take the men from the streets of Seattle and feed them, then once a month they get together and pick the ones that will go to the Care-Net ranch."

Aimee, "Oh, is it a rehabilitation ranch for men?"

Krueger, "Yes, it's a rehabilitation ranch for men. They have another bunkhouse that sleeps three (3) men."

After the evening service, Aimee and Anna Mae Cousart had the following conversation, on the platform, with Don Strong and Dale Carpenter:

Aimee tapped Dale on the back of his shoulder and asked, "May we talk to you two men?"

Dale, "Yes, right here is okay."

Aimee, "Dale, you preached a good message, it was a good sermon. You preach about love, but there are a lot of hurting people in the Kittitas area and have either one of you showed them any love? Have you showed them God's love? A lot of people have been kicked out of church, do you believe it's right to kick people out of church?"

Anna Mae told Dale and Don about the Kittitas Assembly pastor, Gary Jeffery rejecting a young couple because of their ethnically mixed marriage.

Aimee, "Mixed marriage, do you believe it's right to kick people out of church because of mixed marriage? Don, you wrote a hard letter to the Northwest District Attorney."

Don, "No, I didn't."

Aimee, "Are you used to people going around signing your name to letters? I have a copy of that letter. In it you say Pairlee Treat has caused most of the trouble in most of the churches for the past 20 to 30 years. Don, only God knows that, so it's false, that was a hard thing to say."

Don, "You haven't lived here for 20 years and it's in the District records."

Aimee, "It's still not true because God is the only one that knows."

Anna Mae, "You need to listen to Pairlee's story."

Aimee, "Dale, you two need to go home and pray."

Dale, "We have prayed." (Then Dale laughs.)

Aimee, "It's not a bit funny." (The smiles are instantly gone from their faces.)

Aimee, "Don, we gave you some documentation to give to the District and you promised to do so, but you didn't give it to them. I want to tell you something else, Rollin Carlson and Care-Net are operating illegally."

Dale, "How's that?"

Aimee, "They didn't get the proper permit. Warren Bullock has been given some documentation and if you want to know more you can ask him about it."

Dale, "That makes me think, we have discussed how the neighboring pastors did not support us like they should have in our backing the Pastor, maybe you would like to appear before the Presbyters?"

Aimee took this as a threat against Albert's credentials. The Andersons were not in harmony with the Kittitas pastor, Gary Jeffery, and the Kittitas Care-Net Outreach ranch pastor, Rollin Carlson, who was also the pastor of Everett Bethany Assembly of God church, as well as an Executive District Presbyter. Nor did they countenance the Northwest District Officials in all their wrong doings concerning the rejected Kittitas people and the Care-Net ranch.

Aimee, "That wouldn't bother me in the least. I would love to. I would love to meet with the Presbyters." (Aimee thought it would be an opportunity to personally tell the church officials about some of the terrible things that were taking place concerning the Kittitas Assembly cast-out people and Rollin Carlson and Care-Net.)

Dale, (Pauses) "Well, maybe it won't be necessary."

Don, (As he started to walk away to the left, said almost under his breath), "Well, we'll see!"

(Dale went off to the right while at the same time Don went to the left, leaving Aimee and Anna Mae standing there. Then the two ladies, suddenly left standing alone, soon followed Dale, down the aisle.)

Aimee, "Bye, Dale."
Dale, "Bye, Aimee."
Anna Mae, "Bye, Dale." (She held her hand out to shake Dale's hand.)
Dale, "Bye."

March 1, 1994

87. Dick Clever, Investigative reporter for the *Seattle Post Intelligencer* newspaper, phoned around 3:30 P.M. and asked to interview the Andersons. The conversation lasted about one hour. Albert did most of the talking, using the same agenda the Andersons used in their conversation with Warren Bullock on February 26, 1994.

March 4, 1994

88. The final inspection of the residential addition to the existing house by B.B., was filed with the Kittitas County Building Department. This residential addition was already being used in 1992 as the community room for the rehab men, even though the conditional use permit for such a rehabilitation/transitional housing was never obtained by Rollin Carlson and The Care-Net Outreach.

March 6, 1994

89. Iva Steigleder wrote a letter concerning the Kittitas Assembly of God, giving monthly contributions to Mel and Winnie Chapman, and then later to Randy and Vicki Bale. The Chapmans and Bales were considered to be in ministry at the Care-Net Outreach ranch, in Kittitas, Washington under the MAPS program, which is an Assemblies of God home missions program.

The monthly support for Randy Bale, started at $25.00 and later it was raised to $45.00 each month. This contribution, along with other charitable contributions, helped to support Randy Bale and his family during their time of ministry at the Care-Net Outreach ranch.

Church people throughout the Northwest have been led to believe, by word of mouth, brochures, and the Care-Net video, that the Care-Net Outreach ranch is a valid home missions work, while at the same time the Kittitas County records show the property to be a farm/livestock ranch with a residence for a rancher and his family.

March 8, 1994

90. Albert and Aimee had a 9:00 A.M. appointment in Seattle with Dick Clever. After about two hours talking about the Kittitas and Care-Net situation, they left pages of documentation with him.

At 4:30 P.M., on arriving back in Ellensburg they met with David Pitts and John Jewitt about Rollin Carlson and the Care-Net ranch problems. David Pitts said he was going to play the "Devil's advocate" concerning the December 1993 Care-Net ranch brochure the Andersons had received through the United States mail. The Andersons left that meeting feeling like the whole thing was hopeless.

Later in the evening during a meeting at Wanda Cotton's, Jerry Marchel told Albert and Aimee about the Care-Net ranch's purchase of hay from Kennon Forester, who lived at Royal City. The story goes as follows: Rollin asked Kennon to make out two bills, one for the hay and one for the hauling. Kennon made out two bills and when Rollin came to pay for the hay, he brought his own set of bills. The total was the same but the **hay was decreased** and the **hauling was increased. Rollin said he was going to turn the hauling bill into the insurance company since he hurt his wrist in the accident and couldn't haul the hay himself.** Kennon said he told the insurance company, "I think he is trying to take advantage of the insurance company." Also Kennon said the hay bill was written on a bank in Ohio. He had a hard time cashing the check. Since Jerry told the Andersons this incident, they have had personal phone conversations with Kennon Forester, confirming his story.

March 9, 1994

91. Today the Andersons learned that in 1991 Rollin Carlson had applied for a non-profit license for The Care-Net Outreach but apparently failed to completely fill out the application. Thus, the State mailed it back to Rollin refusing

to give him a non-profit license for the Care-Net Outreach or The Care-Net Outreach ranch. Are Rollin Carlson and the Care-Net Outreach attempting to use the umbrella of the Assemblies of God in order to solicit charitable contributions for the illegal/phony Care-Net Ranch ministry at Kittitas, Washington?

QUESTION: If so, why would the Assemblies of God Officials stamp their approval on something so illegal and corrupt as the Care-Net Outreach ranch (phony/deceptive) ministry at Kittitas, Washington? And, especially when they have been given documentation that proves the claim of corruption.

The only logical reason for this cover-up of corruption by the Church Officials, is that the District and General Counsel Officials are deeply involved in the apparent and obvious illegal/fraudulent activities. It would be far better to come clean now where forgiveness and cleansing is possible, than to stand before God with sin uncleansed. This means more than lip service. It means making it right with ministers, churches, and any and all who have been wronged, as well as civil agencies.

> "For there is nothing covered, that shall not be revealed; neither hid, that shall not be known." (Luke 12:2)

ALBERT & AIMEE ANDERSON

March 9, 1994

92. March, 1994, The Great Commission Partners Newsletter, contains a picture of Rollin J. Carlson, as Executive Presbyter, president/pastor of Care-Net Outreach, and pastor of Bethany Christian Assembly, Everett, Washington. The following quotations are taken from that issue:

****

GREAT COMMISSION PARTNERS

NEWSLETTER

1. Page one, **"It's Just Beginning...**
"Expanding program to include Acreage for God on which to grow crops.

"Randy Barton, Foundation president, says, 'The Great Commission Trust will provide the funds for the leasing of land and purchasing of seed for the farmers who set aside acreage for God.' As in the livestock placement program, a minimum of 25 percent of the net gain generated by farmers participating in the acreage for God program is earmarked for college scholarships at Assemblies of God colleges. The remaining 75 percent of the net gain is designated by the farmer to go to the A/G ministry of his choice, whether foreign missions, home missions, benevolences, district ministries, or directly to educational institutions."

2. Page 2, **"EVERYBODY WINS FOR CHRIST!"**
"Missionary Terry Dwelle Applauds Partners Program."

3. Page 3, **"CARING ENOUGH TO ACT!"** By Rollin J. Carlson.
"One person, one church, one organization, or one agency cannot do it alone. The Great Commission Partners program networks concerned

ranchers, churches, district councils, general council, and benefiting Assemblies of God ministries.

"When Howard Hoskins, field consultant for the Great Commission Partners program, sat in my office in Everett, Washington, I felt moved to respond in the affirmative. Howard outlined to me how our Care-Net Outreach, a home mission's project of the Northwest District, could be both a provider for ministry and a recipient of ministry funds.

"He said, 'Dollars raised for ministry can come from sources other than the offering plate.' Our board agreed. We immediately responded.

"Dr. Randall K. Barton and the entire Foundation staff have tremendously assisted Care-Net in establishing a solid foundation of participation. Today, the Care-Net Outreach is networked with others having placed over 300 cows into ministry. Our goal is 550 stock cow units in ministry.

"The plight of homeless, abused, and hurting people is growing more serious each day. Simply recognizing the problem is not enough. CARING enough to act brings new hope and help! CARING enough to feed, clothe, and house is making an impact. CARING enough to give a second chance is infusing meaningful direction in human life! Care-Net is making a difference to human need in a practical way. The Partners program is helping us accomplish this ministry.

"By participating in the Partners program, Care-Net is playing a part in endowing scholarships for young people across our Fellowship. These dollars do not come from the offering plate. They are uniquely identified funds derived from a creative ministry application. People can participate who have not been able to do so in the past.

"A wise man once told me, 'Two men can carry more than twice as much as one man.' So the Partners program networks people and ministry to carry out the Great Commission.

"The Care-Net Outreach is an enthusiastic GREAT COMMISSION PARTNER!"

On this same page it reads as follows: "Go ye therefore into all nations..." Every Day 66,000 people die without hearing about Jesus... Save souls for Christ with a perpetual gift to the Great Commission Partners program. Year after year, you will be multiplying harvest field workers at home and overseas. Bless the Lord today with your contribution, and become a Great Commission Partner in spreading the Lord's Great Commission...

Great Commission Partners.
1600 N. Boonville Avenue
Springfield, Missouri 65803
Please apply my enclosed gift to the Lord's Great Commission:
$1,000___ (1 head of cattle)__ I want to discuss a gift of appreciated property and decrease capital gain tax.
$5,000___ (5 head of cattle) __
Other _____
Name _____
Address _____
City _____ State _____ Zip _____
Phone (_____)

4. Page 4, **"BITS AND PIECES."** From the desk of Howard W. Hoskins, U.S. Field Consultant. Other quotes from this page are:

"When you sell God's cattle, always sell in the name of the Great Commission Partners. This way you will not have to pay income tax or social security tax.

"If you are selling your stock along with the ministry stock and it is convenient, separate ministry stock from your personal stock. If it is not convenient to separate them, then send like animals together through the sale ring.

"Have your marketing agent take the average and make out the check for ministry stock to 'Great

Commission' and then send the check to the GCP office... ...."

Some quotes from the December 1993 issue of the Great Commission Newsletter are as follows: "It was so simple ... I knew there had to be a catch! ... I first heard about the Great Commission Partners program at the 1993 General Council in Minneapolis. Howard Hoskins, field consultant for the GC Partners program, spoke to the Council-in-session on Friday afternoon and showed the Partners program video...

"It's just as the video presents. The Assemblies of God Foundation locates the donors who provide the financial support to purchase the livestock. The Foundation also locates the ranchers and farmers who provide the care and feeding of the livestock. The 25 to 45 percent return from the investments of the donors and the efforts of the ranchers endows scholarships for young people attending our A/G schools and colleges and provides brand new ministry dollars. By 'brand new' money, I mean money that is not taken from another ministry or out of your pockets... By Rick Davis, National Representative, Industrial/Institutional Chaplaincy."

NOTE: If the money is not out of, "your pockets," whose pocket did the money come out of for the purchase of the cattle for both the Care-Net Outreach ranch and the Great Commission Partners? **The above "Great Commission Partners Newsletter" demonstrates the reason why District and General Council officials defended the Care-Net ranch illegal operation. The stamp of approval came from the highest level.**

March 10, 1994

93. The following phone conversation took place between Albert and Aimee and Warren Bullock:
  Warren, "Hello."

Albert, "Hello, this is Albert and Aimee is on the phone too."

Aimee, "Hi."

Albert, "Do you know there is a Deed of Trust for $350,000.00 between the Northwest District and Care-Net?"

Warren, "Yes."

Aimee, "I thought you said you didn't loan Rollin and Care-Net any money in 1993?"

Warren, "That was for the original sale."

Aimee, "Papers are being dug out of the Courthouse and we have a copy of that Deed."

Warren, "Who did you say is doing this?"

Aimee, "Someone."

Warren, "Could you send me those papers? We appreciate all the papers we can get for information."

Aimee, "No, I'm tired of it going one way. Did you ask Rollin any questions?"

Warren, "Yes."

Aimee, "What did he say?"

Warren, "He had his explanations. Does that surprise you?"

Albert & Aimee both said, "No." They both felt it was hopeless to go on any further and with that they all three said their good-byes.

QUESTION: Everyone who engages in illegal/criminal activity, has his or her explanations — does that make evil, right?

March 14, 1994

94. Aimee was told that Jason Ringe, a Counselor at the Care-Net ranch had left.

March 18, 1994

95. CERTIFICATE OF OCCUPANCY, Kittitas County, Washington, Department of Building and Fire Safety. "This certificate is issued pursuant to the requirements of Section 308 of the Uniform Building Code certifying that, at the time of issuance, said structure was in compliance with the various ordinances of Kittitas County which regulate building construction or use. For the following: Use Classification: Residence — Building Permit Number: K-91-1009."

This Certificate of Occupancy was issued for a "Residence" and not for the "Community Room" for rehabilitation purposes.

March 18, 1994

96. Shortly after Albert and Aimee heard that Jason Ringe, the Care-Net Counselor, had left the ranch, they heard that Randy and Vicki Bale and family were also leaving. Was the pressure to move on to something else, laid on Randy and Vicki Bale and Jason Ringe because Rollin Carlson at Bethany Assembly and Randy Bale at the Care-Net Outreach ranch both had received the February 23, 1994 Care-Net violation notice by certified mail?

To our knowledge, no Counselors have lived at the ranch since Jason Ringe and Randy & Vicki Bale left.

QUESTION: Did the Violation Notice scare Rollin Carlson and Randy Bale enough to make them back off? Even so, Rollin and other Northwest District Officials continued to lead the Ministers and laity to believe the false claims, that the Care-Net Outreach ranch was worthy of promotion as a Home Missions — valid/legal, rehabilitation/transitional, housing/ministry for homeless and/or needy men.

March 19, 1994

97. A friend told Aimee a certain individual attended the Raymond Baptist church, (last Sunday) and heard it announced that the Bales (Randy and Vicki and family) were leaving the Care-Net ranch and they, (meaning the Baptist church) would no longer be supporting Care-Net.

March 22, 1994

98. The following phone conversation took place between Aimee and Mel and Winnie Chapman:

Aimee, "How long were you at the Care-Net ranch?"

Mel, "One year."

Aimee, "I'm someone who is very concerned about Care-Net. Did you own some of the Care-Net land?"

Mel, "Yes."

Aimee, "How much did they pay you for it?"

Mel, "It's none of your business."

Aimee, "There are documents."

Mel, "Then go get them from Carlson."

Aimee, "Oh, thank you. Good-bye."

Mel, "Bye."

March 22, 1994

99. Aimee decided to phone the Chapmans back and the following second conversation took place:

Aimee, "Winnie, I'm sorry I was not trying to be snoopy with your husband, just trying to help. There are people who feel you were used by Rollin."

Winnie, "We were willing to be used in starting it in the beginning."

Aimee, "I know you were willing to be used for the Lord. Some feel you were used in the buying and selling of the land."

Winnie, "We were willing for him to use our name. Who are you?"

Aimee, "I'm just an anonymous person trying to help."

Winnie, "Isn't this a bit irregular?"

Aimee, "Well, it is not personal. There is an investigation going on."

Winnie, "I think we better just answer to subpoenas."

We both said our good-byes.

March 23, 1994

100. Aimee phoned the Chapmans early this morning. It did not go as well as the day before. Aimee first talked to Mel and then to Winnie as follows:

Aimee, "Mel, I thought I would phone you back, I don't know if I should talk to you or your wife?"

Melvin, "Just a minute." Then Aimee heard him speak to his wife, "You can take this."

Aimee, "Winnie, there are a lot of people who have been hurt by Rollin. What happened to the money, the difference between $105,000.00 and $260,000.00?"

Winnie, "I don't know who you are or who these people are that have been hurt but why don't you go to the District and let them do the investigation?"

Aimee, "Did you go to the District?"

Winnie, "Of course, we aren't stupid! This is not another Jimmy Swaggart thing."

Winnie then hung up without saying good-bye.

March 23, 1994

101. Aimee found out from the treasurer's office that Care-Net is delinquent with their property taxes. Anita Kazee found more filed documents concerning Care-Net. One was the Deed of Trust, between the Northwest District Council of the Assemblies of God and Care-Net. The Northwest District loaned to Care-Net $135,000.00 in May 1991.

March 24, 1994

102. Aimee phoned the Department of Revenue 1-800-647-7706 and asked if it was all right for Rollin Carlson and other church officials to claim that the "Care-Net Outreach is a Non-profit Corporation licensed in the State of Washington?"

The spokesperson told Aimee that it should be reported to the Police.

Aimee, again reported this to David Pitts. He told Aimee, "We are investigating it... We're working on it... Just hang in there... Hold tight... We're working on it."

April 4, 1994

103. Northwest District Superintendent Frank Cole wrote a letter to Robert Cousart (former pastor of Kittitas Assembly of God and a friend to the excommunicated Kittitas members and adherents) and a copy to Albert Anderson, in which the by-laws relative to scriptural discipline were quoted. The strong inference was that credentials could be in jeopardy unless there was withdrawal from participation in the Kittitas church problems, "whether by meeting, phone or letter..."

April 5, 1994

104. Aimee phoned the IRS 800 number to ask if The Care-Net Outreach was listed as a non-profit corporation? Someone looked for it and said, **"I cannot find The Care-Net Outreach listed at all. It is not in our book."**

April 9, 1994

105. Today is our (Albert and Aimee) 40th wedding anniversary. To God be the glory for our love for Him and beautiful love for each other.

April 12, 1994

106. A friend living in Springfield, Missouri, told Aimee that she could not find Randy Bale's name listed in the MAPS file.

April 14, 1994

107. Albert had a good board meeting this evening, until the "Bomb" was dropped by Dale Ball. He (Dale), Paul Bennett and Oscar Rairdan had talked to **Don Strong**, who **advised them to ask their Pastor to resign**. Albert indicated he would let them know. **The Andersons were absolutely devastated. How could Don Strong do such a thing to them? How could Dale Ball, Paul Bennett, Oscar Rairdan and Erwin Bennett go along with the evil plot against Pastor Albert Anderson, to remove him as Pastor? (It was obvious that District Officials had influenced Albert's deacons to join the District Leaders in their evil deeds.)** Needless to say, the Andersons could not sleep until after mid-night.

April 20, 1994

   108. Larry E. Chase submitted his resignation, as a church deacon, to the church board, because he could not condone the actions of the other two deacons working with District Officials to remove his Pastor.

****

April 20, 1994

To the Board of the Assembly of God Church
Ellensburg:

   As of April 14, 1994, I, Larry E. Chase do hereby resign, due to actions taken on April 14th, in the board meeting. That is, asking our pastor to resign for no reason other than our church isn't growing? Also, that the other two board members went with a non board member to approach Don Strong, without my knowledge, which should not have been done in the first place. Obviously, I am not needed in the decision making of this Assembly.

   I just pray that the board members that are taking action against a man of God, that has done no wrong, will search their own hearts; because you will be accountable to God for how you have acted. I will have no part in this action in trying to destroy a shepherd of the flock.

May God help you!

Sincerely,

Larry E. Chase

****

April 25-28, 1994

109. While attending the Northwest District Council in Everett, Washington (Bethany Christian Assembly), it was revealed that the District was in the red about $3.8 million dollars. The reason stated, "Wrong accounting procedures, with no fraud evident."

Nonetheless, the Care-Net Outreach ranch at Kittitas, Washington, received the following loans from the Northwest District revolving fund (as a home missions project) in the amounts of: $135,000.00 (1991), $350,000.00 (April 1, 1993), and $30,000.00 (July 1, 1993). A total of $515,000.00.

NOTE: The Northwest District Council Officials (with Rollin leading the way), were able to loan over one-half of one million dollars to the illegal/phony Care-Net ranch, deceptive ministry. During this same time, did they loan money to all the needy (legitimate) churches that applied for loans?

May 2, 1994

110. Don Strong phoned and asked, "I would like to talk to you, would it be alright if I come to your home?" Albert replied, "Oh, yes."

During the one and a half hour visit with Don Strong in our home, the following conversation, in part, took place:

Aimee, "We heard Frank Cole could have been fined $10,000.00. Is that right?"

Don, "We all could have, we still can be!"

Albert, "Did you tell Oscar, Dale, and Paul that they should ask me to resign?"

Don, "No, but I can see how they could get that impression."

Albert, "Are there any charges against me?"

Don, "No, there are no charges against you!"

Aimee, "Are there any charges against me?"

Don, "No, there are no charges against either one of you!"

Albert, "I took Frank Cole's letter to Bob Cousart, with a copy mailed to me, as a subtle hint."

Don, "It was not so subtle."

Some days later, two church board members, Dale Ball and Paul Bennett said to Albert, "Don Strong told us to circulate a petition asking for your resignation!" Albert was crushed.

May 4, 1994

111. Jim Brown stopped by the Andersons' home for a visit. During their conversation he said, "Randy Barton is the one who phoned me and asked if I would build the four bunk houses for Care-Net?" Jim told the Andersons he could not do the job because they wanted him to build the bunkhouses on blocks which he said was illegal, instead of on a permanent foundation.

May 4, 1994

112. Aimee phoned the Great Commission Partners, of the Assemblies of God Foundation, 1600 North Boonville Avenue, Springfield, MO 65803-2730. The person with Great Commission Partners said, "The money that is given to the Great Commission is put in a trust fund and cows are given cost free to their ranchers. Care-Net is one of our ranches. It's kind of like a hybrid. It's a ranch and also a rehabilitation ministry for men under IRS Code 501-C-3. The Great Commission Partners was started in 1993 and Care-Net was also started in October 1993."

Interesting! How could the Care-Net Ranch have been started in October 1993, when a Real Estate Excise Tax form filed in Kittitas County, states "Care-Net Outreach, a Washington non-profit Corporation,"—grantee; and the grantor, the United States of America, acting through the

Administrator of the Farmers Home Administration, U.S. Department of Agriculture—was executed May 30, 1990. Or, was the representative, at the Great Commission Partners, indicating that the Care-Net Outreach at Kittitas became one of the Great Commission ranches in 1993? It seems significant that in the March 1994 issue of the Great Commission Partners newsletter, Rollin J. Carlson stated that, "The Care-Net Outreach is an enthusiastic GREAT COMMISSION PARTNER!"

Randall Barton, an attorney, is the president of the Assemblies of God Foundation.

What does Rollin Carlson do with the net proceeds or net profit made from the gifted cows? **Twenty-five per cent** is earmarked for College but where does he choose to put the other **75 per cent?** Also, how about the **15 per cent** earmarked for administration. **Does this add up to 100 per cent or 115 per cent?**

Does he keep the Care-Net profits separate from the Great Commission profits?

May 5, 1994

113. Albert and Aimee Anderson were feeling the stress of the extreme pressure laid on them.

In the 7:00 P.M. board meeting, Dale Ball and Paul Bennett exerted more pressure on Albert to resign as pastor of the Ellensburg First Assembly.

Albert did not feel he should resign at that time and encouraged the men to pray. The two board members tried to reassure Albert by telling him, "It is nothing against you personally, we just think it is time for a change." Albert was informed by the board members, that Don Strong had met with Dale Ball, Paul Bennett and Oscar Rairdan in Yakima, where he told them to circulate a petition among the church members, asking for Albert's resignation.

At various times, Oscar Rairdan, former board member and old-time friend of Rollin Carlson, told Aimee that he had talked to Rollin Carlson and sometimes, he even attended his church services in

Everett, Washington. Also, on June 7, 1994, at the close of the Executive Presbyter's meeting, while standing at the door, Aimee asked Rollin, "Have you talked to Oscar Rairdan?" She indicated that the "talk" to Oscar was about getting Pastor Anderson to resign his pastorate at Ellensburg. Rollin answered, "Yes, I told him to go to Don Strong." (Of course Don Strong would be the one to help take care of things at the Ellensburg and Kittitas Assembly churches, since he was the presbyter for the Yakima section, which section included the Ellensburg First Assembly of God.)

When Don Strong was talking to Albert and Aimee in their home on May 2, 1994, he said to the Andersons, "There are no charges against either one of you." Yet, apparently he told two of Albert's board members and one other member to circulate a petition against Albert as pastor. Surely, Don Strong knew, that circulating a petition against a pastor, would stir up discord, unrest and bring confusion to the church that Albert pastored.

NOTE: We wonder what could possibly have made Don Strong act in such an unchristian manner towards one minister/pastor who had no charges against him and on the other hand stand behind Gary Jeffery, the neighboring pastor, who had many charges against him? Could it be politics or was he afraid to take a stand for what was right and honest? Or, was he trying to save his own skin, because he, himself, was so deeply involved? Earlier, Don had told the Andersons that his church had given Care-Net several thousand dollars and "this could be a big stink."

When the revealing light started to expose the corruption, it must have been rather frightening to all the Northwest District Officials, to think of all the possible ramifications of the alleged illegal activities connected with the Care-Net Outreach ranch, Rollin Carlson, and various other Northwest District officials.

Randy Bale had two pastors: 1. Rollin Carlson was Randy's pastor at the Care-Net ranch and 2. Gary Jeffery was Randy's pastor at the Kittitas Assembly.

Randy was the Care-Net Outreach ranch director; as well as, a board member at the Kittitas Assembly of God and his wife Vicki Bale, was the church secretary/treasurer. One can readily see that **this created a very touchy situation.** Possibly Rollin Carlson, Don Strong, Dale Carpenter and other District Officials knew that Gary Jeffery or Randy Bale, either one or both, could expose some of the illegal activities that were going on at the Care-Net Outreach ranch! **Even so, sin, nor the cover-up of sin, never pays!**

May 7, 1994

114. Albert and Aimee are under heavy pressure and especially Albert is feeling it.

May 9, 1994

115. Albert and Aimee took their "Petition for Investigation" to attorney Jeff Slothower, for his input.

May 9, 1994

116. Dale Ball phoned requesting another board meeting. He asked Albert, "When are you going to resign?" Later, Albert phoned Dale back to give him his answer, "I am not resigning now and will you please pray?" Dale was harassing Pastor Albert Anderson and said, "You haven't told us when you are resigning." Albert stood firm.

May 10, 1994

117. Albert and Aimee sent the "Petition for Investigation" to the General Council Credential

Committee and a copy to the Northwest District Council Credential Committee by registered mail.

May 10, 1994

118. Erwin Bennett phoned and said to Albert, "I would like to talk to you alone." On their way out to the Marchels, Albert and Aimee stopped at Erwin and Ruth's. Erwin talked to Albert in his outside shop while Aimee visited with Ruth. Erwin said to Albert, "I'm not wanting a response from you now, but I wonder if it would be good to publicly, next Sunday morning tell the people you will retire from Pastoral ministry next January when you are 65. I want you to know, I did sign a petition to get you to resign."

Did Erwin have any idea how this cut deep? We wonder how he came up with such a thought? Assemblies of God preachers are not required to retire from public Pastoral ministry when they turn 65. Thus, this seemed like a very strange request, especially when Erwin had been so vocal about what a wonderful preacher Albert was.

The Ellensburg, First Assembly of God church business meeting, January 1994, did not hint in any way, of a petition stating the people wanted a new Pastor.

After this harassment and pressure from Erwin, Albert and Aimee drove on to the Marchels. Albert read the entire Complaint to Jerry, Phyllis, Anita, Wanda and Pairlee (excommunicated Kittitas church members and adherents).

May 11, 1994

119. Albert and Aimee fasted and prayed at the church in the morning. Albert's hearing was becoming impaired, probably because of all the stress he was under.

May 12, 1994

120. Aimee walked into their home study early in the morning and spoke to Albert, who was on his knees praying. He looked up and said, "Honey, my hearing is gone." Albert stood and Aimee reached out her arms; they hugged each other and cried and prayed together.

Then Aimee phoned some ear clinics and doctors' offices for an appointment with no success. A few family members and friends were praying for Albert's healing. Finally, she found a doctor who would see Albert.

Aimee sat in the doctor's office and silently wept while the doctor examined her husband. At this time, Albert's hearing was a little better. Praise God! The doctor said, "You have no infection and no wax. The ear clinic and hearing aids are the next move unless it gets better. If it gets better then you won't need to go to the clinic. Stress can do strange things."

Praise God, Albert's hearing was restored by bedtime! To God be the glory.

May 14, 1994

121. Warren Bullock phoned and asked Albert to meet with him, Elmer Kirschman, Les Welk and Rollin Carlson. Albert responded, "I can meet on that date, May 18, but I would like my wife Aimee to be with me." Warren answered, "I do not know if that would be proper as you are the credential holder, but I will see?"

After Albert thought about it awhile, he phoned Warren Bullock back and said to him, "Since my wife has had more people and more information come to her I think she should be there." Warren responded, "I will set the ground rules." Albert answered, "I am not trying to set the ground rules." Warren emphatically said, "Yes, you are!" Then in conclusion he said, "I will give it some thought."

May 15, 1994

122. Albert and Aimee Anderson and their church congregation experienced a "sovereign move of God" in the morning service. At the close of the meeting, Aimee felt like she could keep standing in the presence of the Lord forever. Some of the people who were excommunicated from the Kittitas Assembly attended the service, and were crying and seeking the Lord. Thank God, He blessed them in such a special way. The breaking and melting lasted until around 12:40 P.M. It was wonderful and refreshing.

May 16, 1994

123. We received 18 pages of documentation, brochures, contract, etc., concerning The Great Commission Partners, from our friend who works at the Gospel Publishing House in Springfield, Missouri. Aimee had asked her if she would go to the Great Commission Partner's office and send her whatever material she could get from that office.

May 16, 1994

124. Geri Hardesty, whose husband passed away January 22, 1994, told us that Paul and Eva Bennett brought a petition to her house for her to sign. She felt pressured to sign it but refused to do so. Also, Lori Lindberg, another good friend of our family was very upset because she was approached as well.

May 17, 1994

125. Beth Rairdan, whose husband passed away April 22, 1994, told the Andersons how she was approached by Paul and Dale and also felt the pressure to sign the petition and refused. She said to the Andersons, "After all you have done for my family, I couldn't think of it."

May 17, 1994

126. Warren Bullock's secretary, Ann, left the following message on the Andersons' answering machine: "Morning! This is Ann calling in behalf of Warren Bullock at the District Office and we are just confirming whether Rev. and Mrs. Anderson will be at the District Office on Wednesday, May 18, at 1:30 and if there is any change in that please let us know. Our number is 206-827-3013."

May 18, 1994

127. Albert phoned the General Council for Brother Trask. He was not in so Albert talked to his secretary. She said the Complaint (Petition for investigation) was sent to the Credential's Committee division, so she transferred Albert to the General Secretary's office for Brother Wood. He was not in so Albert talked to his secretary. She said, "The Complaint will be on Brother Wood's desk for him when he comes back to his office in the morning."

May 18, 1994

128. Albert phoned the Northwest District office and talked to Warren Bullock's secretary. Albert asked, "Have you received our registered complaint?"

Ann, "I can't find it here on the desk."

Albert, "We mailed it by registered mail and the original we mailed by registered mail to the General Council. Brother Trask and Brother Wood were both out of the office but Brother Wood will be back tomorrow and it will be on his desk in the morning. We received your phone message. Are you planning on my wife being with me? We think we should wait until we hear from the General Council."

Ann, "Your wife can come with you. I think this is important so I will have to check with my boss.

Just a minute. His line is busy. I will phone you right back."

In a few minutes Ann phoned back and said, "You both can come."

Albert, "We will either come or I'll phone back."

Later Albert phoned back and told Ann, "Since my wife and I are both complainants we think we should wait until we hear from the General Council Credential Committee.

Ann, "Brother Bullock says that the decision is not yours to make."

Albert, **"First, it was an invitation from Brother Bullock, now it's changed to a demand."**

Ann, "Are you refusing?"

Albert, "Yes, on the grounds that we should hear from the General Council first."

Ann, "All right, I'll get the message to him."

May 20, 1994

129. Aimee phoned the local post office, to find out if they had any knowledge of delivery of the registered packets, containing the complaint, to the Northwest District. Then she phoned the Kirkland post office. The mail lady told Aimee that the Northwest District Council was notified May 12, 1994, but did not pick it up until May 19, 1994, the day after Warren Bullock's secretary demanded Albert to come over for the meeting with Warren Bullock, Les Welk, Elmer Kirschman, and Rollin Carlson. They picked it up only yesterday, seven (7) days after they were notified.

May 27, 1994

130. We received George Wood's response to our "Complaint." It made us feel terrible. It was so unreal!

May 28, 1994

131. Aimee phoned Julius Jepson, Executive Presbyter, and asked him, "Have you read our 'Complaint' or do you even know about it?"

Julius, "No."

Aimee, "We mailed it to you or the executive committee and you should have received it." He acknowledged the fact that he should have read it, but went on to say, "I heard there were some questions and Rollin said he had been investigated by several agencies and had been cleared by them all, including the food commodities. I am surprised that you haven't heard from Warren Bullock because we voted that you both should come and talk to the Executive Committee on their June 7, 1994 meeting. I urge you to go to that meeting and bring along all of your documents and papers."

Aimee responded, "We have put together another letter, with charges against Rollin."

Julius, "I would wait until after this meeting before you do that."

Aimee, "We don't mind talking to you but we have been ignored so long."

Julius, "Believe me, you are not being ignored any more."

May 31, 1994

132. Albert received a certified letter from Elmer Kirschman requesting his presence at their next meeting, "It is urgent that you honor this appointment. Should you choose not to honor our request, further steps will become necessary."

June 2, 1994

133. Albert and Aimee drove to Sunnyside to confer with Manuel Deeds, former Northwest District Parliamentarian and Executive District Presbyter. **After reading the "Formal Charges" Manuel said, "I don't know how anyone could have**

more charges against him ... You are not on trial, but rather the District Officials are on trial."

June 3, 1994

134. The Andersons discovered from the Kittitas County Treasurer's office, that The Care-Net Outreach ranch property taxes are delinquent in the amount of $5,493.97.

June 7, 1994

135. Albert and Aimee drove to the Northwest District office at Kirkland, for their meeting with the Executive Presbytery at 2:00 P.M. They sat waiting in the reception room for one hour past their appointment time. While they were waiting in the foyer Al Baunsgard walked over to them to tell them he had to leave so they gave him his charge packet before he left. Greg Austin came out around 3:00 P.M. and led the Andersons into the room full of District Officials. Those present were: Warren Bullock, Elmer Kirschman, Les Welk, Rollin Carlson, Dale Carpenter, Don Strong, Julius Jepson and Greg Austin.

Albert and Aimee thought this meeting was to discuss Rollin Carlson and his dealings with Care-Net. Not so! Warren Bullock let the Andersons know in no uncertain terms, that they were called in to discuss Albert and his credentials. Rather than being a meeting to consider the "complaint and charges" against Rollin Carlson and Care-Net, the Andersons were very much interrogated. The following conversation took place:

Aimee, "Can we tape this meeting?"

Dale, "Oh, no, we trust everybody around here."

Warren, "We're here to talk about you and your relational problem you have with Rollin and the church. Have you heard the name Dick Clever?"

Albert, "If I answer that, it will just lead to another question."

Warren, "Have you talked to Dick Clever?"

Aimee, "We don't have to answer that."

Warren, (Pointing his finger at Aimee, very quick and apparently very angry) "You be quiet, I'm not talking to you, I'm talking to him." (Then pointing his finger at Albert) "What do you have to say?"

Albert, "The same as my wife. She's right."

Warren, "Well, it looks like we're through then."

Albert, "Yes, I guess we are."

Aimee, (Leaning over towards Albert and reaching for the attache case sitting on the floor) "Honey, before we leave, maybe now is a good time to give their packets to them?"

Albert and Aimee both leaned over and picked up the packets out of the attache case and started passing them out to everyone. The men began to open them.

Warren looked at the men starting to open their charge packets and said, "Don't open those now."

Aimee, "Les, Dale, and this one is unnamed. I'm sorry we did not know your name, Greg Austin. We have filed formal charges like Brother Wood told us to. And the charges sent to the General Council Credentials Committee are against not only Rollin Carlson, but also against Frank Cole, Warren Bullock, Elmer Kirschman, Don Strong, and Dale Carpenter."

Warren, "Why us?"

Albert, "Because you didn't respond to our complaints and check into it like you should have. Because of the way you have handled information about Care-Net, Kittitas and Rollin."

Aimee, "Also, because of the threats we have received. Manuel Deeds said we are not on trial."

Warren, "What does he know. When did you talk to him?"

Albert, "We went to see him recently in Sunnyside."

Aimee, "He read everything, all the charges."

Warren, "Why did you refuse to come to the May 18th meeting?"

Albert, "I told your secretary that we felt we should wait until we received a response from

General Council since you said you wanted to talk about Care-Net."

Julius, "Brother Bullock, maybe I can clear something up. Mrs. Anderson phoned me and I told her to bring everything about Care-Net. Maybe I misunderstood?"

Aimee, "That's right. I told him no one was paying any attention to us and he told us to bring everything. Besides, Manuel Deeds told us we were not on trial."

Albert, "May I say something to Rollin?"

Warren, "Yes."

Albert, "Rollin I'm glad you are here today because I wanted to tell you to your face, that I don't hate you, I don't even dislike you. I love you in the Lord. I just don't agree with some of the things you are doing."

Les, (After turning to Aimee he asks), "If it's as bad as you say, why isn't the County doing something about it?"

Aimee, "For one thing, Rollin tells them something else."

Albert, "May I read a letter from the County?"

Warren, (Nods his head)

Rollin, "What's the date of that letter?"

Albert, "June 3, 1994."

Rollin, "I'm hurt that you didn't come to me first with that."

Aimee, (looking at Warren) "May I read a letter, too?"

Warren, (Nods his head)

Aimee read Kennon Forester's letter about Rollin increasing the price of the hay freight in order to collect more money from the insurance company.

Rollin, "Well, he was just angry because we wouldn't buy any more hay from him."

Dale, "Aimee, you were all upset when you talked to Don and myself about the Kittitas people. What does that have to do with you?"

Aimee, "I talked about Care-Net too and said Rollin and Care-Net were operating illegally."

Dale, "You just talked about the Kittitas situation."

Aimee, "Anna Mae Cousart and I were there and we talked about both Care-Net and Kittitas."

Don, "You lit into us."

Rollin, read from a list the following: "You have condemned me, you have been judge and jury, you have abused ministerial trust, you have falsely accused, you have slandered, you have gossiped and sown discord among the brethren. You have spoken against my family and my father."

The Andersons felt like Rollin was throwing out a smoke screen to get them off the issue and didn't even bother answering the false accusations except the one about his father.

Aimee, "We love your father, and we never even thought about speaking against your father."

Rollin, "Did you have anything to do with this, (holds up '*Beware the Wolves*' pamphlet) I heard you had some input into it?"

Aimee, "We have read it, but we didn't know about it until it was all finished."

Rollin, "We might have to sell the ranch because of what you've done."

NOTE: Why not tell the truth? It is not because of Albert and Aimee exposing the corruption but because of Rollin, and his accomplices' illegal/criminal activity that they "might have to sell the ranch."

Dale, "People from your church are phoning us."

Albert, "About who?"

Dale, "About you." (This was to be expected after the petition was circulated.)

Aimee, "Some of our people said a board member tried to pressure them into signing a petition, but they refused. A couple of our deacons said one of the District Presbyters told them to circulate a petition asking for Albert's resignation, even though there were no charges against him."

NOTE: It is strange that Warren Bullock chose this particular time to close in prayer. Maybe the Andersons were getting too close, for comfort, to the real issue.

Warren, "We are going to close in prayer." He then prayed something about the truth coming out.

Albert and Aimee got up to leave. Everyone stood and Rollin followed them to the door.

Aimee, "Rollin, do you remember in our living room when you asked, 'You believe me, don't you?'"

Rollin, "No, I don't remember that."

Albert, "It wasn't a good testimony for the Care-Net property taxes to be delinquent."

Rollin, "There's nothing wrong with that. A lot of people do that all the time."

NOTE: Paying penalties because of neglecting to pay bills is a waste of God's money and is a Violation of the Northwest District By-laws.

Aimee, "Have you talked with Oscar?"

Rollin, "Oscar talked to me. I told him to go to Don."

Warren, "If you want to continue talking, you'll have to go out."

Albert and Aimee said good-bye and left.

June 8, 1994

136. Before going home to Ellensburg, the Andersons met with Dick Clever for about one hour in the Alderwood Mall in Lynnwood. They sadly told him of their meeting with the Executive Presbytery on June 7, 1994. Albert and Aimee Anderson grew up attending Assemblies of God churches. Albert had preached over (44) forty-four years as an Assemblies of God minister. He was ordained in 1954, ten days after Albert and Aimee were married. Needless to say, they were both heartsick and especially Albert. **They could not believe that the District Officials would countenance illegal actions.**

June 9, 1994

137. Nellie Dees, a dear friend of the Andersons, was lingering between life and death. Some of the Dees family talked to the Andersons about funeral arrangements for their mother. One of Nellie's sons was also approached about getting his mother to sign the petition against Pastor Anderson. Needless to say, Nellie's son denied the deacon his request. It was hard to believe anyone could even think of doing such a thing, especially to someone on their deathbed.

June 9, 1994

138. Tonight, at the church board meeting, Dale and Paul virtually demanded Albert's resignation or announce next Sunday that a special business meeting would be held on June 21. Albert indicated he would probably resign Sunday or have someone else read his resignation.

The cruelty of all the pressure was affecting his health. All the threats from District Officials and now threats from his two board members was too much. Albert and Aimee felt sick at heart.

June 10, 1994

139. After breakfast Albert phoned Erwin and requested the board to put in writing their demands; also, to see a copy of the petition.

June 10, 1994

140. This afternoon, Erwin Bennett hand delivered the requested letter to Albert. It reads as follows:

****

June 10, 1994

Rev. Albert Anderson:

At the regular board meeting held on 4-14-94 at First Assembly of God Church we asked you verbally to resign because, though we have nothing personally against you we feel that the church is failing and that the time has come for a change.

According to the church constitution and By-laws Article Ten, page nine, any voting member has the right of Initiative; therefore we have contacted the members of said church as to how they feel about a pastoral change and the majority thought that the time has come.

This letter is a formal request for your resignation.

According to Article Nine Section two-B business meetings can be called by a majority of the official board (b). We stated at last night's board meeting (6-9-94) that a special business meeting should be announced from the pulpit on Sunday's 6-12-94 and 6-19-94 and the meeting which is to be chaired by a district official be on 6-21-94 - 7:00 P.M. for the sole purpose of voting on the pastor.

We sincerely hope this meeting will not be necessary.

As we were writing this letter a district official called and we asked him about showing you the petition and he said we didn't have to.

In Christ,

Dale S. Ball_____
Paul Bennett_____

The final, verbal demand for a business meeting, as stated in the above letter, to be chaired by a District Official, for the "sole purpose" of trying to remove Pastor Anderson from his pastorate, took place two days after the Formal Church Charges were hand delivered, June 7, 1995, to the Northwest District Officials by Albert and Aimee Anderson. The next day, Erwin Bennett, hand delivered to Albert, the June 10, 1994 letter addressed to Rev. Albert Anderson by Dale Ball and Paul Bennett that states, "As we were writing this letter a district official called and we asked him about showing you the petition and he said we didn't have to."

NOTE: It is quite evident who the District Official was helping and who the District Official was working against.

These men were acting strange and bold. No doubt, they were being used by certain District Officials to get rid of the Andersons, (even though there were no charges against them) because they had filed charges against some of the District Officials. The Andersons' understanding of the church By-laws is that, **there is no right to circulate a petition requesting the Pastor's resignation, when there are no charges against him. Furthermore, all of the members were not shown the petition or even contacted about signing it**

The Andersons could feel the unkindness in the letter. Both Albert and Aimee were suffering physically from all the threats and pressure put on them by some of the Northwest District Council Assemblies of God officials. Also, their son Jonathan, was suffering. He had been assisting his father in Pastoring the church; leading the worship service, driving the Sunday School bus, teaching a Sunday School class, sometimes helping with the sound system and in general a real blessing and help to his parents and the church. Their daughter and her husband Larry and family were suffering, as well, from the cruel attacks against their parents. They too, were such a blessing and help, especially with the music. Deborah was the church pianist and choir director. Larry and Deborah directed the Children's Church, drove the Sunday School bus. Larry ran the sound system and was a deacon, who had been voted in by the church members, until he resigned because of the way three board members (along with the Northwest District Officials) cruelly treated his Pastor, his wife's father, his father-in-law, and grandfather of his children.

****

WHITED SEPULCHRES

ALBERT AND AIMEE
Sitting on beach - LAKE CLE ELUM, WA

ALBERT & AIMEE ANDERSON

JONATHAN
View from STEPTOE BUTTE, WA

WHITED SEPULCHRES

MATTHEW, DEBORAH, LARRY, LARISSA

Now the cruel and unjust threats against Albert and Aimee were reaching into their church congregation. Consequently, Albert did not believe it would be helpful to the church to stay and fight for his rights. Thus, he felt the leading of the Lord to resign as Pastor of Ellensburg First Assembly of God. It was very difficult to make this decision after putting ten (10) years of their lives into this place of ministry. It not only hurt Albert and Aimee, but their son, Jonathan, and their daughter Deborah and her husband Larry, who, as stated above, assisted their Father in the ministry; worship service, children's ministry, bus ministry, sound system, and in any other needed area of ministry. They too, had given several years of their lives to this church; helping and blessing those in need.

June 11, 1994

141. Albert met with the church board, Paul Bennett, Dale Ball, and Erwin Bennett, to clarify when he would resign, whether he would minister any more at Ellensburg Assembly, and asked about his vacation pay, etc. He then left them alone to discuss it. They would phone him when they had reached their conclusion. A short time later, they phoned for Albert, and asked him to join them again. They asked him to make **June 19, 1994, FATHER'S DAY,** his resignation service and conclude his ministry as Pastor of the church with the evening service, as they indicated it would be easier on all concerned.

June 19, 1994

142. Albert resigned this morning, on Father's Day, as Pastor of the First Assembly of God Church due to the threats and the extreme pressure put on him. Most of Albert and Aimee's dear family came home and attended the morning service. They gave support and love to their Dad and Mom on this heart-breaking occasion. It was a very sad Father's Day, but oh — so wonderful — to hear <u>our dear family sing again</u>, several beautiful songs of Praise to the Lord. They blessed their parents and the church congregation, one more time, with their <u>songs of triumph</u>, even though <u>their hearts were breaking</u> and <u>their eyes were full of tears</u>. <u>Praise God for the Victory</u>!

ALBERT & AIMEE ANDERSON

**ALBERT & AIMEE ANDERSON & FAMILY
(1999 - Almost 5 years later)**

The following was Albert's written resignation:

****

Albert E. Anderson, Pastor
FIRST ASSEMBLY OF GOD
Capitol Avenue and Walnut Street
Ellensburg, Washington 98926

RE: Pastoral resignation from Ellensburg First Assembly of God.

June 19, 1994

TO: The members and friends of First Assembly of God:

It is now ten years since we came to minister as Pastors of Ellensburg First Assembly of God. During that time, we have sought to be faithful to God and to each one to whom we had opportunity to minister. In His faithfulness, God has blessed in saving souls, filling believers with the Holy Spirit, healing the sick, and lifting up the fallen. Without HIM we can do nothing.

The time has now come to resign as Pastors of First Assembly of God in Ellensburg. Separation from ministry responsibilities is never easy, given the best set of circumstances. This today is no exception. As always, there are mixed emotions on the part of many.

The reasons for resigning at this time are varied. Due to extenuating circumstances — some beyond our control — we shall be closing out our ministry today at Ellensburg First A/G.

We express our gratitude publicly for the opportunity of ten years of ministry in this Assembly. Our future and yours is in God's hands. It is to Him that each one of us shall give an account.

We close with the words of the Apostle Paul to the Corinthian church: "The grace of our Lord Jesus Christ be with you all. My love be with you all in Christ Jesus. Amen" (I Corinthians 16:23, 24).

Because of Jesus,

Albert & Aimee Anderson

      ****

June 27, 1994

143. Aimee phoned the General Council to talk to one of the executives, hoping to find out what was being done about the charges. Apparently, no one was there to take her call, so she phoned Julius Jepson and asked him what was taking place. Julius Jepson told Aimee, "A sub-committee had been appointed with Les Welk as the chairman."

June 28, 1994

144. The Andersons learned that, apparently no vehicles are registered in Rollin Carlson's or his wife's name and that the vehicles they use are registered in Care-Net's name. The Lincoln car Helen Carlson drives for her own personal use is registered in Care-Net's name.

July 27, 1994

145. An article came out in the Seattle Post Intelligencer about the District Council's financial difficulties, by Dick Clever, investigative reporter for the P.I.

September 7, 1994

146. Julius Jepson phoned the Andersons and asked Aimee for Rachinskis' phone number. She told him that Rollin Carlson was trying to collect on another deceitful insurance claim. He asked her, "Is that with All State too?" Aimee said, "No, this is with another insurance company." Because the Andersons had another appointment, she asked if he could phone back later in the day and she would tell him about it.

Julius Jepson phoned the Andersons later, as was agreed. She told him about the Loafing shed blowing over at the Care-Net ranch and Rollin Carlson trying to collect insurance money for it, from Preferred Risk, even though the loafing shed was not insured. She also let him know that the loafing shed anchor posts were not buried in four feet of sand or gravel as the County Code required but about two feet of dirt and rocks.

Aimee's search for the insurance company that had paid Rollin Carlson and Care-Net money for the deceptive claim, using Myron Rachinski and Kennon Forester, was over. It was All State!

After learning that **All State was the insurance company that Rollin Carlson filed his deceptive claim** with, (Using Rachinski and Forester as a means for collecting money) Aimee phoned the fraud division of All State, which resulted in several different phone conversations with John Quigley. In the initial conversation, she had with him, John told Aimee that he would send for the file from Marysville and try to find out what happened.

Some time later, after days of waiting for John Quigley to receive the file from Marysville and time for him to be able to read it, Aimee had the following phone conversation with John Quigley:

John Quigley, "I pulled up both Myron Rachinski and Kennon Forester's names from the file. The accident happened the end of 1991 at which time Rollin Carlson hurt his wrist. One check, from All State, was written to Rollin Carlson and one check was written to Care-Net."

Aimee asked, "Was the payment over $10,000.00?"

John Quigley answered, "Yes."

Aimee asked, "Was it a substantial amount?"

John answered, "Yes."

Aimee said, "I beg you to become involved. Would you become involved if you knew you would get your money back?"

John answered, "Yes."

Aimee understood him to say, "It was a third party liability; All State's agent didn't verify everything and wasn't thorough enough in his investigation." She reminded him that everybody's insurance keeps going up because of such deceptive claims. And again, she begged him to get involved. He did tell her he would keep the file available for awhile.

September 7, 1994

147. Albert and Aimee met Tom and Jeanne Mahon for the first time at their home. Jerry Marchel had set up the appointment. Eventually, the Andersons began to show the Mahons documentation of irregularities relative to the Care-Net ranch.

September 9, 1994

148. Albert and Aimee bought some more copies of building permits relative to Care-Net, from the Building Department. (Loafing shed and daylight basement home).

Aimee phoned and talked to Ken Dunn, with the fraud department of Preferred Risk, currently the Everett Bethany Christian Assembly church's insurance company.

Aimee asked, "Are you interested in hearing about the deceitful insurance claims and he said, "Nope."

Aimee responded, "Really!"

Ken Dunn answered, "Just two preachers fighting."

Aimee wondered if Rollin Carlson or Jim Arneson, Preferred Risk insurance agent for Everett Bethany Christian Assembly, had told him that.

September 12, 1994

149. Aimee phoned and talked to the Vice President of Preferred Risk Insurance, Jack Kelly, and told him about the above conversation with Ken Dunn, fraud division. On this occasion she also mentioned to Mr. Kelly about the loafing shed blowing over and not being insured. The Andersons were told that Jim Arneson, a Preferred Risk insurance agent, took pictures of the blown-over shed, and apparently Rollin told Jim Arneson that he just assumed the shed was insured.

NOTE: Jim Arneson is an Assemblies of God member who is the Preferred Risk agent for a number of Assembly of God churches, including the Care-Net Ranch.

In a later conversation with Jack Kelly, he told Aimee, "I put a stop to it and Rollin Carlson and the Care-Net Outreach did not collect any money on the loafing shed claim as it was not insured." He also said he was keeping his conversation with Aimee out of the record because Aimee did not want it to get back to Rollin or Ken Dunn that she had talked with Jack Kelly about the deceptive insurance claims.

NOTE: As noted in our new book, **A GENERATION OF VIPERS**, the 2001 sequel to **WHITED SEPULCHRES**, **Jim Arneson came under the fire of the Northwest District Council of The Assemblies of God Church Officials, when he came to the defense of the Lynnwood Assembly of God church board and members. District Officials threatened Jim with loss of his business because he was trying to help save the Lynnwood Assembly. District Officials fired the board and took over the church. Some call it stealing, "They stole our church from us."**

September 13, 1994

150. The Andersons spent about two and one-half hours with the Mahons at the Care-Net ranch talking about various concerns and events.

September 15, 1994

151. Albert and Aimee went to the Kittitas County Building Department and purchased more copies of Care-Net building applications. They talked to Michael Burntness about code violations relative to the loafing shed. (CODE: Anchor posts are to be buried in either four feet of sand or concrete). They were, in fact, buried in about two feet of dirt/rock. The Andersons personally observed the blown-over loafing shed and the obvious depth of the anchor posts.

September 16, 1994

152. Albert and Aimee Anderson prepared and mailed letters to Thomas Trask, George Wood, and Members of the Credentials Committee regarding the Northwest District not taking action in 90 days, concerning the Formal Charges of unchristian Conduct of Assemblies of God Ministers in the Northwest District Council. Copies were also prepared and mailed to the Northwest District.

September 16, 1994

153. Aimee returned a call to Jean Rachinski concerning Myron's interview with Les Welk on September 15, 1994. Myron told the Andersons that **Les Welk had said the charges were serious enough,** that **if** they were found to be **true, Rollin Carlson and some of the others involved would lose their credentials.**

NOTE: What happened? Who manipulated the documented Charges to prevent any Northwest District Official from losing his credentials? *The only one who lost his Assembly of God credentials was the one (Albert Anderson) who cried out against the "Corruption" and brought the "True" Charges.*

September 19, 1994

154. George Wood, General Secretary, of the General Council of the Assemblies of God, sent a letter to Albert & Aimee Anderson concerning bringing the Formal Charges before the General Council Credentials Committee on November 14-16, 1994.

September 20, 1994

155. Tom & Jeanne Mahon were evening dinner guests in the Andersons' home. They discussed Care-Net problems. Tom expressed his concerns about all the deception taking place with Rollin Carlson and the Care-Net ministry.

September 21, 1994

156. Tom Mahon phoned the Andersons today and informed them of his conversation with Rollin Carlson, who bad-mouthed the Andersons.

September 24, 1994

157. The Andersons received a letter from George Wood, General Secretary, of the Assemblies of God, indicating he was requesting Warren Bullock, District Superintendent of the Northwest District Council of the Assemblies of God, to respond to the General Council in writing.

September 28, 1994

158. Albert and Aimee Anderson mailed a letter to Rev. George Wood thanking him for his response.

September 29, 1994

159. Tom Mahon stated that thirty head of calves were brought to the Care-Net ranch from the coast today, and fifteen more were scheduled to come tomorrow.

October 14, 1994

160. Leslie Welk, Northwest District Assistant Superintendent, sent a letter to Albert and Aimee Anderson informing them that the Northwest District Presbytery had sent their findings concerning the Formal Charges to the General

Council Credentials Committee. In his letter he stated, "A report of findings was formulated and forwarded to the District Presbytery during the course of their regular meetings on October 10-12. At that point the report became the ownership of the District Presbytery."

A few days before the October Northwest District Council Executive Presbyters' meeting, while in a phone conversation with Julius Jepson, Executive Presbyter, Julius said to Aimee, "I just arrived home from Canada and found a twenty (20) page findings of the investigation in my mail but I have not been able to read it through. I hope to finish reading it tomorrow on my way to the Presbyters' meeting." Then after the Presbyters' meeting he told Aimee over the phone, "Les Welk will be phoning you and sitting down with you and go over each of the charges with you and your husband."

The Andersons have never seen that report nor have they been told anything about its contents. The only official word received from the Northwest District Council Officers was Les Welk's October 14, 1994 letter in which he made the above statement.

NOTE: No one has ever gone over any of the charges with Albert and Aimee Anderson.

October 27, 1994

161. Tom Mahon gave Aimee the following information over the phone: (On another occasion, during a visit in their home, Aimee asked if she could look at the check register to see the large deposit entries herself. Tom handed her the check book and Aimee and Albert saw the following entries:)

   1. June 24, 1994, Care-Net was paid $19,607.00 for cattle sold.
   2. July 22, 1994, Care-Net was paid $21,646.00 for cattle sold.

3. August 19, 1994, Care-Net was paid $32,640.00 for cattle sold.

(This last information was given to the Andersons at a later time.) The Great Commission was paid about $3,000.00 for cattle sold.

November 4, 1994

162. Albert and Aimee are looking forward to flying to Israel with their friends, Stan and Myra Chester. They are scheduled for an eight-day visit with Stan and Myra as guides. It was a refreshing thought to look forward to, as they very much needed a change. Praise God for his blessings.

November 12, 1994

163. Ruth Townley brought to the Andersons her notarized statement telling about Randy Bale asking her to cook for men who were supposed to be living at the Care-Net Outreach in the rehabilitation/transitional housing program.

November 14, 1994

164. The General Council Executive Presbyters began their bi-monthly meeting in Springfield, Missouri today. The Formal Charges against Rollin Carlson and other Northwest District Officials are scheduled to be on the agenda.

November 14, 1994

165. Jeanne Mahon told Aimee that 40 cows and 40 more calves would be coming to the ranch soon.

November 15, 1994

166. Jeanne Mahon told Aimee that they had around 300 head of cattle up at the Care-Net ranch. She said, "Yesterday they brought over 40 cows and 40 calves. Rollin is going to sell around 100 calves real soon."

November 18, 1994

167. Aimee phoned the General Council to speak to George Wood or Thomas Trask. Neither one was available so she consented to talk to Charles Crabtree, Assistant General Superintendent, when the following conversation took place:

Aimee, "Did you have your presbyters meeting this week?"

Charles Crabtree, "Yes."

Aimee, "Did you consider the Charges against, Rollin Carlson and Care-Net?"

Crabtree, "Yes, you should be hearing from the Northwest District. If you don't hear from the District, let us know. The ones charged have been exonerated."

Aimee, "Really!" (Aimee was indeed shocked.)

Crabtree, "You can appeal it, but I don't know where it would go, or you can just leave it with the Lord."

November 22, 1994

168. George Wood mailed a letter to Albert and Aimee Anderson informing them that the Northwest District Presbytery and the General Council Credentials Committee totally exonerated the individuals charged without addressing any of the issues or charges brought by the Andersons.

November 26, 1994

169. Albert and Aimee went to the Jerry Marchel's home to pick up Jim Boswell's statement and then to Tom and Jeanne Mahon's home for about a two-hour visit.

January 8, 1995

170. In a phone conversation with Ms. Blake, of All State Insurance, Aimee told her about the deceptive insurance claims by Rollin Carlson. The conversation, in part, continued as follows:

Aimee, "I told John Quigley, with the fraud division of All State, all about it."

Ms. Blake, "You should report it to the insurance company and then they take it from there."

Aimee, "John Quigley told me that he pulled the file from Marysville on Rollin Carlson's car accident. He told me that the accident happened the later part of 1991. He also said that All State paid Rollin on his claim, with two checks; one check was written to Rollin Carlson and another check was written to Care-Net. He said he pulled Myron Rachinski's and Ken Forester's names up on the computer."

Ms. Blake, "He was not supposed to do that." It was quite evident Ms. Blake was not too happy about Aimee receiving this information.

Aimee, "I asked John Quigley if All State paid out over $10,000.00 to Rollin Carlson on the accident claim and he told me, 'Yes.'"

Ms. Blake, "He was not supposed to tell you that."

Aimee does not recall telling Ms. Blake, that she had also asked John Quigley, "Was Rollin Carlson paid a substantial amount?" John answered, "Yes." Aimee asked, "Would you get involved if you knew you could get your money back?" John responded, "Yes."

January 8, 1995

171. About one hour after Aimee's phone conversation with Ms. Blake, she phoned John Quigley and the following conversation took place:

Aimee, "I talked with Ms. Blake about Rollin Carlson's 1991 car accident and his claims. I related to her what you told me, point by point."

(After Aimee tried to tell him all she said to Ms. Blake, she asked, "Is that correct?")

John Quigley, "Yes."

Aimee, "Ms. Blake wasn't too happy about your giving me any information. I hope it doesn't cause you any problems."

John Quigley was very courteous. He never denied any of the various things that Aimee reviewed with him.

More than one time Aimee has begged John Quigley to become involved; reminding him that insurance fraud affects everyone. He has indicated that All State's agent did not do a thorough job of investigation.

Aimee, "Rollin Carlson, while sitting in our home, admitted receiving an insurance settlement involving Myron Rachinski. Rollin said, 'I told them all about it and the insurance company said it was okay.'"

The night Rollin visited the Andersons, they were unaware of Rollin inflating Kennon Forester's freight bill and decreasing the cost of the hay, in order to collect more money from the insurance company.

In the Northwest District Office on, June 7, 1994, Rollin told the Andersons and all the District Officials present, "I have the insurance papers right here before me."

Just what insurance papers was he referring to?

January 11, 1995

172. Albert received his Ministerial Credential renewal today.

January 14, 1995

173. Aimee had the following phone conversation with John Mustered at Cedar Springs Camp near Lake Stevens:

Aimee, "Hello, is this John Mustered?"

John, "Yes."

Aimee, "I understand you have worked with the Care-Net Ranch and I know someone who needs help. I was wondering if they are still taking in men for rehabilitation?" (The Andersons were personally acquainted with a man in Ellensburg, who very much needed rehabilitation.)

John, "Yes. It's more to give men a new beginning. I really don't get into the administration part of it. I haul hay and do other things."

Aimee, "How many men do they have there now?"

John, "One."

Aimee, "Why don't they have more?"

John, "They only have a small bunkhouse and they had to go far away to another area for their kitchen and dining facilities. They are just about done with a bigger house that will accommodate more men where they can have them all together and have their kitchen right there."

Aimee, "How do you get there?"

John, "There is quite a screening process. Then men are picked who can work on the ranch."

QUESTION: What was the real reason for wanting a rehabilitation/transitional ranch for housing men — to really help needy men or for <u>free-labor</u> in a <u>ranching operation?</u>

Aimee, "Did you help build the house?"

John, "I put in the septic tank last year."

Aimee, "Do you think it's a good rehabilitation ranch for the men?"

John, "I think so. You need to contact the President of the Corporation."

Aimee, "Who is he?"

John, "Rollin Carlson."

Aimee, "What's his phone number?"

John, "339-3303."

Aimee, "Is that his home or place of business?"

John, "It's his church he's pastoring."

Aimee, "Okay. Thank you. Good-bye."

John, "Good-bye."

January 15, 1995

174. Aimee had the following phone conversation with Julius Jepson:

Aimee, "Why was Rollin Carlson exonerated concerning the Charges?"

Julius, "Oh, no, that's not the way it was; he wasn't totally exonerated. He was admonished concerning the charges in some areas." (If indeed Rollin was admonished, why didn't Albert and Aimee hear about it from the District officials? Why were they threatened instead and told that Rollin was "cleared by all the agencies?")

January 16, 1995

175. Aimee and Julius Jepson had the following phone conversation:

Aimee, "Why have we not received any word from Les Welk concerning the charges?"

Jepson, "Haven't you heard from him?"

Aimee, "No."

Julius, "I will phone Les Welk and then phone you back."

Aimee, "Do you know anything about the brief letter from Les Welk, informing us that the findings were sent to the General Council? And do you know that the General Council, also, sent us a letter, stating that the 'individuals charged, were exonerated?'"

Julius, "No."

January 17, 1995

176. Julius Jepson phoned and talked to Aimee and Albert, for about 30 minutes, concerning Rollin and Care-Net. Julius said, "After going over the material, they decided there was not enough to move against Rollin Carlson's credentials but he was admonished. I felt we were rather hard on him. I left a message with Les Welk's secretary to have Les Welk phone you, but I urge you to please phone Les yourselves."

January 18, 1995

177. After lunch, Albert and Aimee decided to heed Julius Jepson's advice and phoned Les Welk. The following conversation took place:

Aimee, "Why did you exonerate Rollin Carlson?"

Les Welk, "The October 1994 letter is our response, nothing further is needed. The quote in the General Council letter was not the Northwest District's quote but the General Council Credentials Committee's quote."

(Les let the Andersons know in no uncertain terms that, the Northwest District did not have any obligation to talk to the Andersons or communicate any further with them concerning the charges.)

Aimee, "Brother Crabtree said we would be hearing from the District concerning the charges."

Les, "Brother Crabtree was out of line." (Previously, Charles Crabtree had told Aimee in a phone conversation, "You should be hearing from the Northwest District concerning the charges and if you don't hear from them let us know.")

Aimee, "Do you condone your Ministers engaging in illegal and fraudulent activities?"

Les, "Now I feel like you are attacking me. You don't know me."

Aimee, "That doesn't have a thing to do with it. I am talking about the charges."

Les, "If you choose to pursue this, the ramifications will be felt."

Aimee, "Is that a threat?"

Les, "That's the way it is."

Aimee, "What is the Care-Net ranch for?"

Les, "It's a Transitional Housing for men."

Aimee, "How many do they have there?"

Les, "I don't know."

Albert, "There has not been any men there for months and there has been no retraction by the District. It is not a legal rehabilitation ranch for men or transitional housing for men, but they are still soliciting funds for it as indicated in the last communication from the District. It's going to hurt the whole Assemblies of God."

Les Welk made no comment to Albert's statement but ignored it as though he didn't even make it.

Aimee, "Will you phone us back?"

Les, "I just want to bring closure to the whole thing."

Aimee, "Warren Bullock told us that the Northwest District did not loan Rollin and Care-Net any money in 1993."

Les, "I don't want to discuss Brother Bullock."

Aimee, "Did you know that somebody made $155,000.00 on the sale of the property to Care-Net in 1993?"

Les, "We have all the papers." He informed the Andersons that they were knowledgeable about what was going on.

NOTE: If they all were so knowledgeable, then why did Frank Cole, Warren Bullock, Elmer Kirschman, Don Strong and Dale Carpenter all act so uninformed about what was going on concerning Rollin Carlson and the Care-Net ranch, when the Andersons talked to them about it?

Aimee, "How about the insurance claims by Rollin?"

Les, "We got statements from the agent and his supervisor." (Later, Aimee was told by John Quigley, with All State Insurance, "We never gave Rollin Carlson or anyone else any such statement or letter. It probably was from the Preferred Risk agent, [Jim Arneson] who maybe wrote some kind of statement about the Loafing Shed.")

The Vice President of Preferred Risk, told Aimee that he stopped them from paying Rollin Carlson and the Care-Net Outreach for the loafing shed because it was not insured.

Aimee, "I've talked to the fraud department of the insurance company and I know the story." (Afterwards Aimee wished she would have asked if the agent was Jim Arneson.)

Les, "If you take this any further, there will be ramifications involving Albert's credentials."

I believe it was at this point that Albert and Aimee decided to say good-bye because it was obvious that Les had no intention of going over the charges with them.

Possibly one of the reasons why Les Welk was so upset at the Andersons is because he is the Home Missions Director by virtue of his new office of Assistant Superintendent. And, in his November 20, 1994 letter that was mailed to the ministers, he still solicited funding and volunteer labor for the Care-Net ranch.

Jeanne Mahon told the Andersons that in October, 1994, Les Welk along with some men from the church he pastors, did some work on the four (4) bedroom daylight basement house on the ranch. It would seem he could not help but notice there were no men there for rehabilitation.

January 18, 1995

178. After Albert and Aimee related their phone conversation with Les Welk to Julius Jepson, Julius responded, "I talked to Les this morning and he told me that since the findings were sent to General Council they chose not to talk to you further."

Aimee, "If we are wrong why can't they sit down with us and show us?"

Julius, "I wish they would. May I pray for both of you?"

Albert, "Yes." Albert and Aimee were both broken in spirit while Julius prayed for them. They felt like they had been attacked and beat up in battle during their conversation with Les Welk and it was good to hear someone intercede in prayer in their behalf.

January 20, 1995

179. In a phone conversation, Jeanne Mahon told Aimee that someone from Rollin's church gave her the following information and advice:

1. Where the Care-Net money is going should be posted and it is not.
2. Gaylord Pearson is in it with Rollin.
3. You are in a bad spot. When this thing all goes, you don't want to be in it. You better escape now.

Also Jeanne told Aimee, "Rollin is asking Tom to haul 70 head of cattle over to Marysville, two at a time, in pairs. One time Tom asked Rollin, 'What do you do with all the money?' and he said, 'That's none of your business.'"

NOTE: And why not? Are not the affairs of a public church supposed to be open?

January 20, 1995

180. Aimee phoned and talked to the Kittitas County Prosecutor, Greg Zempel. After telling him very briefly about Rollin Carlson and the Care-Net ranch, he gave Albert and Aimee a 3:00 P.M. appointment for Tuesday, January 24, 1995 to go over the Care-Net alleged illegal activities with him.

January 23, 1995

181. Aimee phoned Debbie Randall, Assistant Planner with the Kittitas County Planning Department and asked if the Andersons could come in and see her about Rollin Carlson and the Care-Net Outreach ranch? They met in Debbie's office and discussed the Care-Net problems. They told her that they had an appointment with the Prosecutor, Greg Zempel, concerning Rollin Carlson and the Care-Net ranch.

Debbie gave the Andersons some Care-Net documents and phoned Patty, building enforcer and told her to pull the Care-Net file and the violation file for the Andersons.

Albert and Aimee went to see Patty McLean Johnson, Kittitas County Building Planning Code Enforcement Inspector. They paid her for copies from her file, which included the February 23, 1994 violation of the Kittitas County Zoning Code by Care-Net Outreach. This is the first time Albert and Aimee had any knowledge of the written violation notice by the Kittitas County Department of Building and Fire Safety.

January 24, 1995

182. Greg Zempel's secretary phoned and postponed the appointment with the prosecutor to January 26, 1995. Aimee was very thankful as she was not feeling well.

January 24, 1995

183. Aimee has not been feeling well since their disturbing conversation with Les Welk on January 18, 1995. Finally, she went to the Doctor for treatment of an infection. Aimee believed all the stress helped to break down her defenses.

January 25, 1995

184. Aimee phoned Greg Zempel's secretary and postponed her appointment scheduled for the next day since she was not completely well. The Andersons are relieved because they felt they needed a little more time before they expose it all.

February 7, 1995

    185. George Wood mailed to Albert the following letter:

****

THE GENERAL COUNCIL OF THE ASSEMBLIES OF God
1445 Boonville Avenue
Springfield, Missouri 65802-1894

February 7, 1995

George O. Wood	Phone:	(417) 862-2781
General Secretary	Fax:	(417) 863-6614

Reverend Albert E. Anderson
— — — Avenue
Ellensburg, WA 98926

Dear Brother Anderson:

    Greetings in the Lord!

    You have now reached the age of sixty-five and we wish to express our deep appreciation to you for your dedication, ministry, and labor through the years! We also rejoice with you in anticipation of the rewards for faithful service!

    "In respect and honor to those ministers who have given years of service to the Fellowship, senior status shall automatically be given to all credential holders who have reached the age of 65, whether they continue in full-time ministry or not" (Bylaws Article VII, Section 7).

    Since you have reached this age, we are listing you as a senior-active minister. Senior ministers who are not fully active may file a request with their district to be listed in one of the other two following categories:

    1. Senior-active: Those who continue to serve ¾ to full time in the ministry.

2. Senior-semi-retired: Those who continue to be active, but half time or less.
3. Senior-retired: Those who have ceased to engage in any regular appointed ministry.

All senior ministers are still required to renew annually. Senior-active and senior-semi-retired are required to designate $10.00 monthly to the support of the General Council. Senior-retired ministers have no further financial obligation.

We pray that God shall yet give you good health and strength so that you may be able to continue your ministry as He opens doors of service.

Sincerely yours in Christ,

George O. Wood
General Secretary

GOW:lr
cc:Elmer E. Kirschman

****

February 10, 1995

186. In a phone conversation, Mark Severn, Department of General Administrative Division of Commodity Redistribution (D.G.A. - D.C.R.) related the following things to Aimee:

1. Winnie Chapman was the one who originally came in and set up the transitional housing food commodity program. The original had something to do with people in crisis.

2. After Aimee had told Mark Severn, on March 25, 1994 and then on April 11, 1994, about the stockpile of food commodities at the ranch, he decided to check with Rollin Carlson.

3. Mark Severn visited Rollin and his church on April 4, 1994, then later went to the Care-Net ranch for inspection. Rollin Carlson showed him the community room that was almost bare of any food commodities.

4. Rollin said the County only allowed him to have up to 10 men at the ranch."

NOTE: A total fabrication. County Code forbade any such "ministry."

Aimee asked Mark Severn, "Did Rollin tell you why the County would not let him have more men?"

Mark answered, "He, (meaning Rollin) said something about not having enough beds."

NOTE: Another total fabrication from Rollin!

Mark Severn indicated to Aimee that in 1994, when he questioned Rollin about the number of men at the ranch, (10+ needy, later changed to 20 needy, and then again changed to 45 needy) that Rollin said something about getting it mixed up with the number of meals served at the Everett ministry, but he said, **"That didn't wash either."**

NOTE: In fact, the food requisition forms were changed on more than one occasion; that is, from 10 to 20 to 45.

Mark seemed very concerned and expressed that with the government changes there might not be any food to give away in the near future. Aimee responded, **"It's a shame when the system is abused."**

February 12, 1995

187. In a phone conversation with Jeanne Mahon, Jeanne made the following statements:

1. When we (Tom and Jeanne Mahon) arrived at the Care-Net ranch on April 1, 1994, there were three (rehab) men at the ranch.
2. One man received a DWI and had to leave sometime in August, 1994.
3. Another man, left in August or maybe the first of September. He didn't like being paid under the table and told the Mahons that someone said to him, "The can of worms was going to explode, so he better get out." He left and went back to Whidbey Island. (Tom and Jeanne Mahon have told the Andersons on several different occasions that there have been no men for rehabilitation at the ranch since August or September, 1994.)
4. The third man, Jeff left sometime in July or August. On an earlier occasion, in a phone conversation Jeff told Aimee he had a drinking problem. He indicated that he would probably be there for several more months. Apparently, it was very soon after their conversation that he was gone.

February 13, 1995

188. Aimee phoned the Prosecutor's office and made an appointment for Albert and Aimee to meet with Greg Zempel for one hour on February 16.

February 16 or 17, 1995

189. Aimee had the following phone conversation with Vi Lien, Rollin Carlson's secretary:
Vi, "Hello, this is Vi."
Aimee, "Hi, I was wondering if they are taking in any more men at the Care-Net ranch?"
Vi, "Not for 30 days, they are in a building project, but we are still taking applications."
Aimee, "Will they be taking in more men after 30 days?"
Vi, "Yes, we are still taking applications."
Aimee, "How many men do they have there now?"
Vi, "I don't know. Why?"
Aimee, "Just wondering. Bye."
Vi, "Good-bye."

February 17, 1995

190. Albert and Aimee Andersons met in the Prosecutor's office with Greg Zempel for over one hour concerning Rollin Carlson and the Care-Net issues.

February 17, 1995

191. Aimee had the following phone conversation with Tom Mahon:
Tom, "Rollin says he is going to be sending (5) five men plus a counselor to the ranch. I told him, 'the Anderson have shown me the Violation Notice that Care-Net received from the Kittitas County and you don't have a right to send men to the ranch for rehabilitation.' Rollin said, 'that's not true. I wish I could take you to the Courthouse and show you.' I said, 'let's go.' Rollin said, 'I don't have time.'"

On another occasion, **Jeanne Mahon told Aimee,** "I was a witness to the three men loading boxes and boxes of government food onto a truck and driving it away from the Care-Net ranch, before Rollin Carlson came with another man (Mark Severn) for inspection. She also, indicated to Aimee that the three men were, Tom Mahon and the two rehab men at the ranch. The inspection took place in 1994, after Aimee had informed Mark Severn (USDA FOOD COMMODITIES).

February 17, 1995

192. In a phone conversation, Jerry Marchel told Aimee that he asked Rollin, "Are you still taking in men up at the ranch?" **Rollin's response to Jerry was,** "There are no men there now until the house is completed and all the lies over there are taken care of."

NOTE: Is Rollin making a personal confession and referring to all the lies he has told by word of his mouth, his letters and on other documents?

February 20, 1995

193. Aimee had the following phone conversation with Don Strong, a Northwest District Presbyter:
Don, "Rollin said the County went out to the ranch with him and 'approved the whole ministry project;' and even after the charges, he took them out there again and it was approved."
Aimee, "Did you see the document saying so?"
Don, "No, but they read it to us."
Aimee, "Was it the 'Certificate of Occupancy'?"
Don, "I don't know!"
Aimee, "Did you know Rollin received a violation notice?"
Don, "No."
Aimee, "Did you know there haven't been any men for rehabilitation, at the ranch since about August?"
Don, "No."

Aimee, "Someone talked to Erwin Krueger recently and he said the men were there for six months and Care-Net had a high success rate."

Don, "That's what I keep hearing. Why doesn't the County do something?"

Aimee, "I believe they are going to."

February 22, 1995

194. Aimee identified herself to Mark Severn, with the Department of General Administration of Commodity Redistribution. Albert and Aimee had a long phone conversation with him about Rollin Carlson and the Care-Net ranch receiving Food Commodities under false claims. Mark, over and over apologized to the Andersons for hurting them in any way, by not checking into the situation properly months earlier. Aimee had started talking to Mark in March of 1994, concerning the deception surrounding Rollin Carlson and The Care-Net Outreach ranch receiving Food Commodities. Finally, Joyce with KCAC (Kittitas County Action Council) talked Aimee into phoning Mark Severn and identifying herself to him. She told Aimee to tell him the whole story. Joyce was very understanding and helpful to Aimee.

Aimee told Mark Severn, "We have taken the documents and information to the Prosecutor, Greg Zempel."

Mark Severn said, "We will fully co-operate with the Prosecutor in their investigation."

Mark Severn also indicated to the Andersons, that after Rollin and Mark went to the Care-Net ranch to check on the food commodities there, that Rollin Carlson dropped the needy number from 45 back to the original number of 10 homeless or needy men at the Care-Net ranch to receive the food commodities.

NOTE: Rollin had no legal right to have even "one (1) man" at the ranch for rehabilitation – yet, Rollin still applied for Government food commodities for "needy men" at the Care-Net ranch

in Kittitas, Washington. Whether it was for 45 or 10 men, it was illegal and wrong. And, to make this a double tragedy, the "needy men" appeared to be missing from the ranch. Where did all the Government Food go?

(As indicated above, Jeanne Mahon told Aimee that she is a witness to the men loading boxes and boxes of USDA surplus food onto a truck and driving it away from the Care-Net ranch before Mark Severn came for inspection.)

Aimee asked Mark Severn, "Did Rollin tell you how many men he can have up at the ranch?"
Mark Severn answered, "Rollin said the County allowed him to have up to ten men at the ranch (For rehabilitation/transitional housing purposes)."
Aimee asked, "Did he tell you why he can only have ten (10) men up at the ranch?"
Mark answered, "He said something about they didn't have room for enough beds."

February 24, 1995

195. Aimee had another phone conversation with Mark Severn. He indicated that he was going to do everything he could to help clean up the mess. The Andersons said they would mail him a few of the documents so he could see for himself that Rollin Carlson did not have a Conditional Use Permit for the Care-Net ranch. He was still very apologetic and said he would fully co-operate with Greg Zempel in an investigation.

March 2, 1995

196. After breakfast, Albert phoned Don Strong. He was not available at the time. Later, when he phoned back, Aimee answered and talked to him a few minutes before giving the phone to Albert. The following conversation took place:
Aimee, "Have you seen the Violation Notice?"

Don, "What notice?"

Aimee, "You know. I told you about it the other day."

Don, "Oh, yes. Well he's been approved by the County and Rollin is keeping the County posted on everything that's going on. He's told them there are no men there now and won't have any more for awhile until they finish their house."

NOTE: What <u>absolute hypocrisy</u>! Neither Rollin nor Care-Net had any legal right for <u>even one man</u> — for Rehabilitation Ministry – to live at the Care-Net ranch.

Aimee, "How many men can he have up there?"

Don, "I don't remember. I know there's a limit, it's so many needy men per acre that they can have there."

NOTE: The deception continues. The limit was zero! None!

Aimee, "What's the name of it?"

Don, "I don't remember."

Aimee, "How can you solicit funds for something you don't even know the name of? Is it Care-Net?"

Don, "Oh, oh, yeah, that's what it is. They can have a counselor. It's a ministry."

NOTE: <u>More fabrication</u>! Neither Rollin, nor Care-Net, nor the Northwest District Officials, had any<u> legal right</u> for a Counseling, Rehabilitation/Transitional Housing ministry at the Care-Net ranch.

Aimee said good-bye and gave the phone to Albert.

QUESTION: Why are the Northwest District Officials parroting these lies? Is it because they are trying to save their own skin and do not care about who they hurt in the process?

March 3, 1995

197. After several tries, Aimee finally reached John Quigley by phone. The following conversation took place:

Aimee, "I plan on giving your name and number to the Prosecutor today. If the Prosecutor calls you, are you going to deny it? If I have to, I will tell what you have told me in court. We have two letters, from Rachinski and Forester concerning the claims."

John, "I didn't tell you how much."

Aimee, "I asked you if it was over $10,000.00 and you said, 'Yes;' and I asked you if it was a substantial amount paid, and you said 'Yes.'" (This was concerning the amount of money Rollin and Care-Net received from Rollin's insurance claim.)

Aimee, "I was told that the insurance agent and supervisor gave Rollin Carlson some statement clearing him."

John, "We didn't give anybody any letter. It's probably his own agent concerning that loafing shed."

Aimee expressed her concerns about people getting by with insurance fraud. She reminded him that everyone's insurance bill keeps going up because of insurance fraud.

March 3, 1995

198. Jeanne Mahon came by in the early afternoon feeling terribly sick with pain on her left side, and requested the Andersons to pray for her. Shortly after prayer, she laid down on the floor and cried out in pain. Aimee phoned Jeanne's doctor, but by that time she was feeling better. She sat down in the kitchen and began pouring out her heart to Aimee and Albert. Some of the things Jeanne said are the following:

1. Mark Porter is Rollin's cattle buyer.

WHITED SEPULCHRES

2. Matt Chambers, a real nice minister from Whidby Island, said to the Mahons, "Rollin wears many hats."
3. Mel Konsmo, a volunteer laborer, worked up at the Care-Net ranch this past weekend working on the new daylight basement house.
4. Two men have been working up the ground near the house. I think they are getting it ready to sell. Tom is planning on quitting the first of April.
5. We can't stand any more of this deception.
6. One of the neighbors told Tom he would help fix the road into Care-Net. He piled a bunch of rocks in the road, making it impossible for cars to go by. Tom asked him what he did that for and he told Tom, "To stop the men from going up and down the road." Tom then told him there were no men up at the ranch.
7. The cattle that die are dumped into the gravel pit (apparently owned by the Government) and left uncovered. Several cattle have died since they came to the ranch on April 1, 1994.

March 5, 1995

199. Aimee had the following phone conversation with Tom Mahon:

Tom, "Rollin says he can have five men in the new house and a house on every twenty acres. He said, 'Calculate that, Tom, to see how many men we can have here.'"

Aimee, "The Violation Notice says a family can mean five (5) unrelated individuals, but it does not mean an organized ministry, such as Rollin is trying to do."

Tom, "Oh, now it's starting to click, that's where he's getting this. He should be stopped."

Albert and Aimee indicated to Tom and Jeanne that Rollin would not be able to carry on with this deception forever.

March 6, 1995

200. In conversation with Milton Lewis, he made the following statement: "In the men's meeting in Yakima in 1992, when Rollin was making his appeal for $70,000.00 for the Care-Net ranch, he said, 'some of you here can write a check for $70,000.00 yourself.'"

Later Albert and Aimee reviewed the 1992, seven page, promotional mailing that Rollin had sent to "All Northwest District Pastors." Again, they read about Rollin's appeal for 100 cows at $700.00 per cow, a total of $70,000.00, for the needed therapy project at the Care-Net Outreach ranch.

March 9, 1995

201. The following phone conversation took place between Aimee and Don Strong:

Aimee, "Did you see the violation notice or tell Warren Bullock or any of the District officials about it?"

Don, "What violation?"

Aimee, "You know, Care-Net."

Don, "Oh, Care-Net. No, I just talked to Rollin about it."

Aimee, "Does the Care-Net money received for the ranch go through the Northwest District books or Everett Bethany Christian Assembly books or does it only go through the Care-Net books?"

Don, "No, it goes through its own books, Care-Net, but they give a monthly report. They are just about done with the house."

Aimee, "Les says it's 'Transitional Housing.' Is that right?"

Don, "I don't know, but it is a home missions ministry."

Albert, "Are they contributing the $15,000.00 that was projected in the beginning?"

WHITED SEPULCHRES

Don, "They are giving substantial amounts and some to Teen-Challenge. Actually they are doing real well."

Aimee, "Are they going to be bringing men to the ranch?"

Don, "They are almost done with the house. They are expanding. Sunday there was a couple at the Kittitas Assembly. So things are moving ahead."

Aimee, "Don, do you think it's really on the up and up?"

Don, "I think so." After a few more words, the conversation was ended.

March 10, 1995

202. Jeanne told Aimee, "Rollin promised Tom five heifers for Christmas 1994, and he never gave them to him. Then he promised him the heifers for our anniversary, April first and we still are waiting." (At a later date, Jeanne told Aimee that Rollin Carlson finally gave Tom the five heifers.)

March 11, 1995

203. Tom phoned the Andersons and told them, "Rollin told me to write up a proposal of what I want from Care-Net." Tom indicated that Rollin still could have men at the ranch for rehabilitation but because of all the fuss, Rollin will let Tom and Jeanne move into the new home. He will then rent out the old house that Mahons are living in now; then use the money for Transitional housing at Everett. Tom said he is fed up with it all and hopes to get on with his life.

March 23, 1995

204. Aimee and Vi Lien had the following phone conversation:

Aimee, "When are they going to be sending more men, needing rehabilitation, to the Care-Net ranch?"

Vi, "After the building program is complete. I'm not going to use that word, we use 'Transitional Housing.'"

March 24, 1995

205. Jeanne Mahon told Aimee they will be through at Care-Net April 1, 1995.

March 27, 1995

206. Albert received a certified letter from Elmer Kirschman demanding his presence at their Presbyters meeting. It was a very difficult time for both Albert and Aimee. Later today, someone told the Andersons, "They have already deprived you of your pulpit, what more do they want but your credentials?"

March 27, 1995

207. After the Fellowship meeting at Wapato, Albert asked the evening speaker, Les Welk, Northwest District Assistant Superintendent, "What precipitated the letter of request at this time?"
Les, "We want to bring it to closure."
Albert, "Is the ranch going to be just a District investment?"
Les, "No, it's Transitional Housing. There are no men there now. We told Rollin not to send any more men there until things get cleared with the County. It looks like it has been taken care of this past month and men will be going there soon."

QUESTION: County Code had not changed. Why this continued fabrication?

March 28, 1995

208. The following phone conversation took place between Elmer Kirschman and Albert and Aimee:

Aimee, "I am my husband's wife, I am his secretary, and I am his partner, thus I want to tell you that we have a former commitment for April 4." He let Aimee know that it would be to their best interests for Albert to appear.

Elmer, "The charges are dead and gone and the letter was sent to Albert and we are going to deal with him. It's now a credentials matter."

Albert, "My wife and I have been married for almost 41 years, and if I come, she will come with me."

Elmer, "She can come with you, but she won't be allowed to speak." Later in the conversation Elmer said, "You will have to be approved by Warren Bullock, because Warren said that Aimee would not be allowed to come."

Aimee, "You said I could come. What do you have against women?"

Elmer, "You are unreasonable."

Aimee, "Why, because I want sin and corruption to be exposed? If you don't want to talk to me, maybe you will be forced to in court someday, not that I want to."

Elmer, "It looks like you are not going to drop it."

Aimee, "No, not until it's cleaned up."

All three agreed the conversation was over and said good-bye.

March 29, 1995

209. The following phone conversation took place between Aimee and James Bridges:

Aimee, "Have you heard about the formal charges brought against Rollin Carlson, Care-Net and other district officials?"

Bridges, "I don't know what you are talking about."

Aimee, "Have you seen the charges?"

Bridges, "No, maybe it will be coming up at our next meeting."

Aimee, "Are you part of the Executive Presbytery?"

Bridges, "Yes."

Aimee, "We sent a letter to you, the Executive Presbytery and you did not receive it or know anything about it?"

Brother Bridges further indicated he did not know anything about the charges or what she was talking about and said he would have Brother Crabtree phone Aimee.

March 29, 1995

210. Albert and Aimee had a phone conversation with Loren Triplett. He said, "I don't know anything about the charges." He sounded like he was deeply concerned. He indicated he was not at the November Presbyters' meeting but still he should have a copy of the charges and some knowledge of what was going on concerning them.

March 30, 1995

211. Albert and Aimee sent off their letter, by certified mail, appealing the decision concerning the Formal Charges, to Trask, Crabtree, Bridges, Wood, Triplett and copies by Certified Mail to Warren Bullock, Northwest District Council Credentials Committee in care of Elmer Kirschman.

April 3, 1995

212. In a brief phone conversation, Brother Crabtree, (Assistant General Superintendent) said to Aimee, "You mean you haven't heard from the District concerning the charges?"

Aimee, "No official notice has come, only the demand for Albert to appear. Brother Bridges (General Treasurer) told me that he did not know anything about the charges. We have decided to appeal the decision concerning the charges. We are sending you a copy of it."

Crabtree answered, "Alright."

April 3, 1995

213. After talking to Crabtree, Aimee phoned and talked with George Wood. (General Secretary) His secretary said, "Didn't you already talk to Brother Crabtree?"

Aimee, "Yes, but I would like to talk to Brother Wood about something different."

Secretary, "Isn't it the same subject?"

Aimee, "Yes, but something different that only he can answer."

Secretary, "Brother Wood is a very busy man."

Aimee, "Is he too busy to talk to someone about something important enough to affect the whole Assemblies of God?"

Secretary, "Just a minute."

Wood, "Hello."

Aimee, "Hello. Both Brother Bridges and Brother Triplett told me that they didn't know anything about the charges."

Wood, "Brother Triplett is a very busy man and is in and out of the meetings. Brother Bridges is usually pretty good with his memory but I can't understand why he doesn't know anything about the charges."

Aimee, "Did you give a copy of the charges to the General Council Credentials Committee members?"

Wood, "No." He further indicated to Aimee that he gave a brief review of it to the committee.

Aimee, "You mean to tell me we went to all that expense and work for nothing? Will you please mail a copy of the charges and a copy of the appeal, that we are sending to you, now, to the men, or do we have to send it to them?"

Wood, "I will make it available to the brethren."

Aimee, "Albert refused to appear at the Northwest District Executive Presbyters meeting, due to a prior commitment."

Wood, "That weakens Albert's position."

Aimee, "The men did not want to talk to me about the charges."

Wood, "It probably is because they figured the charges were over. Do you hold credentials?"

Aimee, "No, but Brother Wood, if some woman in the church brought charges against you, would you face her and talk to her?"

Wood, "Probably."

Aimee, "We will be mailing out the appeal and expect you to give it to the Credential Committee members." They said good-bye.

April 3, 1995

214. In a phone conversation this evening with Loren Triplett, (Executive Director, Division of Foreign Missions) Aimee asked, "Have you received the certified package containing the charges and appeal?"

Triplett, "Yes." Aimee sensed the difference in his attitude from the previous March 29, 1995 conversation.

Triplett, "I think you are missing something. I feel so sorry for you. It saddens me to see you try so hard but I think you are missing something. I know these men. I've heard them pray."

Aimee, "Brother Triplett, if you knew these charges were one hundred per cent correct, would they be serious?"

Triplett, "Yes, they would be serious."

Aimee, "They are absolutely one hundred per cent correct. They are true."

NOTE: We have had objective professional men, who know the law, read the charges with documentation. They very quickly saw the illegal activities, nor did they view them of little consequence.

April 7, 1995

215. George Wood sent a letter to Brother and Sister Anderson informing them that the Formal Charges would be on the agenda for the May 31 to

June 1, 1995, meeting of the Executive Presbytery for another review.

April 8, 1995

216. Aimee and Julius Jepson (Northwest District Executive Presbyter) had the following phone conversation:
Aimee, "Brother Jepson, were you at the Presbyters' meeting last week?"
Jepson, "Yes, it was the Executive Presbyters' meeting."
Aimee, "Did you receive a copy of our letter?"
Jepson, "Yes, I have a copy with me."
Aimee, "Good. I was not going to put your name in the letter but I finally decided it would be all right."
Jepson, "Yes, I think so too."
Aimee, "We really appreciate you and your spirit. You have always been nice to us. I just wished they would believe us."
Jepson, "It's now in the hands of the General Council."

April 10, 1995

217. Aimee and Brother Brandt (Northwest Region Non-Resident Executive Presbyter) had the following phone conversation:
Aimee, "Brother Brandt, do you know about the charges?"
Brandt, "No." He further indicated that he wanted her to tell him about it. After telling him some about the charges, he said, "I was at the November 1994 Presbyters meeting, but I did not hear anything about the charges. Would you send them and the appeal to me at my home address, so I can be aware of what is going on?" He further expressed his sorrow and concerns about it all. He was very pleasant to talk with. Thank God.

April 11, 1995

218. Early this morning the following phone conversation took place between Aimee and Brother Hackett: (Executive Director, Division of Home Missions.)

Aimee, "Brother Hackett, do you know anything about the charges against Rollin Carlson and Care-Net?"

Hackett, "I do not know anything about the charges. I was at the November 1994, Presbyters meeting but I did not hear anything about the charges." He let Aimee know in no uncertain terms but in a very nice way that he had no knowledge of the Complaint, the formal Charges, or any of the letters concerning the whole thing. He also, requested that Aimee send him the charges and appeal letter. "So I can know what's coming up in the next Presbyters meeting in May."

April 12, 1995

219. Albert and Aimee sent a letter, appealing for help, to Robert Brandt and Charles Hackett. They enclosed in both of those letters, a copy of the charge packet.

April 13, 1995

220. Albert and Aimee mailed the letters today to Robert Brandt, Charles Hackett and to each of the other General Council of the Assemblies of God, Credential Committee members. Also, today they received George Wood's April 7, 1995 letter informing them that the Charges would be reviewed again in their May 31-June 1, Presbyters meeting.

April 19, 1995

221. Albert and Aimee had a 1:30 P.M. appointment with Greg Zempel.

April 21, 1995

222. George Wood sent a letter to Brother and Sister Anderson letting them know that he had received the copy of their letter to Robert Brandt and Charles Hackett and would provide copies of their correspondence to the General Council Executive Presbyters.

April 24, 1995

223. The secretary at the Everett Bethany Christian Assembly confirmed over the phone that there is a ranch for men who need help.

She said, "It's a rigid screening process to go through. They have to be drug and alcohol free."

April 24, 1995

224. Jeanne told Aimee, "We probably will move into the new house next week. (The daylight basement house, referred to as "bunkhouse" that is almost finished, that will house (9) or (10) men.) We are cleaning up around this house before we move into the new house. I hope it all works out all right. Rollin promised not to send any men to the ranch."

(Tom quit working for Rollin Carlson and the Care-Net ranch and somehow Rollin talked him into going back to work for him and the Care-Net ranch.)

Aimee asked Jeanne, "Have you received the five heifers yet?"

Jeanne answered, "Not yet." (Later Jeanne told Aimee that Rollin finally gave them the five heifers.)

April 25, 1995

225. Aimee phoned Everett Bethany Assembly and had the following phone conversation with Shirley Pearson:

Aimee, "When I phoned and talked to, I believe, Vi, in February about the possibility of taking in needy men at the Care-Net ranch, she said they were in a building project and they would be taking in men again in about thirty days. Is it too late or do you have room for any more?"

Shirley, "They are still working on the house. It takes a long time because it is all volunteer labor. It's quite a screening process they go through. They have to be free of drugs and alcohol and be tested for aids."

Aimee, "How many men do they have at the ranch?"

Shirley, "They have one."

NOTE: We were told that Rollin stopped sending rehab men to the ranch in 1994. Yet, Shirley, wife of Gaylord Pearson, Care-Net board member, told Aimee that they had one man at the ranch, on the above date. John Mustered told Aimee on January 14, 1995, there was one rehab man at the ranch. See #173.

Aimee, "Is he alone?"

Shirley, "Yes, they have to be so careful about that."

Aimee, "How many men can they have at the ranch?"

Shirley, "I don't know. They have two main houses; the old one with a basement they (rehab men) used, although the family that lived there had such a large family they used it too, and the new house with three bedrooms and a basement. They will be doing some counseling. The basement will be used for that. I believe they also have three bunkhouses. Pastor Carlson is away at District Convention and you need to talk to him. You can phone him next week."

QUESTION: Where are the (3) three bunkhouses? When the Andersons have toured the ranch on different occasions, they have NEVER seen three bunkhouses.

May 24, 1995

226. Aimee and Vi Lien, Rollin Carlson's secretary, had the following conversation:

Aimee, "Are you still taking in men at Care-Net?"

Vi, "We are still taking applications."

Aimee, "I talked to you several months ago and you said they were in a big building project."

Vi, "They are. It's not completed. They are still working on it."

Aimee, "Then you will be taking in men again?"

Vi, "Oh, yes."

Aimee, "I heard that possibly it was going to be sold?"

Vi, "Even if it is, there will be other arrangements made for the transitional housing. But nothing has taken place yet."

Aimee, "Then the applications should be sent to Bethany?"

Vi, "Yes, but send it to my attention, Vi Lien, so it won't be waylaid."

Aimee, "Thank you. Bye."

Vi, "Bye."

May 25, 1995

227. Aimee and Brother Brandt had the following phone conversation:

Aimee, "Brother Brandt, this is Aimee Anderson. We brought charges against Care-Net and I wanted to know if you received the charge package from Brother Wood? His secretary said she was sending it to all the ministers."

Brandt, "Yes."

Aimee, "Good, that's what I wanted to know. You are having your executive meeting this next week?"

Brandt, "Yes. (few moments pause) I've read through it and I don't see anything that's worth anything. I think you've made something out of nothing. And why isn't your husband doing this?"

QUESTION: How could anyone read the documentation and make such a statement?

Aimee, "What do you have against women. How about Esther and Deborah? I believe God has chosen me."

Brandt, "Your husband is supposed to be the head of the house and why isn't he doing this?"

Aimee, "Because he wants me to."

Brandt, "I'm sure! Did you do this because you were voted out of a church?"

Aimee, "No! My husband resigned this last June because of threats, after we had already filed the charges."

Brandt, "I know these men."

Aimee, "Let me tell you something: if some one came into my home and stole my piano, no matter how godly that man was and no matter how godly the brethren were who said that man did not steal my piano, I would know better because I saw him steal it. We have first-hand knowledge of the corruption that has been taking place. There is some real dishonesty taking place here."

Brandt, "Will you abide by the brethren's decision?"

Aimee, "If you will pray and seek God and do an honest investigation, I believe the decision will be right."

Brandt, "Are you saying the brethren are not honest?"

Aimee, "I have revered you. That is why I have come to you. If you will pray and do an honest investigation I believe it will be right."

Brandt, "I sensed a wrong spirit in what I've read. You picked up on everything and made something out of nothing."

Aimee, "Even if the spirit was wrong, would it give the other person a right to be dishonest?" (Aimee does not believe the Andersons' spirit was or is wrong, she just did not want to argue the point with him.)

Brandt, "No, two wrongs don't make a right."

Aimee, "I thought our leaders were supposed to be honest."

Brandt, "That's your judgment. You are not considerate. I know these men."

Aimee, "So do I. I think I have known them longer than you. How about Jimmy Swaggart and Jimmy Bakker? I used to listen to Jimmy Swaggart and cry. Fact is I did not even want to go to church sometimes in the morning because I wanted to listen to him. I thought he was the best preacher in the world, next to my husband. **The District Officials doing the investigation is like the fox guarding the hen house."**

Brandt, "I guess there's no point talking if you are not going to abide by the decision. We are supposed to be in submission one to another and you are coming against a lot of godly brethren."

Aimee, "I'd rather obey God than man. Have you heard from me before?"

Brandt, "No."

Aimee, "My husband and I have been married forty-one (41) years and this is the first time for this. How about Esther and Deborah? I have six (6) grown children who love the Lord and you can talk to any of them. If you men will pray and do an honest investigation yourselves, I believe the decision will be right. This is why I've come to you."

Brandt, "I see your point."

Aimee, "We are praying. Bye."

Brandt, "Bye."

June 1, 1995

228. George Wood wrote a letter to Brother and Sister Anderson letting them know that both the Northwest District Presbytery and the General Council Credentials Committee, "determined that no charges should be filed against the ministers accused; and, that the General Council Credentials Committee concurs with the district action and regards the matter as closed."

June 23, 1995

229. Jeanne Mahon told Aimee that Rollin Carlson had put the Care-Net land up for sale. She thought Bob Kelly was listing it. Aimee phoned and was told that it was indeed for sale. There seemed to be some uncertainty as to the price and terms.

July 3, 1995

230. Aimee phoned the Kittitas County Treasurer's Office and asked who paid the taxes the last half of 1991, 1992 and first half of 1993. She was told that the Kittitas County Title Company paid them. She then phoned the Kittitas County Title Company and learned that the taxes for the two years that Chapmans had the land in their name were paid on April 1, 1993, by the Kittitas County Title Company and that they were unable to give out who put up the money.

Later Albert and Aimee went to the **Treasurer's Office** for more information. The lady told Albert and Aimee that the **tax bills were mailed to Everett Bethany Church during the two years that Chapmans were the "Owners of Record."** (This was the address listed as Chapmans permanent address on the Real Estate Excise Tax form #031500 with Chapmans listed as the owners of record.)

July 5, 1995

231. Aimee phoned the National Hotline number (800) 835-6422 (by accident, not knowing what the number was for). She decided to ask them about All State not wanting to be involved in exposing the false insurance claims. Aimee was transferred to The National Insurance Crime Bureau. She told Bob Chambers, Manager of Property and Casualty, about Rollin Carlson's deceptive insurance claims and asked, "If an insurance company does not want to take care of insurance fraud, do you do something about it?" Bob Chambers said, "Yes." He also, told Aimee, "We will be glad to help in any way we can." He seemed very willing to work with Greg Zempel, the Prosecutor.

July 5, 1995

232. Thayne Rich, from the government office in Moses Lake, Washington, returned Aimee's July 3rd phone call. When Aimee first started talking to Thanye Rich, he mentioned the Park Creek Ranch.

Aimee, "This is another ranch named the Care-Net Outreach." (Thayne Rich, is the man who signed the February 25, 1991 Real Estate Excise Tax affidavit on document #031500, Melvin L. Chapman and Winnie Chapman, 2715 Everett Avenue, Everett, WA 98201, as Buyer/Grantee.)

Aimee asked him about Melvin and Winnie Chapman using the Everett Bethany church's address as their own personal permanent address on the Excise Tax form. Thayne Rich told Aimee that Rollin Carlson wanted to buy the land parcels #17-20-0400-0006, #17-20-0400-0014, and #17-20-0500-0017.

Thayne Rich said, "I never met the Chapmans, Rollin Carlson is the only one I dealt with."

Aimee, "Did Rollin want to buy the land for himself?"

Thayne Rich, "Rollin said he wanted to buy the land for the church, but said he didn't have enough money, so he found someone in his church, the Chapmans, who put up the front money and purchased the land in their name." Thayne Rich told Aimee that he would be willing to visit with the Prosecutor, Greg Zempel, and also willing for the records to be subpoenaed.

He seemed surprised to hear that on April 1, 1993, the Care-Net Outreach, Rollin Carlson, President/Pastor, bought the land for $260,000.00, supposedly from Melvin and Winnie Chapman.

Aimee's understanding is, according to Thayne Rich, that on February 25, 1991, Rollin Carlson bought the three parcels of land for the church, for $105,000.00, using Chapmans' name and their front money. If this is correct, how could Rollin Carlson buy the three parcels of land for the church, again, a second time, in less than 26 months, on April 1, 1993, for $260,000.00, a profit of $155,000.00?

ALBERT & AIMEE ANDERSON

Rollin Carlson was appointed in 1992 as the Finance Chairman for the Northwest District Council. The Northwest District loaned Rollin Carlson and the Care-Net Outreach ranch the $135,000.00, on February 25, 1991. Then, again, on April 1, 1993, when Rollin Carlson was the Northwest District Council Finance chairman, the Northwest District Council made another loan of $350,000.00 to The Care-Net Outreach. Further search has revealed a third Deed of Trust, July 1, 1993, for $30,000.00, between the Northwest District Council of the Assemblies of God and the Care-Net Outreach. Apparently, all three of these loans came from the District church loan fund for the Care-Net Ranch at Kittitas, Washington. This sounds like a conflict of interest.

QUESTION: Who was the recipient of the $155,000.00 gain on the property purchased by the Care-Net Outreach, at Kittitas, Washington, on April 1, 1993?

Rollin was the President/Pastor of the Care-Net ranch ministry and finance Chairman of the Northwest District Council. Thus, he was overseer of the money ($350,000.00 and $30,000.00) that he borrowed (1993) from the Northwest District Council Church Loan Fund for the Care-Net ranch. Apparently, a large percent of this "Church loan" was used for the questionable $155,000.00 gain that Rollin helped himself to and/or helped someone else make. This sounds like a big conflict of interest! And it sounds like misappropriation of funds and to put it more bluntly, just plain <u>stealing from the church</u>.

July 7, 1995

233. Jim Bryant, with State Farm, Regional Claims, returned Aimee's July 3, 1995 phone call. After some minutes of checking in the file, Jim Bryant told Aimee that the State Farm claim #472558139, was the correct number for Everett

Bethany Assembly's accident on December 10, 1991. The church's vehicle involved was a 1986 Ford van, which was driven by Michael Helin and State Farm Insurance only paid out for property damage.

Is this the same accident that Rollin collected a substantial amount of money from All State by deceitfully using Rachinski and Forester or a different claim?

July 7, 1995

234. After her conversation with Jim Bryant of State Farm, Aimee decided to phone John Quigley with All State. She found out that he now has changed from Special Investigative Unit to Casualty and Claim Manager.

John Quigley was not at liberty to give Aimee any more information concerning Rollin's 1991 accident.

Aimee asked, "You can't say anything because of what happened with Ms. Blake?"

John Quigley said, "Yes."

July 16, 1995

235. Albert and Aimee traveled to Lynnwood to take care of their daughter's home while she, her husband and family spent a week at Lake Chelan.

July 18, 1995

236. The following certified letter, post marked July 18, 1995, was sent to Albert Anderson:

****

NORTHWEST DISTRICT COUNCIL of the
ASSEMBLIES OF GOD

Warren D. Bullock, Superintendent
Leslie E. Welk, Assistant Superintendent
Rollin J. Carlson, Secretary-Treasurer

July 14, 1995

Rev. Albert Anderson
— — — Avenue
Ellensburg, WA 98926

Dear Brother Anderson:

Warm Christian greetings!

I trust that you are having a restful and profitable summer. Judi and I have had opportunity to be at Silver Lake Camp and we certainly did enjoy that.

Brother Al, I am writing to invite you to meet with the Executive Presbytery on September 6 at 10:00 a.m. I believe that such a meeting is needful and will be helpful to all concerned. Thank you in advance for your response to this invitation and your willingness to meet with us.

Blessings on you.

Sincerely,

Dr. Warren D. Bullock
District Superintendent

WDB:at

cc: Rollin Carlson
     Les Welk

July 19, 1995

237. At six o'clock A.M. Albert started having chest and arm pains while watering the lawn. He did not say anything to Aimee about it but continued watering the lawn and flowers. Around 11:30 A.M., he told Aimee, "I'm tired and want to go upstairs and lay down awhile."

Aimee, "How about lunch?"

Albert, "Do I have to eat? Oh well, you can call me when it's ready."

Aimee decided to wait with the preparations for lunch until Albert was through resting. She did not have long to wait, as Albert called from upstairs. "Honey, come here."

Aimee knew something was wrong and called to her husband as she hurried up the stairs, "What's wrong?"

Albert answered, "I don't know!"

Aimee's feet took flight, as she flew up the rest of the steps, not knowing what to expect. She definitely knew something was wrong. Her heart quickened when she found Albert lying on the bathroom floor. "Honey, what's wrong."

Albert answered, "I have pain in my chest and arm and I almost passed out." (Albert could not sleep so arose to shave; and while he was shaving, he almost blacked out. Immediately he got down on the floor. He tried to get up and continue shaving but broke out in a cold sweat and ended up on the floor calling for Aimee to help him.)

Immediately Aimee laid hands on Albert's head and started praying for him; simultaneously she reached for a damp washcloth to wipe off some of the shaving cream still on Albert's face. Her touch discovered he was cold and clammy and his tee shirt was drenched with perspiration. Before she was through praying Aimee asked, "Shall I phone 911?"

Albert said, "I don't care!"

Aimee knew his physical condition had to be serious for Albert to respond this way. This was the response Aimee needed and she took command of the situation. She felt weak and shaky but gathered strength from above for the strenuous hours and days ahead of her.

The 911 operator was very kind, patient and gentle with her as he reassured her that the ambulance and paramedics would be there right away. He told her, "I will stay with you on the line until they arrive. Do not let your husband go to sleep. Keep his head down."

Aimee thought the 911 operators only talked to little children this way and other people in very dire emergencies. She was so grateful and thankful to him for his kindness to her.

Aimee said, "I can't even tell you how to come to our daughter's house." (Fact is, she had to get the address from her husband who was lying on the floor). The operator answered, "That's all right, I have it right here on the computer. The men will be at the door any minute."

The paramedics and ambulance arrived in about five minutes. The four men immediately started administering IV's, to Albert, while taking blood pressure, pulse and whatever else was necessary. They transported Albert as quickly as possible to Stevens Hospital in Edmonds, Washington. The head paramedic told Aimee that she could ride in the ambulance with them.

Not long after Albert was admitted to the hospital, since the pain would not cease, but went from one arm to both arms besides his chest, it was diagnosed as a heart attack. The pain left shortly after the clot buster was administered to him. He was put in the intensive coronary care unit with a cot provided for his wife to help take care of him, according to his wishes and request.

July 20, 1995

238. During lunch, Aimee looked up to see Rollin Carlson and Les Welk standing in the doorway of the Intensive Coronary room. Her heart quickened and she wondered if Albert would be able to stand the added stress of their appearance at this time. About the first thing Rollin said was, "We met one of the requirements, there's two of us." (The other requirement for the intensive care unit was only family members.)

After a few minutes of conversation, Rollin reached to take hold Albert's hand and his other hand took Aimee's hand, while Les, on the other side of the bed, took Albert's other hand. Then Les led in prayer. Soon after, they said good-bye and left the room.

Albert told Aimee that he was warned, by the Lord, that possibly someone from the District office would come in to see him.

The Doctor had to be told about some of the stress the Andersons had been under for almost three years and about the uninvited visitors. The Doctor indicated that the nurse would take care of things by limiting the visitors to only Albert and Aimee's children and screening all calls.

July 21, 1995

239. Albert was moved from the Intensive Coronary Care Unit to the Progressive Coronary Care Unit, both units being the two Critical Care Units.

Among the beautiful flowers that started coming in, was a most gorgeous, large bouquet. As Aimee opened the card and began reading what it said, tears started filling her eyes. She shared the following card with her husband, Albert:

****

ALBERT & AIMEE ANDERSON

```
          07/24 Mon 00010461   West
               STADIUM FLOWERS

ALBERT ANDERSON
STEVENS HOSP.
RM 322 BED 1
EDMONDS WA 98026

             Best Wishes For
             A Speedy Recovery.
                   From,
             Warren & Judi Bullock,
              Les & Darcie Welk,
             Rollin & Helen Carlson &
             The District Office Staff
```

****

While Aimee was trying to keep from crying, Albert said, "Let's talk about it." Aimee expressed her hope and desire for the flowers to be given out of love, but only God knew the real motive of those who gave the gift. After a few minutes discussing our emotions in relation to the flowers, Aimee said, "The flowers didn't do anything wrong, they are God's flowers, so I'm going to enjoy them. From that point on, the flowers became a joy and blessing to both Albert and Aimee, when they took them as a gift from God.

July 21, 22, 23, 1995

240. Drs. Althouse and Hubbard both gave approval for Albert and Aimee's children to visit with their father in the Critical Care Unit. Fortunately, the room was fairly large and very accommodating for the Anderson family. There were many tears shed and hugs given, as this was a shock to their dear family.

WHITED SEPULCHRES

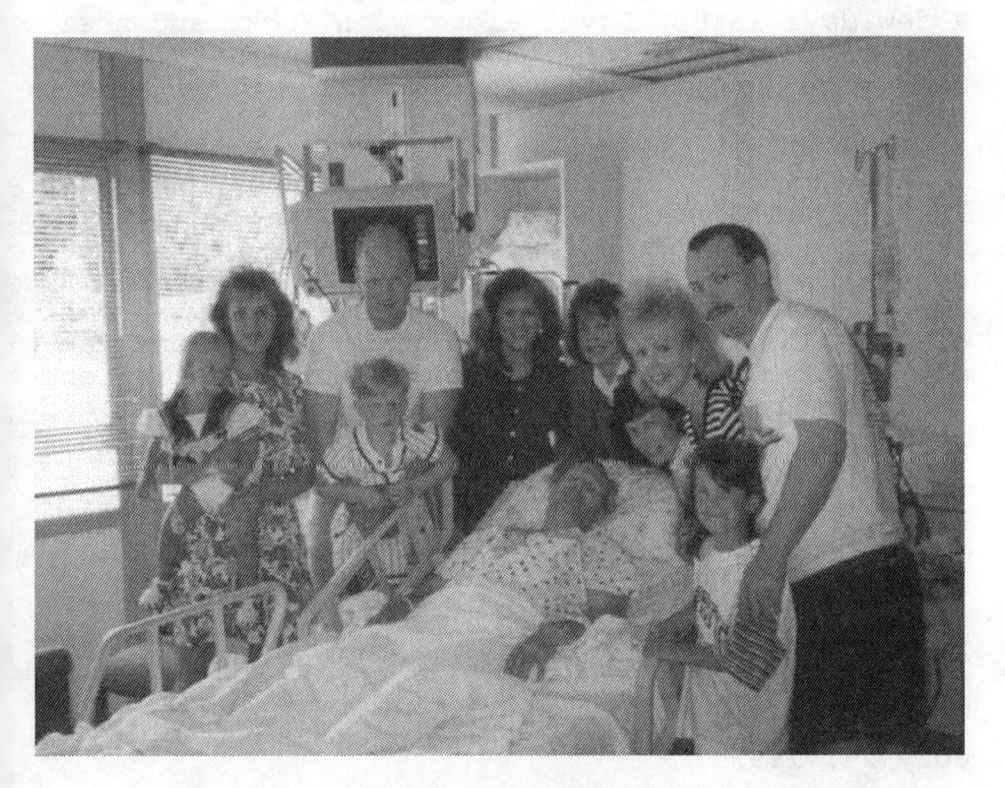

ALBERT - IN THE HOSPITAL
MARY, MARK, REBECCA, AIMEE, DEBORAH, EUNICE, JONATHAN
BREANNA, JORDAN, KRISTINA

ALBERT & AIMEE ANDERSON

The Andersons' oldest daughter Debbie, and her husband Larry, and two children, Larissa and Matthew; their second daughter Becky, (Becky's husband Dave was back East on a business trip, but a few days later, Dave, along with Becky and their five children, Charity, Starr, Benjamin, Tyler and John came to see their father and grandpa in the hospital); their third daughter Mary, and her husband Joe, and their four children, Jordan, Joseph, Jameson and Kendrin; their fourth daughter Eunice, and her husband Emil and their three children, Emil, Kristina and Breanna; their oldest son Mark, and his oldest son Jordan; (Mark's wife Emily, stayed home with their baby Zackary) and of course Albert and Aimee's youngest son Jonathan, all came to see their father in the hospital and lend support and love to both their father and mother.

This tearful and emotional, yet very wonderful family reunion in the hospital, included, Bill Roberts, a very close friend of the Anderson family. The Andersons were so grateful that the Doctors did not limit the number of children and grandchildren that could be with their Dad and Mom in the hospital room at one time.

July 24, 1995

241. Doctor Althouse performed an angiogram on Albert at the Stevens Hospital. Later he came to the room and gave his report to Albert and Aimee. One place in Albert's heart artery was 80 per cent closed. The Doctor advised angioplasty (balloon) to take care of the problem. He informed the Andersons of the various risks involved in this procedure. Albert took the Doctor's advice and said he would do what he felt best. Aimee told the Doctor, "I believe you are God's gift to us. Thank you so very much!" Both Albert and Aimee felt the ever-abiding presence of the Lord with them at all times and knew God was the one who really was in control. Praise the wonderful name of Jesus. Thank the Lord for His wonderful miracle of love and grace!

July 25, 1995

242. Around 7:00 A.M., Albert was moved by ambulance to the Providence Hospital in Seattle. Again, according to Albert's desire and request, Aimee rode along in the ambulance.

July 25, 1995

243. The angioplasty did not work on Albert. When the balloon was removed, the artery collapsed to 90 per cent closed. Thus Doctor Althouse, after consultation with other surgeons, implanted two stainless steel stents in Albert's heart artery.

July 25 through July 28, 1995

244. Albert spent these days in the critical care unit at the Providence hospital with his wife, Aimee, close by his side, reading the Bible to him, praying for his recovery and doing what she could to assist the doctor and nurses. Albert and Aimee so keenly felt the sweet presence of the Lord with them all the time.

ALBERT & AIMEE ANDERSON

July 27, 1995

245. A personal card, postmarked July 27, 1995, was mailed to Al Anderson. The hand written (the Andersons believe the hand-writing was Warren Bullock's) part of the card read as follows:

****

Bro. Al

So sorry to learn of your illness. You are regularly in our prayers. Keep looking up.

Warren & Judi Bullock

****

July 28, 1995

   246. A certified letter, post-marked July 31, 1995, was mailed to Rev. Al Anderson, which read as follows:

****

Northwest District Council of the Assemblies of God
Warren D. Bullock, Superintendent
Leslie E. Welk, Assistant Superintendent
Rollin J. Carlson, Secretary-Treasurer

July 28, 1995

Rev. Al Anderson
— — — Avenue
Ellensburg, WA 98926

Dear Brother Anderson:

   Warm Christian greetings!

   We were so saddened to hear of your recent heart attack. We are praying for you that God will fully restore you to good health.

   I need to offer a correction to the previous letter we sent regarding the executive presbyters' meeting. The date of the meeting is September 7 rather than September 6. Forgive that error but my mind slipped a cog. We would not want this meeting to be an interruption of your physical recovery. Please keep us posted as to your availability to meet with us.

   We love you, brother. Keep looking up. Blessings on you.

   Sincerely,

Dr. Warren D. Bullock, District Superintendent

WDB:at

7001 220th Street SW, Suite 101
Mountlake Terrace, WA 98043-2164
Telephone (206) 640-0222

ALBERT & AIMEE ANDERSON

Fax (206) 640-0333

July 28, 1995

247. This evening, Albert was moved out of the Critical Care Unit to another recovery room, hopefully to be released tomorrow morning.

July 29, 1995

248. After Doctor Althouse took Albert for a short walk around the hospital hall, he released him to go home to their daughter Eunice's home in Lynnwood, with the instructions to come back to the Doctor in two days, then again two days later, and once each week for the next few weeks, for a check-up. Their daughter's home was very close to the Doctor's office and the Stevens hospital, which was a real help in going to the Doctor for the follow-up examinations.

July 30, 1995

249. Jonathan spent the week-end alone with his father and mother in Lynnwood.

WHITED SEPULCHRES

Jonathan, Aimee & Albert
Mt. Rainier, WA

July 31, 1995

250. Jonathan drove his father to the doctor for his first blood check.

July 29 through August 11, 1995

251. Albert and Aimee stayed two weeks in their daughter's home in Lynnwood, while Albert was recuperating from his heart attack and making his weekly visits to the doctor for the follow-up examinations. They had a few scares along the way but sensed the sweet abiding presence of the Lord at all times.

August 11, 1995

252. Albert had his last follow-up check by the doctor and was released to go back home to Ellensburg to continue his recuperation.

August 18, 1995

253. Aimee's mother went home to heaven early this morning. The next few days were filled with phone conversations with the members of her family making funeral arrangements.

The family asked Albert to preach the funeral message. The cardiac nurse told Aimee that the doctor said Albert should not go to the funeral, that Aimee should stay home and take care of her husband, because both Albert and Aimee had been under a lot of stress.

Thus, it was decided that Albert would preach a short message on tape and both Albert and Aimee would sing the song, "He the Pearly Gates Will Open," on casette tape, to be played at the funeral along with other songs and messages by other preachers.

****

August 25, 1995

254. The following taped song and message was played at **Aimee's mother's (Minnie) funeral**:

****

"Due to my recent heart-attack Aimee and I are sorry that we are unable to attend this memorial service in honor of Aimee's mother, Minnie.

"Two years ago this summer, Aimee and I spent nine days with her mother while she was in the hospital. During this time, as never before, we both were able to gain an insight into Minnie's heart and soul.

"Minnie placed her life and future in God's hands. When told of her condition and faced with the possibility of death, her reply was, "It's up to God." No fear, just trust and confidence in her Lord.

"On another occasion, as Aimee sat by her bed, her mother looked at her and said, 'Aimee, that other chair is more comfortable and will be better for your back.' In Minnie's weakened condition, her thoughts were not selfish or self-centered, but rather of concern for her daughter's comfort and well-being. This character trait was so strong in Minnie that even in her hour of need, others came first.

"Again, because Mom's rose garden was being neglected, she taught me (while she lay in her hospital bed) how to trim the rose bushes so they would bloom again that summer. Her instructions were: 'Albert, move down the rose stem to where there are five leaves and cut the stem just above that point.' Because of what she taught me I was able to trim some of her rose garden.

"Recently, just a few days before Minnie's death, when she was barely able to speak, the last words Aimee could hear her say were, 'Thank you.' Again, the inner person shone through; for she was the soul of graciousness."

****

HE THE PEARLY GATES WILL OPEN

(Albert)
1. Love Divne, so great and wondrous,
   Deep and mighty, pure, sublime!
   Coming from the heart of Jesus,
   Just the same thro' tests of time.

(Chrous)
   He the pearly gates will open,
   So that I may enter in,
   For He purchased my redemption
   And forgave me all my sin.

2. (Swedish, Verse & Chorus)

(Duet, Albert & Aimee)
3. Love Divine, so great and wondrous,
   All my sins He then forgave!
   I will sing His praise forever,
   For His blood, His pow'r to save.

(Chorus, Duet)

(Duet, Albert & Aimee)
4 In life's eventide, at twilight,
   At His door I'll knock and wait;
   By the precious love of Jesus
   I shall enter heaven's gate.

(Chorus, Duet)

By: Fred Blom
Translated:by
Nathaniel Carlson

****

"The Apostle Paul exhorted in Romans 13:7, 'Render therefore to all their dues: ... honour to whom honour.' Likewise the Apostle Peter declares, 'Honour all men...' (I Peter 2:17). While reviewing another pilgrim's life, we can be instructed and challenged.

"Minnie's spiritual warfare is over; the battle has been won. Victory through personal faith in Jesus Christ has again been demonstrated. For her, Biblical truth has become personal and eternal reality.

"The promises of God are not vain empty words. God's Word is true, He has prepared a place for those who love Him. Our Lord and Saviour, Jesus Christ said, 'I go to prepare a place for you... that where I am, there ye may be also.' There is comfort and consolation in God's Word, but there is also exhortation and challenge for those of us who remain.

"Our lives must be lived out each day. Each of us is still in the race for the prize 'of the high calling of God in Christ Jesus.' Each of us must still determine what the record of our lives shall be — whether the testimony of faithfulness in holy godly living — or that of compromise and failure. No one else can live our lives for us, no one else can make the multitude of daily decisions determining eternal destiny; all of these are personal and individual responsibilities.

"The Apostle declares in Hebrews 12:1,2: 'Wherefore seeing we also are compassed about with so great a cloud of witnesses, let us lay aside every weight, and the sin which doth so easily beset us, and let us run with patience the race that is set before us. Looking unto Jesus the author and finisher of our faith, who for the joy that was set before him endured the cross, despising the shame, and is set down at the right hand of the throne of God.'

"Minnie Filan, having now become part of that 'cloud of witnesses,' would urge each one here today to do what the Apostle exhorts. As I can attest from recent experience, we all are just a *breath away from eternity. Therefore, look unto Jesus; follow closely the 'Good Shepherd,' count every earthly thing of no value in comparison to knowing, loving, and serving Him.*

"Again, the Bible says, 'Be thou faithful unto death, and I will give thee a crown of life.' Each day draw near to Jesus, let nothing and no one come before or between you and the Saviour. Build your life each day on the solid rock, Christ Jesus. Then one day you too, by His grace, can hear these wonderful words spoken by our Saviour, '... Well done, good and faithful servant: . . enter thou into the joy of thy Lord.' (Matthew 25:21) AMEN!"

****

WHITED SEPULCHRES

AIMEE'S MOTHER - MINNIE FILAN in CASKET
CARRIED BY JONATHAN and MARK
AND AIMEE'S NEPHEWS

August 28, 1995

255. Aimee phoned the Northwest District office and asked to speak with Warren Bullock. The conversation was in part as follows:

Aimee, "Yes, may I speak to Brother Bullock, please?"
Ann, "May I help?"
Aimee, "He's not in? Do you know when he'll be in?"
Ann, "Tomorrow."
Aimee, "Tomorrow? This is Aimee Anderson, I would like to talk to him. Is he out of town?"
Ann, "Yes. How's your husband doing?"
Aimee, "Oh, he's coming along. I want to thank you for the flowers, they were beautiful."
Ann, "Will your husband be home tomorrow, if you are away?"
Aimee, "He won't be answering the phone."
Ann, "I see."
Aimee, "Do you know what that September 7th meeting, is about?"
Ann, "You have the letter."
Aimee, "It didn't say anything. Absolutely nothing. Both letters. There was nothing in either one of them."
Ann, "It's good for the brethren to get together and talk."
Aimee, "For what? This is what we would like to know."
Ann, "The investigation."
Aimee, "I thought they said they brought closure. Les Welk said this and others said it too. Les Welk said it and the last letter from General Council stated the same."
Ann, "Let me see if I can find the letter."
Aimee, "There was nothing in the letter at all. At this time, I just want to talk to Brother Bullock. I know they don't feel I should be the one to do the talking. Okay. I'll just plan on calling at 10:30. Okay? Thanks, Ann. Bye, bye."
Ann, "Bye."

August 29, 1995

256. Aimee phoned the Northwest District office and asked to speak with Warren Bullock. She tape-recorded her part of the conversation. She did not tape what Warren Bullock had to say, but made notes during the conversation and typed what he had to say shortly thereafter. The conversation was in part as follows:

Aimee, "Yes, is Brother Bullock in?"
Secretary, "Just a moment please."
Ann, "May I help you?"
Aimee, "Yes, this is Aimee. Is Brother Bullock available?"
Ann, "Yes, just a moment, please."
Aimee, "Thank you."
Warren, "Hello."
Aimee, "Hi there."
Warren, "How are you?"
Aimee, "Oh, doing fine. First, I want to say thank you for the beautiful flowers. We still have not mailed a thank you, but plan to do so."
Warren, "How's your husband doing?"
Aimee, "Well, he's coming along. He is supposed to have another exam by the doctor this week. He would like to know what this meeting is for and why is it needful? No reason is indicated in the letter. I know you don't care to talk to me, but that's the way it is."
Warren, "It's about the investigation."
Aimee, "Oh. Well, I thought they have already brought closure to the whole thing. That is what Les Welk said, to the whole thing. Are you talking about a new investigation?"
Warren, "The Assemblies of God by-laws allow for an investigation."
Aimee, "Like what? I thought you already brought closure to the whole thing."
Warren, "The by-laws require us to do an investigation of alleged violations of Assemblies

of God principles. We are not dealing with Rollin but with Brother Anderson."

Aimee, "Alleged violations against Assemblies of God principles?"

Warren, "Yes, we tried to do something months ago, but you circumvented us, went around us and over us to the General Council."

Aimee, "And so you're saying that the charges, there's nothing to any of those charges, they aren't a Violation against Assemblies of God principles? The charges against Rollin?"

Warren, "Rollin went to all the agencies and was cleared by all of them."

NOTE: We have been told that this is not true! We cannot understand how Rollin Carlson and some of the other Northwest District Officials can sleep at night while living and telling lies.

Aimee, "So in other words, - oh - okay. What are you going to do now, when the doctor says it's not medically advisable for him to meet with you?"

Warren, "I'd have to see that in writing."

Aimee, "Oh, the doctor said he would put it in writing."

Warren, "I'd have to see it."

Aimee, "That's why - - - -. This whole thing has about done him in. **This is the thing I do not understand, how you and the whole General Council could whitewash the charges that we have brought against Rollin Carlson. We could never begin to understand, because it is clearly evident there is so much evidence to prove, so much documentation to prove, our charges are correct. We cannot understand how you could whitewash that and then come against the one who brought the charges.** And both of us have brought everything, understand that?"

"**How could you turn around and say the one who brought the charges (Which should include me) is under investigation, instead of the one who really is guilty**? Now that I don't understand."

"And there's one other thing I don't understand, too. Maybe you can answer this. We both are very puzzled as to why you said you did not loan Rollin Carlson any money, (in 1993) and then did. We have never been able to understand why you said that?"

Warren, "I don't remember saying that, because I know we did loan him some money."

Aimee, "At the University you told us. You brought that up yourself. You said, 'If it will make you feel better, Rollin came to us and wanted to borrow money (in 1993) and we turned him down.' After that, the documents were put in our hands, and we called you. Remember that conversation, when we asked, 'We thought you told us, you didn't loan Rollin any money?' You said, 'It was on the original sale.' You never wanted to sit down and go over the original charges. There are a lot of things we don't understand."

Warren, "You brought charges against me."

NOTE: We believe this was a personal confession coming from Warren Bullock as to why he was fighting so hard, to cover the ungodly and illegal/criminal activity regarding Rollin Carlson and the Care-Net Ranch phony ministry.

Aimee, "But before that, no one seemed interested in ever sitting down, talking to us, and going over anything. I guess there is nothing more to say then. **What you are saying is that Brother Anderson is under investigation.** Is that what you're saying, and not Rollin, but Brother Anderson, because you feel he's violated Assemblies of God principles?"

Warren, "Yes."

Aimee, "Like what? **Because he brought charges against someone who has done illegal things?** Is that what you are saying? We will try to get something in writing to you and we plan on sending a thank you. It's quite evident that you are saying, as far as you are concerned and the General Council is concerned, the charges are over?"

Warren, "Yes, Rollin has been cleared. Rollin went to all the agencies and was cleared by all of them."

NOTE: If so, why the need of an on-going (Criminal) "Grand Jury Case?"

Aimee, "Do you really believe before God that you did what was right?"
Warren, "Yes."
Aimee, "And you feel he is innocent of all. Do you feel this is a legitimate Care-Net ministry over here, this ranch?"
Warren, "In the beginning, it was."

NOTE: More falsehoods! From the very beginning, the entire Care-Net Ranch Ministry (Home Missions) for needy men and/or called the Rehabilitation/Transitional/Housing Ministry for needy men (Kittitas, Washington) was <u>never</u> legally approved by Kittitas County!

Aimee, "Was it ever, with the County?"
Warren, "Yes."

NOTE: <u>The lying continues</u>.

Aimee, "You really, truly believe that? You are going to find out that what we have said is one hundred per cent true. I am sorry that I have to say that. I am very, very sorry, very sorry. I am very sorry, because, I cannot believe. See, what you have chosen to do, is - you have chosen to believe Rollin and disbelieve us. Without getting in there and digging out the truth yourself. And that is what makes us really feel bad. You have chosen to take one man's word against another. In addition, the Bible does not even teach that. In other words we do not understand why you did't get in there and do something yourself? It would not have hurt you. I'm not being disrespectful."
"My husband feels you owe me an apology for talking to me the way you did in the District

office, (June 7, 1994). He said, 'No man should ever talk to my wife that way.'"

"I'm not trying to be disrespectful, but I believe before God, it was your duty to come over here, and check with the County yourself, instead of taking one man's word against another. Someday you are going to find it out, I know you will. It will be too late then. I am sorry, I really am. I have nothing against you, I have never had anything against you. (Aimee meant by this statement, she did not hold any personal grudge against Warren Bullock.) I love your wife. I am sorry this has happened. I should let you go, and we will see what happens. Bye-bye."

Some of the strange and/or false things Warren Bullock said to Aimee in their phone conversation are as follows:

1. The by-laws require us to do an investigation of alleged violations of Assembly of God principles. We are not dealing with Rollin but with Brother Anderson.
2. Rollin went to all the agencies and was cleared by all of them.
3. In the beginning, Care-Net was a ministry but not now.
4. When Aimee told Warren, "The doctor said it is not medically advisable for Albert to go to the September 7, 1995, Executive Presbyters meeting," Warren responded, "I'd have to see it in writing!"

August 31, 1995

257. Albert went in for his first treadmill test and follow-up examination by Doctor Althouse. Albert is gaining strength. The Andersons are so grateful to God for giving them Doctor Althouse.

August 31, 1995

   258. A Sympathy card was postmarked August 31, 1995, and mailed to Al and Aimee Anderson. The handwritten message read as follows:

                ****

        Aimee and Al

        So sorry to hear of the death of your mother. Our love and prayers are with you. May you know God's comfort.

                Warren and Judi Bullock

                ****

September 1, 1995

259. A letter postmarked September 2, was mailed to Dr. Warren D. Bullock with a copy mailed to Albert E. Anderson, from Doctor Ralph G. Althouse. It read as follows:

****

STEVENS CARDIOLOGY GROUP

Stephen R. Yarnall, M.D.
Cardiology/Internal Medicine

Stephen T. Hubbard, M.D.
Cardiology/Internal Medicine

Richard A Crone, M.D.
Cardiology/Internal Medicine

Ralph G. Althouse, M.D.
Cardiology/Internal Medicine

September 1, 1995

Dr. Warren D. Bullock
District Superintendent
Northwest District Council of the Assembly of God
7001 220th Street S.W., Suite 101
Mountlake Terrace, WA 98043-2164

    RE: Albert E. Anderson

Dear Dr. Bullock:

I am taking care of Mr. Anderson following his myocardial infarction. In order to recuperate fully from this recent heart attack, I have instructed him not to take part in any business or church related activities over the next months. I will see him again at the end of the year for repeat treadmill testing and reassess his suitability to return to full time work at that time.

Yours faithfully,

Ralph G. Althouse, M.D., F.A.C.C.

RA/ecm

ALBERT & AIMEE ANDERSON

CC: Albert E. Anderson

September 05, 1995

   260. Albert and Aimee mailed a letter to Warren Bullock that read as follows:

****

REV. ALBERT E. ANDERSON
– – – Ave.
Ellensburg, Washington 98926

September 05, 1995

Rev. Warren D. Bullock, Superintendent
7001 220th Street, S.W., Suite 101
Mountlake Terrace, WA 98043-2164

Dear Brother Bullock:

   Christian Greetings!

   We are in receipt of your July 14, 1995 and July 28, 1995 letters. Your invitation for Albert Anderson to meet with the Executive Presbyters, per these two letters, is being declined at this time, as the doctor said, "It's not medically advisable." Also doctor Althouse said he would send you a letter stating this fact.

   Will you please mail to me the purpose and agenda for requesting my meeting with the Executive Presbyters? I would appreciate this very much.

   Thank you!

Sincerely,

Albert E. and Aimee D. Anderson

AEA/ada

Enclosure: Thank you note!

==

EVANGELIST - BIBLE TEACHER - PASTOR
SPECIAL EVENT SPEAKER

****

(The thank you note enclosed in the September 05 letter reads as follows:)

****

REV. ALBERT E. ANDERSON
− − − Ave.
Ellensburg, Washington 98926

September 5, 1995

THANK YOU!   THANK YOU!

Warren and Judi Bullock
Les and Darcie Welk
Rollin and Helen Carlson
The Northwest District Office Staff

FOR

Your prayers, cards, and the beautiful flowers!

Sincerely,

Albert E. and Aimee D. Anderson

==
========
EVANGELIST - BIBLE TEACHER - PASTOR
SPECIAL EVENT SPEAKER

****

September 12, 1995

261. Warren Bullock's response to Albert and Aimee's September 5th letter, with a letter postmarked September 13, 1995, which read as follows:

****

Northwest District Council of the Assemblies of God
Warren D. Bullock, Superintendent
Leslie E. Welk, Assistant Superintendent
Rollin J. Carlson, Secretary-Treasurer

September 12, 1995

Rev. and Mrs. Al Anderson
— — — Ave.
Ellensburg, WA 98926

Dear Brother and Sister Anderson:

Warm Christian greetings!

Thank you for your letter as well as the letter from your physician. We shared them with our Executive Presbytery. Our prayers certainly are with you that God will give you a full and complete recovery.

You asked for what items would be under discussion should the Executive Presbytery wish for you to come in at a later date. Those items would be the same as I discussed with Aimee over the phone.

May the Lord richly bless you, friends.

Sincerely,

Dr. Warren D. Bullock
District Superintendent

WDB:at

WHITED SEPULCHRES

NOTE: It is indeed strange that Warren Bullock does not seem to want to put in writing the Northwest District Council Executive Presbyters' and District officers' concerns and intentions, which in phone conversations said they were now "dealing with Albert's credentials" and not the "charges of illegal activity" that Albert and Aimee brought against Rollin.

Apparently, the Northwest District Council of the Assemblies of God officers and presbyters are not pleased with Albert and Aimee exposing the alleged illegal activities of Rollin Carlson and The Care-Net Outreach ranch at Kittitas, Washington; as it involves so many of the Northwest District Council of the Assemblies of God officials and the National General Council of the Assemblies of God officials.

October 15, 1995

262. Warren Bullock was the guest preacher at the Kittitas Assembly of God.

October 22, 1995

263. Rollin Carlson was the guest preacher at the Ellensburg First Assembly of God.

October 23, 1995

264. The Yakima Sectional Fellowship meeting was held at the Ellensburg First Assembly of God. James Stephens, pastor of the Kittitas Assembly of God was the afternoon speaker. Rollin Carlson, Secretary/Treasurer of the Northwest District was the evening speaker.

In the early evening Jerry and Phyllis Marchel came to the Andersons' home where they shared the following information:

ALBERT & AIMEE ANDERSON

Jerry Marchel had attended the afternoon fellowship meeting and evening dinner, when the following conversations took place between Jerry Marchel and Don Strong and between Jerry and Rollin Carlson:

Jerry, "Don, Rollin still hasn't paid that chip bill."
Don, "Rollin says he's not going to pay it because he doesn't owe it."
Jerry, "I wouldn't be telling you this if he didn't owe it."
Jerry Marchel had hauled several loads of wood chips to the Care-Net Ranch in 1993. Following is the bill he referred to:

CANYON LOG HOMES
Route 3, Box 395
Ellensburg, WA 98926
(509) 968-3638

NAME Randy Bale
Date 1/22/93
Qty. Description
5 loads chips del by Jerry

	Price	Amount
	30.00	150.00
Tax		11.25
Total		161.25

Received by Care-Net Care of Rollin Carlson - unpaid No.0000209.
All claims and returned goods must be accompanied by this bill.
Thank you

****

Jerry stepped out of the meal line to wait for Rollin, at which time the following conversation took place:
Jerry, "Rollin, you still haven't paid that chip bill."

Rollin, "I only received it a couple of days ago."

Jerry, "I gave it to you three weeks ago." (It was Albert and Aimee's understanding that Canyon Log Homes had also mailed the bill to the Care-Net Outreach.)

Rollin, "I turned it in a few days ago and maybe they've already paid it."

Jerry, "I wouldn't be telling you except that it has not been paid. God's going to hold you responsible for the damage that's been done."

After dinner Rollin motioned for Jerry to come over and sit by him, at which time the following conversation took place:

Rollin, "Did you get enough to eat?"

Jerry, "No."

Rollin then pulled out of his pocket two one hundred dollar bills ($200.00) and handed them to Jerry along with his own personal card, that read on one side as follows:

>Northwest District Council of
>The Assemblies of God
>Rollin J. Carlson, Secretary-Treasurer,
>7001 220th Street SW, Suite 101,
>Mountlake Terrace, WA 98043-2164
>PHONE: (206) 640-0222
>FAX: (206) 640-0333

>***************

The other side of the card Rollin Carlson wrote the following information and instructions:

>200. - Cash
>mail change and receipt marked
>Paid to address on the card.
>Thank you. Rollin

>***************

Rollin then told Jerry, "I went to the bank and cashed a check. This is my own personal money. I will get reimbursed for it."

A little while later Jerry told Don, "Rollin paid the bill."

Don responded, "Praise the Lord." Earlier Don told Jerry that Rollin was not going to pay the bill because Rollin said he didn't owe it and now he tells Jerry, "Praise the Lord" because he hears that Rollin paid the bill.

Jerry told the Andersons, "I considered standing up and exposing it publicly." Maybe Rollin had an idea Jerry might do just that and rather than risk it, he paid the bill even though he paid it in a very questionable way.

Jerry's story was verified by Bob Cousart, who told the Andersons that Rollin told him about it.

October 24, 1995

265. Aimee talked to both Tom and Jeanne about their leaving the ranch and moving to Montana where Tom's folks live. They both seemed relieved to be through as of November 1, 1995.

October 26, 1995

266. Jerry told the Andersons that the Real Estate agent said Rollin and the Care-Net Outreach were selling the ranch because the County wouldn't allow them to have the Care-Net Outreach there.

NOTE: Yet, the Northwest District Officials and the General Council Officials will not acknowledge to Albert and Aimee Anderson that their charges against Rollin Carlson and the Care-Net Outreach are correct. Nor will they acknowledge to the churches and ministers that the Care-Net Outreach ranch ministry at Kittitas, Washington, was an illegal operation. Nor will they acknowledge to the ministers and churches that the charges the Andersons brought against Rollin Carlson, The Care-Net Outreach, Frank Cole, Warren Bullock, Les Welk, Elmer Kirschman, Dale Carpenter, and Don Strong, were/are true and accurate.

October 27, 1995

267. Bob Cousart told the Andersons, "Rollin said he asked Jerry if the chip bill was paid. He said he just received the bill a few days ago. He told us he went to the bank and cashed a check and paid the chip bill with his own personal money."

QUESTION: Is this the manner in which a minister of the Gospel and a District Officer should conduct the financial affairs of God's Kingdom? The office of District Secretary/Treasurer is an awesome responsibility and demands the highest level of integrity.

October 28, 1995

268. Aimee had the following conversation with Tom and Jeanne Mahon:

Aimee, "Hi. So you are almost ready to leave?"

Tom, "Hi. Yes, we are getting ready."

Aimee, "May I speak with Jeanne?"

Tom, "No, she's not here. (Pause) She's outside."

Aimee, "Oh, now Tom, I'm sure! She's outside in the dark all by herself?" (About this time Albert picked up the other phone.)

Tom, "No, she's not. I told her next time Aimee calls, she cannot talk to you. Rollin said he heard from the Andersons that he's run us off."

Aimee, "I didn't tell Rollin that. I haven't even talked to Rollin about it. May I talk to Jeanne a little bit and tell her good-bye?"

Tom, "Okay."

Aimee and Jeanne had a very brief conversation and said their sweet, but sorrowful, good-byes. Then Jeanne said Tom wanted to speak to her again.

Tom, "I'm sorry I lied to you." Tom told Aimee several times that he was sorry he lied to her. Aimee accepted his apology.

Tom, "Thank you for praying for us."

Tom and Albert and Aimee said their sad good-byes.

NOTE: Isn't it a breath of fresh air to hear a common layman quickly confess, he lied and ask for forgiveness? Please contrast this with the behavior of some of these <u>professed "Godly" leaders of the Assemblies of God, who speak one lie after another, with seemingly no twinge of conscience</u>.

> "And herein do I exercise myself, to have always a conscience void of offence toward God, and toward men."
> (Acts 24:16)

Failure to follow Paul's example will ultimately produce a "Seared Conscience."

October 31, 1995

269. Albert and Aimee were told that Rollin Carlson and the Care-Net Outreach ranch owed several bills around the area. Aimee phoned one place and asked the bookkeeper, "Does Rollin and the Care-Net Outreach Ranch owe over one thousand dollars?" She answered, "Oh, yes, several times over that." Aimee asked, "How old is the bill?" The bookkeeper answered, "Since June, 1995. He said he was going to come in and take care of things but never showed up. If he does this with us, I'm sure he does it with others." The Andersons were finding out that, this last statement was very true.

November 29, 1995

270. Aimee phoned the same company mentioned above, and was told, "Rollin came in today and paid some on the bill." Is this the kind of testimony Northwest District officials are giving to the world? What kind of example are they setting for other ministers to follow?

December 13, 1995

271. Very early this morning, while driving over to the Care-Net Ranch, Rollin Carlson phoned Jerry Marchel. He asked Jerry if he would bring his tractor and loader to the ranch and help him haul some machinery, cattle, etc. Even though Jerry has not approved of some of Rollin's wrong dealings, he felt he should help him, and answered, "Yes." He understood Rollin's request was for one or two hours. Instead, Jerry worked eight straight hours, 9:00 A.M. to 5:00 P.M., using his own tractor and loader. This, after the shameful way, Rollin and other Northwest District officials have treated him, in relation to the Kittitas Assembly of God conflict.

Shortly before 5:00 P.M., when checking up on his father, Chris Marchel let Rollin Carlson know he was appalled at his gall, to ask his father for help, to move the machinery, cattle, etc., from one section of the Care-Net Ranch to another section, after the way he (Rollin) had mistreated his Dad.

Chris related to Aimee, the following conversation:

Chris, "Have you seen my Dad?"

Rollin, "Your dad?"

Chris, "Yah, Jerry."

Rollin, "He just took a load across the hill."

Chris, "I hope you guys are going to pay him for the work he is doing today."

Rollin, "That's none of your business, that's between your dad and me."

Chris, "That's where you are wrong. That's my Dad and that makes it my business. I can't believe the gall you have, asking my Dad for help. You see that's the kind of man my Dad is."

December 14, 1995

272. Jerry worked several more hours, hauling at the Care-Net ranch, for Rollin.

A few days later, Jerry received a check for, "Tractor/time=moving expense," from The Care-Net Outreach. The December 15, 1995 check was signed by William Handley. The return address on the envelope was (From Rollin Carlson) "RJC, 2715 Everett Ave., Everett, WA."
With the check, the following note was enclosed: "Jerry: Thanks for your help. I really appreciate your time and tractor. Rollin Carlson."

December 15, 1995

273. A STATUTORY WARRANTY DEED was filed with the Kittitas County Title Company. This document, "conveys and warrants to LARRY SHOPBELL and PATRICIA SHOPBELL"... from, "THE CARE-NET OUTREACH, a Washington non-profit corporation. By William R. Handley, President ... By Gaylord M. Pearson, Secretary."

According to the treasurer's office, apparently all of the Care-Net property was sold to Shopbells except about five (5) acres and the original house that Bales and Mahons lived in. This would be the residential house with the garage addition that was used as a community room for the rehab men.

(Sometime after the alleged illegal activities of the Care-Net Outreach Ranch at Kittitas, Washington were exposed, the ranch property was put up for sale.)

December 15, 1995

274. A REAL ESTATE EXCISE TAX AFFIDAVIT, filed with the Kittitas County Treasurer, reads in part as follows: "SELLER/GRANTOR - THE CARE-NET OUTREACH, a Washington non-profit corporation, 2715 Everett Avenue, Everett, WA, 98201 - BUYER/GRANTEE - LARRY SHOPBELL and PATRICIA SHOPBELL, husband and wife, 15215 212th St. SE, Monroe, WA, 98272 ... Date of Document 12/11/95 - Gross Sale Price $390,000.00 - (less) Personal Property (deduct) $5,850.00 - Taxable Sale Price

$384,150.00 - Excise Tax State 1.28 $4,917.12 - Local (tax) $960.38 - Total (tax) $5,877.50."

Apparently, the Personal Property, $5,850.00, was moved on December 13-14, 1995, over to the unsold (about) five (5) acres, as noted above in #271 and #272.

December 26, 1995

275. Another **"Deed of Trust"** was discovered in the Kittitas County files. It reads in part as follows:

"This Deed of Trust, made this first day of July, 1993, between THE CARE-NET OUTREACH, a Washington non-profit corporation, GRANTOR, whose address is 2715 Everett Avenue, Everett, WA 98201 — CHICAGO TITLE INSURANCE COMPANY, a corporation, TRUSTEE, whose address is 1800 Columbia Center, 701 Fifth Avenue, Seattle, Washington 98104 and THE NORTHWEST DISTRICT COUNCIL OF THE ASSEMBLIES OF GOD, a Washington non-profit corporation whose address is P.O. BOX 699, KIRKLAND, WA 98083, witnesseth: Grantor hereby bargains, sells and conveys to Trustee in Trust, with power of sale, the following described real property in Kittitas County, Washington: ... This deed is for the purpose of securing performance of each agreement of grantor herein contained, and payment of the sum of ($30,000.00) Thirty Thousand and no/100 — Dollars ... THE CARE-NET OUTREACH, Rollin J. Carlson, President." The file number is 565116, found in Vol. 348, page 763.

This is the third Deed of Trust that has been found, between the Care-Net Outreach and The Northwest District. May 20, 1991, Deed of Trust for $135,000.00, April 1, 1993, Deed of Trust for $350,000.00 and July 1, 1993, Deed of Trust for $30,000.00. The total for the three is $515,000.00.

A **FULL RECONVEYANCE** of the May 20, 1991, $135,000.00 was filed on April 19, 1993. File number 558742, Vol. 341, page 978. In the Northwest District Church Loan Fund Prospectus, dated August 4, 1994, under EXHIBIT A, entitled CURRENT BORROWERS, The Care-Net Outreach, is listed with two outstanding loans from the Northwest District Church Loan Fund.

Apparently, these two outstanding loans are the April 1, 1993, $350,000.00, Deed of Trust, to the Northwest District, and the July 1, 1993, $30,00.00, Deed of Trust, to the Northwest District. To date, our search has not produced a reconveyance to the above two loans.

In conclusion, some serious issues arise. Financial problems were surfacing in the Northwest District as early as 1991; yet on May 20, 1991, a Deed of Trust for **$135,000.00**; another Deed of Trust on April 1, 1993, for **$350,000.00**; and another Deed of Trust on July 1, 1993, for **$30,000.00**, were executed between The Care-Net Outreach (ranch) and the Northwest District - **evidently from the Assemblies of God Northwest District Church Loan Fund.**

The stated specific purpose of the Northwest District Church Loan Fund according to the prospectus is, "... to provide financing for Assemblies of God church property acquisition and construction within the Northwest District in the United States ... The church construction activities financed through the issuance of Promissory Notes (the "Notes") described in this Prospectus, include capital expansion projects, particularly the construction and renovation of Northwest District **sovereign church** facilities and the financing of sites upon which new mission church facilities can be constructed, and establishment of new Northwest District congregations."

Significantly, The Care-Net Outreach Ranch at Kittitas, Washington, did not receive monies for the construction of a church building, nor is there any indication that the acquisition of the property was for the purpose of building a church. **Clearly, church loan fund monies were used in Violation of the stated purpose.** Yet the Care-Net Outreach has all along been promoted by Rollin Carlson and the Northwest District officials, as a valid Home Missions satellite church, worthy of charitable contributions. **This is <u>unethical</u>, <u>dishonest</u>, and surely a <u>gross Violation of Biblical, civil, (County, State, and Federal) and Assemblies of God principles</u>**.

Who is going to do the investigation of the Northwest District of the Assemblies of God officials and presbyters, who have clearly violated Biblical, civil, and Assemblies of God principles, when the church has failed? **It seems apparent that there has been an obstruction of justice in The Assemblies of God, at both the District and National level.**

The Bible records that God often used those "outside" to chasten and correct His people when they refused to walk in obedience to His will. **Sadly, God too often finds it necessary to use the civil authorities in this dispensation to judge His church because the church has miserably failed to cleanse itself.** This ought never to be, but **God will have a church "without spot, or wrinkle" by whatever means is necessary.**

With no malice or hatred toward any Northwest District Official nor General Council Official, our heart cry is that the passion of the church today (including the Assemblies of God) will be for righteousness rather than worldly success; approval before God more than acceptance by the world; and "... <u>holiness, without which no man shall see the Lord.</u>"

****

CLEANSE ME

Search me, O God, and know my heart today;
Try me, O Saviour, know my thoughts, I pray;
See if there be some wicked way in me:
Cleanse me from ev'ry sin, and set me free.

I praise Thee, Lord, for cleansing me from sin:
Fulfill Thy word, and make me pure within;
Fill me with fire, where once I burned
with shame:
Grant my desire to magnify Thy name.

Lord, take my life, and make it wholly Thine:
Fill my poor heart with Thy great love divine;
Take all my will, my passion, self and pride;
I now surrender: Lord, in me abide.

O Holy Ghost, revival comes from Thee:
Send a revival, start the work in me:
Thy Word declares Thou wilt supply our need:
For blessing now, O Lord, I humbly plead.

By: J. Edwin Orr

****

Section 4.

LAW OF THE HARVEST

WHITED SEPULCHRES

"Search me, O God, and know my heart:
try me, and know my thoughts:
And see if there be any wicked way in me,
And lead me in the way everlasting."
...Psalms 139:23,24

"Examine yourselves, whether ye be in the faith;
prove your own selves..."
...II Corinthians 13:5a

"But let a man examine himself..."
...I Corinthians 11:27a

"Sanctify them through thy truth:
thy word is truth."

...John 17:17

LAW OF THE HARVEST

The Bible teaches that the Church is a living organism with Jesus Christ as it's head. Though comprised of many people, yet, it is one body.

> *"And hath put all things under his feet, and gave him to be the head over all things to the church,"*
>
> *"Which is his body, the fullness of him that filleth all in all."*
> (Ephesians 1:22-23)
>
> *"And he is the head of the body, the church: who is the beginning, the firstborn from the dead; that in all things he might have the preeminence."*
> (Colossians 1:18)
>
> *"So we, being many, are one body in Christ, and every one members one of another."*
> (Romans 12:5)

While claiming allegiance to Jesus Christ -- and relationship to one another -- we Christians often forget the potential power of influence for good or for ill within our grasp. The root problem, of course, is our ingrained selfish motives, intents, and desires.

Like it or not, our lives do affect others; both in the Christian community and also the world outside the church. We often, in fact, are the only Bible some people read. The poet has captured this truth in simple yet profound words.

****

****

"Isn't it strange that princes and kings,
And clowns that caper in sawdust rings,
And common folk like you and me
Are builders for eternity?

To each is given a set of tools,
A shapeless mass and a book of rules,
And each must be 'ere time be flown,
A stumbling block or a stepping stone."
...Author Unknown

It is inescapable, our lives do influence others -- Christians and non-Christians. Each day we are sowing seeds which ultimately produce a harvest. The law is rigid and certain.

> *"Be not deceived; God is not mocked: for whatsoever a man soweth, that shall he also reap."*
> (Galatians 6:7)

How we live leaves a telling mark on those about us. It is true that we are to be witnesses for Christ, but too often this responsibility is relegated only to our words. In reality, it is the things we do, the way we live, the manner of our relationship with "the butcher," "the baker," "the candlestick maker," that makes us a "stumbling block" or a "stepping stone." All too often, little emphasis is placed on this aspect of Christian responsibility.

Jesus spoke sobering words about "offending" a little child.

By the strong words He used, offending a little child must be one of the greatest sins.

> *"But whoso shall offend one of these little ones which believe in me, it were better for him that a millstone were hanged about his neck, and that he were drowned in the depth of the sea."*
>
> *"Woe unto the world because of offences! For it must needs be that offences come; but woe to that man by whom the offence cometh!"*
> (Matthew 18:6-7)

However, while being careful about not offending "little people," we must also be on guard not to offend the "weak" believer or the "babe-in-Christ."

Paul, the Apostle, admonished his son in-the-Lord, Timothy,

> *"Let no man despise thy youth; but be thou an example of the believers, in word, in conversation, in charity, in spirit, in faith, in purity."*
> (I Timothy 4:12)

The word example here means, "model, image, ideal, or pattern." "Conversation" is the word "behavior" and "charity" means "love." While these words were written to a spiritual leader, surely there is responsibility here for every believer. We cannot escape it, our lives are on display, and God has ordained it so. Again, Jesus said,

> *"Ye are the light of the world. A city that is set on an hill cannot be hid."*
>
> *"Neither do men light a candle, and put it under a bushel, but on a candlestick; and it giveth light unto all that are in the house."*
>
> *"Let your light so shine before men, that they may see your good works, and glorify your Father which is in heaven."*
> (Matthew 5:14-16).

Clearly, Jesus is referring here to the kind of lives we live before an unbelieving world. **The Christian is to be different. Oh, how many believers rebel at the mere thought that they must live by a higher and exalted standard — separate from the ways and philosophy of a Christ-rejecting world.** An old adage has it something like this: "What you are speaks so loudly, I can't hear a word you're saying." Sadly, I have heard fellow believers say they would rather do business any day with a sinner than with a Christian. Such a testimony and way of life sorely grieves the Holy Spirit!

It is Paul who adds to what Jesus said in His sermon on the mount which again is directed to followers of the Lord:

> *"Do all things without murmurings and disputings:*
>
> *"That ye may be blameless and harmless, the sons of God, without rebuke, in the midst of a crooked and perverse nation, among whom ye shine as lights in the world;"*
> (Philippians 2:14-15)

Blameless...harmless! What a testimony. In the things we say, in the things we do, let us at all times seek to model the life of Jesus. The chief priests and elders sought false witness against Jesus, but could find none. Mark simply says, "their witness agreed not together." He was crucified nonetheless, but not because of any wrongdoing on His part. As Peter declares,

> *"Who did not sin, neither was guile found in his mouth."*
> (I Peter 2:22)

Let this be our passion and goal, "blameless, harmless," even though we may suffer for doing/being right in God's sight.

Again, Peter adds,

> *"For it is better, if the will of God be so, that ye suffer for well doing, than for evil doing."*
> (I Peter 3:17)

What peace, what rejoicing, when we know we have lived above reproach before God and man.

Paul adds his personal goal when he says,

> *"And herein do I exercise myself, to have always a conscience void of offence toward God and toward men."*
>
> (Acts 24:16)

There is a time and a place for verbal testimony. We are to "confess" Jesus Christ as our Lord and Saviour. The confession of our lips is a divine requirement. But what about our truthfulness or lack of it? What about our business dealings; are they honest in every respect? Or are we devious in order to **"get the best of the deal?"** Will our conduct be such that lost souls will long to drink from the same living water that satisfies our thirst? Or will they say, "If that's what it means to be a Christian, I will never be one?"

Should any believer want to know what is expected of him; how he should live, what he should do or not do, let him ask a sinner — he knows! But God forbid that we should need to be told by an unbeliever. The Word of God is very clear, "the book" will tell us in no uncertain terms. Usually the problem is not so much lack of knowledge, as failure to apply the truth.

Jesus strongly warned His disciples against the leaven of hypocrisy; that is, pretending to be something they were not. Why? The reason is direct and simple,

> *"For there is nothing covered, that shall not be revealed; neither hid, that shall not be known."*
>
> (Luke 12:2)

Exposure is certain, whether in this life or in eternity; therefore, so live,

> *"And now, little children, abide in Him; that, when he shall appear, we may have*

> *confidence, and not be ashamed before him at his coming."*
> (I John 2:28)

There may be many reasons why there is too often a separation between what we say and how we live. Let us consider some of the possible causes for lack of spiritual integrity.

Fundamental to our relationship with God is the understanding that we are in a spiritual battle where eternal destinies are at stake. The enemy of our souls labors to cause believers to water down or compromise eternal truth. He is the master of deception and skilled at mixing a bit of error with a good deal of truth. Anything in order to turn the children of God from the "narrow way" to the "broad way."

An age-old doctrine, which rears its ugly head periodically, is the lie of **Antinomianism**. This word is formed from two Greek words, anti (against) and nomos (law); thus literally "against law." Though various forms of this false teaching had been around for centuries, it was the well known reformer, Martin Luther, who first coined the term.

In practical terms, **Antinomianism** teaches that faith is everything. Because our salvation is by grace through faith, obedience to the commands of Christ is not necessarily required. In application, this means that one who is saved may continue in sin, and possess eternal life with no fear of divine judgment. To state it differently, this means that living a holy, sinless life before God is optional for the believer. We personally heard it preached from the pulpit (several times in the year 2000 and also, preached and strongly contended for in the year 2001) that Christians are **"Sinners and Saints"** at the same time. While it may be true that believers on occasion do sin, living a sinful life, habitually sinning, is never the will or plan of God. Consider what John the beloved Apostle declares:

> *"My little children, these things write I unto you, that ye sin not. And if any man sin, we have an advocate with the Father, Jesus Christ the righteous."*
> (I John 2:1)

Note the words, "if any man sin." Let us say it differently, yet with the same meaning: "Do not sin." However, if, or when sin is committed, we do have an advocate, Jesus Christ. Again, in I John 3:4-10, John makes it very clear that **"practicing" sin, living a life of sin, is inconsistent, yes, impossible, for one who is "born of God."** In this passage, John is not speaking of never committing an "act" of sin, but that it is impossible for one "born of God" to habitually practice sin.

The Apostle Paul agrees with John when he says in the book of Romans:

> *"What shall we say then? Shall we continue in sin, that grace may abound?"*
>
> *"God forbid. How shall we, that are dead to sin, live any longer therein?"* . .
>
> *"...Let not sin therefore reign in your mortal body, that ye should obey it in the lusts thereof."*
>
> *"Neither yield ye your members as instruments of unrighteousness unto sin: but yield yourselves unto God, as those that are alive from the dead, and your members as instruments of righteousness unto God."*
> (Romans 6:1, 2, 12-13)

As Christians, we too often forget that the strong statements of the Apostles regarding sin with its consequent judgments were written to **BELIEVERS**, members of the churches of that day. Paul even goes so far as to say in his letter to the Galatian church (after naming the works of the flesh),

> **"That they which do such things shall not inherit the kingdom of God."**
> (Galatians 5:21b)

Risking redundancy, to whom was Paul writing such terrible words? The sinner? True, "they which do such things" includes the sinner, but Paul here was addressing **CHRISTIANS**.

Was Paul then saying that "professing" believers who practice sinning, or to use his words, "do such things," "shall not inherit the kingdom of God?" Exactly that! Yet, those teaching and believing the false notion of **Antinomianism** would have us believe that it really does not matter how you live, or what you do, just so long as you have "faith."

It was exactly at this point that Jesus was at odds with the Scribes and Pharisees of His day.

> **"Then spake Jesus to the multitude, and to his disciples,**
>
> **"Saying, The scribes and Pharisees sit in Moses' seat:**
>
> **"All therefore whatsoever they bid you observe, that observe and do; but do not ye after their works: for they say, and do not."**
> (Matthew 23:1,2)

Where they represented Moses, the Pharisees were right on target, teaching sound doctrine which the disciples were to follow. But they were not to "do" after their works, for they taught one thing and did another. And for this evil — being unrepentant — they were condemned. Matthew 23:13-36 contains the strongest censure by Jesus of the Scribes and Pharisees. Some of his parting words to them were, "...how can ye escape the damnation of hell?" (Matthew 23:33b)

The answer to Jesus' question is found in simply turning from sin to the Saviour to walk in obedience to Him. This business of obeying Biblical commands is disturbing to many modern, as Finney called them, "professors of religion." But Jesus was very clear on this issue as well.

> *"If ye love me, keep my commandments." (Some translations read, "ye will keep my commandments."*
>
> *"He that hath my commandments, and keepeth them, he it is that loveth me ..."*
> (John 14:15, 21a)

Luke quotes Jesus as saying,

> *"And why call ye me, Lord, Lord, and do not the things which I say?"*
> (Luke 6:46)

Good question. Moreover, Jesus says some of the most awful words he ever uttered in His Sermon on the Mount:

> *"Not every one that saith unto me, Lord, Lord, shall enter into the kingdom of heaven; but he that doeth the will of my Father which is in heaven."*
>
> *"Many will say to me in*

> *that day, Lord, Lord, have we not prophesied in thy name? and in thy name have cast out devils? and in thy name done many wonderful works?"*
>
> *"And then will I profess unto them, I never knew you: depart from me, ye that work iniquity."*
> (Matthew 7:21-23)

Will more awful words ever be uttered? The tragedy of such words necessarily being uttered is indescribable. But as sure as Jesus said these words, such judgment will come upon those who have "believed," yet did not "DO" His will. Yes, we are saved by grace through faith — human merit or goodness can never avail. Yet, it is equally true that saving faith will always be expressed through obedience to the commands of God and the precepts of the moral law. The reformer, Melanchthon, said it clearly and exactly, "It is faith, alone, which saves; but the faith that saves is not alone." Much more could be said on this subject; the New Testament abounds with admonitions in the Epistles to believers, requiring obedience to clear commands of the living God.

It is not our purpose here to discourage any "babe-in-Christ" or any honest struggling Christian longing to do all the will of God. And there are many such. However, we do live in an age of exceeding iniquity with the worldly thinking, standards, and philosophies daily bombarding the believer in Christ. And Jesus said,

> **"And because iniquity shall abound, the love of many shall wax cold."**
> (Matthew 24:12)

Thus, we are all warned of our need to stay close to the written Word of God and the living Word, Jesus Christ. Love for Jesus Christ must be more than mere lip service; there must, as well, be a sincere willingness to do, to obey, and to keep His Word.

Once more, in His sermon on the mount Jesus declared that,

> *"Therefore whosoever heareth these sayings of mine, and doeth them, I will liken him unto a wise man, which built his house upon a rock."*
> (Matthew 7:24)

Note especially the word, "doeth," which speaks of response and of obedience. Believing, but not doing, is to build our spiritual houses upon the sand, "...and it fell: and great was the fall of it." (Matthew 7:27)

The grace of God is sufficient for every person to live a life acceptable to God. Victory over sin is promised to the believing, obedient child of God. Our Lord is not a "taskmaster," nor is He unjust. Our heavenly Father is fully aware of the temptations and pressures which daily press in upon the twentieth and twenty-first century believer. But, nowhere in the Scripture are we given the slightest hint that God is a respecter of persons; in fact, just the opposite, for the Bible states emphatically, "God is no respecter persons."

> *"Then Peter opened his mouth, and said, Of a truth I perceive that God is no respecter of persons:"*
> (Acts 10:34)

> *"For there is no respect of persons with God."*
> (Romans 2:11)

> *"And, ye masters, do the same things unto them, forbearing*

> ***threatening: knowing that your Master also is in heaven; neither is there respect of persons with him."***
>
> (Ephesians 6:9)

He will not change the rules for the believer today.

We often quote the Scripture, when claiming some needed promise. Too often, we forget that He is just the same today in His hatred of sin and iniquity.

> **"Jesus Christ the same yesterday, and today, and forever,"**
>
> (Hebrews 13:8)

This brings us to another reason why compromise of Christian integrity too often occurs. The infinite holiness of God, His awesomeness, the greatness of Who and what He is, has largely been lost by the Western church today. Paul said it of the Gentile world of his day,

> ***"There is no fear of God before their eyes."***
>
> (Romans 3:18)

True then; true now. And, when the fear of God is lost from the church, not only does the church suffer, but the world at large suffers as well. When we lose the wholesome fear of God, it really does not matter what we do or how we live. When accountability and responsibility to God have been lost, when the certainty of personal judgment is no longer a living reality, when fervent love for Christ and righteousness grows cold, we are fair game for the fatal attack of the enemy.

Perhaps someone is thinking at this time, "But don't we need a Gospel of comfort and consolation; not a Gospel of coming judgment and divine wrath against sin?" It is significant, in response to this question, to note the Scripture:

> *"And I saw another angel fly in the midst of heaven, having the everlasting gospel to preach unto them that dwell on the earth, and to every nation, and kindred, and tongue, and people,"*
>
> *"Saying with a loud voice, Fear God, and give glory to him; for the hour of his judgment is come: and worship him that made heaven, and earth, and the sea, and the fountains of waters."*
>
> (Revelation 14:6,7)

During the most troubled times in the history of mankind, do we find a "soft" gospel; a gospel that tickles the ears and caters to the flesh? Quite the contrary, the message preached by the angels flying through the midst of heaven is, "Fear God, and give glory to Him...and worship him..."

It should be stated here that those who truly love God and His righteousness never tire hearing about the **Holiness of God** and their responsibility to walk "the narrow way." Actually, they long to hear and know more of their God because of their intense love for Him and desire to please Him. And, in troublous times they experience what the New Testament Christians experienced. Saul of Tarsus had given his vote to kill those of "the way." Times were dangerous for believers. But notice these words following his conversion:

> *"Then had the churches rest throughout all Judaea and Galilee and Samaria, and*

> *were edified; and walking in the fear of the Lord, and in the comfort of the Holy Ghost, were multiplied."*
>
> (Acts 9:31)

There you have the divine recipe: walking in the fear of the Lord, we have the comfort of the Holy Ghost. Nothing can compare to the peace and comfort that comes when we are walking in obedience to God according to the Word of God. Wonderful are the words of the Psalmist to the heart longing after God and His righteousness;

> **"Like as a father pitieth his children, so the Lord pitieth them that fear him.**
>
> *"For he knoweth our frame; he remembereth that we are dust."*
>
> (Psalms 103:13,14)

The church of today could well use a fresh vision of the living God in His infinite holiness. The prophet Isaiah saw the Lord "high and lifted up." He heard the awesome words,

> *"And one cried unto another, and said, Holy, holy, holy, is the Lord of hosts: the whole earth is full of His glory."*
>
> (Isaiah 6:3)

Result? He said, "Woe is me, for I am undone..." Good place to be, convinced of our need, crying for mercy, drawing near to God in willing humility and surrender, bowing in heart and spirit before the great God of the universe. Here we find rest for our souls and strength to walk with Him in the Spirit. Is there any other place to live?

Again, it was Job after being enlightened by a fresh vision of God, who said:

> *"I have heard of thee by the hearing of the ear: but now mine eye seeth thee."*
>
> *"Wherefore I abhor myself, and repent in dust and ashes."*
>
> (Job 42:5,6)

Multitudes of people know "about God," but all too few actually "know" God. The experience of salvation from sin through faith in Jesus Christ because we have been drawn by the Holy Spirit — is but the beginning of a relationship designed to cause us to "know" God. To begin a race does not necessarily guarantee arrival at the goal.

Personal knowledge of God is acquired only in/through association or relationship with God. And, like it or not, time and effort is absolutely essential. It is not (at least to the flesh) as easy as falling off the proverbial log. Coming to "know" God will take TIME. One, two, three, five minutes a day with God will never produce spiritual giants. And, sadly, surveys indicate this is about the amount of time many American Christians give to God daily (this includes Bible reading, prayer at meals, and any other praying).

Every day, each one of us is given a gift of 1440 minutes. They cannot be stored for future use, nor held in trust; they must be spent. Individually, we choose what we shall do with this gift of God. It is interesting and generally true that most of us do essentially what we "want to do." Do we want to "know" God? Then the choice will be made to take/make time to be alone with Him. We are very astute in planning our days in order to make a living; how wise are we in our plans to "know" God and prepare for eternal service in the coming kingdom of God?

What has all this to do with integrity in Christian leadership and, in fact, among all Christians? Just this. When personal relationship with the living God is pushed to the periphery of our lives, we are fair game for the enemy to attack us at our most vulnerable point. In reality, we are depending upon human strength -- in which we will miserably fail -- rather than relying upon divine strength and thus being open to the aid and direction of the Holy Spirit. Years ago it used to be said, if you are too busy to pray, you are too busy. But, "waiting" on God has largely become a lost art. Everything must be done "now" -- except praying. We do not have time to wait on the Lord. What utter folly! Some years ago I actually heard one of our ministers say, "I've been so busy, I haven't even had time to talk to God." What a confession! Indeed, a sad revelation of priorities. Yet, I fear, not the exception; but perhaps more widespread than we would like to know.

Following the example of Jesus in all of this would be wise for each of us as believers:

> *"And in the morning, rising up a great while before day, he went out, and departed into a solitary place, and there prayed."*
> (Mark 1:35)

While the early morning hours may not be possible for all believers, surely, we would agree, that in order to "know" God, we must give time to Him in some segment of the day. Again, we generally do what we "want to do." It is my firm conviction that God has implanted a hunger, a desire for Him within every human heart. Our problem is not so much lack of hunger; rather, it is misunderstood fulfillment sought in the wrong places. Spiritual hunger and thirst for God must be nurtured and strengthened by deliberately seeking after God. Failure to do so may dull desire's power and influence within us. Feeding the inborn desire for God by prayer and God's Word -- waiting in His presence — will produce an increasing knowledge of God. Does your soul hunger, thirst, long for the living God? Consider the words of the Psalmist:

> *"As the hart panteth after the water brooks, so panteth my soul after thee, O God."*
>
> *"My soul thirsteth for God, for the living God: when shall I come and appear before God?"*
> *(Psalm 42:1-2)*
>
> *"O God, thou art my God; early will I seek thee: my soul thirsteth for thee, my flesh longeth for thee in a dry and thirsty land, where no water is;"*
> *(Psalm 63:1)*
>
> *"My soul longeth, yea, even fainteth for the courts of the Lord: my heart and my flesh crieth out for the living God."*
> *(Psalm 84:2)*

God made us for Himself, as Saint Augustine said centuries ago; and our hearts will be restless until they find rest in a living vital relationship with the living God. Seminars, tapes, books, experts in "deeper life" abound in the Christian world today. And yet! In the American church, at least, the moral level of living is often no higher than the unbelieving world about us. What is wrong? Simply, knowledge without personal application is worthless.

We must take/make time for God. And then follow through with daily commitment to Him. Keep short accounts with God. Sweeping guilt and wrong under the rug will only create spiritual weakness and future failure. It seems there is little conviction in many areas today. I wonder if guilt and the conviction of the Holy Spirit are often misunderstood.

Conviction, in spiritual matters, is the convincing, reproving work of the Holy Spirit, designed by God to bring the sinner, or the Christian who has sinned, to admission of guilt and ultimate repentance. **Guilt** is the product of conviction when we admit to wrongdoing, with the hopeful end in repentance and departure from that sin. The Christian who has sinned ought to feel conviction and if, he/she will advance in God, must accept and own their guilt. The Holy Spirit is faithful, we are the ones who too often defend our actions, rationalize and excuse; thus dulling the convicting work of the Holy Spirit. And, if persisted in by us, a gradual **"hardening"** of heart and conscience takes place.

Preach it from the pulpit, shout it from the housetop. There is freedom from guilt and condemnation for those in Christ Jesus; but it can only be so when God's conditions are met. **Confession of sin (which is admission of guilt) to God, followed by sincere repentance (which is turning from that sin to God) and making restitution, will produce the peace of God and the abiding presence of the Holy Spirit.** But, telling people they are free from condemnation and guilt without declaring God's means is utter folly. If we would have God's marvelous blessings, we must also secure them by His means.

The provision by God of potential salvation for every person cost God more than we are adequately able to comprehend. For Deity to humble Himself to assume human flesh and blood and then bear the sins of all mankind, is a price beyond human understanding.

We must allow the Holy Spirit the opportunity to reveal to our stubborn hearts what it cost God to save us from our sins. Only so will personal sin become the one intolerable in our lives. **God's Word tells us what our Lord and Saviour purchased for us and what it cost Him. Righteousness and righteous living are not cheap.**

"Be not deceived; God is not mocked: for whatsoever a man soweth, that shall he also reap.

"For he that soweth to his flesh shall of the flesh reap corruption; but he that soweth to the Spirit shall of the Spirit reap life everlasting.

"And let us not be weary in well doing: for in due season we shall reap, if we faint not."
(Galatians 6:7-9)

****

WHITED SEPULCHRES

ALBERT & AIMEE ANDERSON'S
GRANDCHILDREN on Playground

JOE, MARY - DAVID, REBECCA
LARRY, DEBORAH - JONATHAN
MARK, EMILY - EMIL, EUNICE
(Albert & Aimee's adult children)

WHITED SEPULCHRES

ALBERT & AIMEE & grandchildren - 1999
Larissa, Joseph, Jordan, Jameson, Benjamin, Emil, Matthew
Charity, Starr, Kendrin, Kristina
Tristan, Breanna, Alexa, Zackary
Tyler, John, Jordan

ABOUT THE AUTHORS

Albert Emmanuel Anderson, the son of Albert and Hazel Anderson, was born near Crocker, South Dakota in Clark County and graduated from Clark High School. In 1952, he graduated with a B.A. degree in Bible from Central Bible College in Springfield, Missouri. Upon graduation, he began Evangelistic ministry. Albert married Aimee Filan on April 9, 1954 in Walla Walla, Washington. He was ordained as an Assemblies of God minister, while on their honeymoon, in his home church at Clark, South Dakota. With his wife, Aimee, they traveled together for almost three years, holding Evangelistic meetings, until taking their first church in February 1957, shortly after their first child Deborah Dawn was born.

Albert has held Sectional District offices; including Sunday School Representative, Youth Director, Camp Speaker, and Presbyter. On June 19, 1994, he resigned as Pastor of the Ellensburg First Assembly of God, after a ten-year pastorate there.

Aimee D. Filan Anderson was born at Hay, in Whitman County, Washington, the daughter of Olaus and Minnie Filan. She grew up on a wheat ranch.

She attended grade school and graduated from Wa Hi in Walla Walla, Washington. She attended Northwest College in Kirkland, Washington.

On April 9, 1954, she married Albert E. Anderson, an evangelist and minister of the Assemblies of God. Together they traveled, holding evangelistic meetings throughout the United States of America, until they accepted their first Pastorate in 1957.

For more than forty-seven years (as of this 2001 edition), Aimee has been a minister's wife, serving as a Sunday School Superintendent, church pianist, and a leader in church organizations. Together, Aimee has helped her husband pastor nine different churches throughout the State of Washington over the past years. When their six children were still living at home, the Anderson family gave numerous musical concerts.

Aimee authored her first book **<u>BROKEN, YET TRIUMPHANT,</u>** in 1983. Soon thereafter, she began working on **SUNSHINE THROUGH CLOUDS**, forthcoming 2001 sequel to **BROKEN, YET TRIUMPHANT**. Aimee has signed a movie contract on both books. Since that time she and Albert, have co-authored **WHITED SEPULCHRES** and forthcoming 2001 **sequel A GENERATION OF VIPERS.**

Recently Aimee returned to working on **SUNSHINE THROUGH CLOUDS**. Her husband, Albert, has now joined her as co-author of **SUNSHINE THROUGH CLOUDS.**

Albert and Aimee are dedicated Christians; their greatest desire is to please the Lord. They are so thankful for the beautiful love they have for each other as husband and wife. Also, they are grateful to the Lord for giving them six beautiful children, who all love the Lord as well. Their family has grown to four married daughters, two sons (one married), seventeen grandchildren (one married), and one great-grandchild — with a second great-grandchild on the way. All praise be to God!

Albert and Aimee Anderson (married over 47 years) are the type of Pastors who, when they see righteous principles violated take a stand and remain steadfast on eternal and unchanging Truth. Their experience (Albert has held ministerial credentials for 51 years) has proven that "wolves" are within church structures, not just predators from outside. And, because the Andersons' have had the courage to expose corruption, they have been caught in the crossfire of defensive officials covering their wicked deeds.

When someone with a flashlight finds a cockroach in their house, should they kill the bug or "kill the light" and let the bugs roam free? Those in authority have seen fit to squash the Andersons and try to sweep them out instead of the corruption. They have been threatened to be silent. However, they won't be silent; conscience forbids it. They have opted to stir up dust amid powerful people who prefer things be left dusty.

Albert and Aimee Anderson heard cries of the wounded (as true shepherds do) and personally became involved in mending wounds. In so doing, they found that the price was extremely high and they became wounded.

Yes, their David-and-Goliath struggle against denominational powers (unscrupulous and unethical conduct by church officials) has taken its toll. They could have accepted an easier road, pretended not to notice, perhaps been "bought off", chosen comfort instead of sacrifice and commitment to Scripture. But for them, righteousness forbids it.

Printed in the USA
CPSIA information can be obtained
at www.ICGtesting.com
LVHW052104221124
797416LV00003B/3